Praise for eBusiness Technology Kit For Dummies

"The *eBusiness Technology Kit For Dummies* is required reading for today's entrepreneurs as well as established business leaders. Today, *all* businesses are ebusinesses and must be comfortable incorporating technology into their everyday activities. In readable, friendly, and engaging 'non-tech' language, Dr. Allen and Mr. Weisner provide the core knowledge all businesses must have to accomplish this, while guiding us past the pitfalls, like service disruptions and 'hardware envy.' At JNS, the 'e-Kit' book has become a reliable and indispensable guide for implementing technology to our operational and strategic advantage."

— Kenneth G. Jordan M.D., F.A.C.P., President, Jordan NeuroScience, Inc., a Neurotelemedicine Company

"Provides a road map, strategies, tactics, and tips to build and execute a killer technology plan."

— Courtney Price, Founder, FastTrac Entrepreneurial Training Program

 ™

References for the Rest of Us!™

eBusiness Technology Kit

FOR

DUMMIES®

eBusiness Technology Kit

FOR

DUMMIES®

by Kathleen Allen, Ph.D., and Jon Weisner

IDG Books Worldwide, Inc.
An International Data Group Company

Foster City, CA ◆ Chicago, IL ◆ Indianapolis, IN ◆ New York, NY

eBusiness Technology Kit For Dummies®

Published by
IDG Books Worldwide, Inc.
An International Data Group Company
919 E. Hillsdale Blvd.
Suite 400
Foster City, CA 94404
www.idgbooks.com (IDG Books Worldwide Web site)
www.dummies.com (Dummies Press Web site)

Library of Congress Control Number: 00-104216

ISBN: 0-7645-5261-9

Printed in the United States of America

10 9 8 7 6 5 4 3 2 1

1B/TR/QY/QQ/IN

Distributed in the United States by IDG Books Worldwide, Inc.

Distributed by CDG Books Canada Inc. for Canada; by Transworld Publishers Limited in the United Kingdom; by IDG Norge Books for Norway; by IDG Sweden Books for Sweden; by IDG Books Australia Publishing Corporation Pty. Ltd. for Australia and New Zealand; by TransQuest Publishers Pte Ltd. for Singapore, Malaysia, Thailand, Indonesia, and Hong Kong; by Gotop Information Inc. for Taiwan; by ICG Muse, Inc. for Japan; by Intersoft for South Africa; by Eyrolles for France; by International Thomson Publishing for Germany, Austria and Switzerland; by Distribuidora Cuspide for Argentina; by LR International for Brazil; by Galileo Libros for Chile; by Ediciones ZETA S.C.R. Ltda. for Peru; by WS Computer Publishing Corporation, Inc., for the Philippines; by Contemporanea de Ediciones for Venezuela; by Express Computer Distributors for the Caribbean and West Indies; by Micronesia Media Distributor, Inc. for Micronesia; by Chips Computadoras S.A. de C.V. for Mexico; by Editorial Norma de Panama S.A. for Panama; by American Bookshops for Finland.

For general information on IDG Books Worldwide's books in the U.S., please call our Consumer Customer Service department at 800-762-2974. For reseller information, including discounts and premium sales, please call our Reseller Customer Service department at 800-434-3422.

For information on where to purchase IDG Books Worldwide's books outside the U.S., please contact our International Sales department at 317-572-3993 or fax 317-572-4002.

For consumer information on foreign language translations, please contact our Customer Service department at 1-800-434-3422, fax 317-572-4002, or e-mail rights@idgbooks.com.

For information on licensing foreign or domestic rights, please phone +1-650-653-7098.

For sales inquiries and special prices for bulk quantities, please contact our Order Services department at 800-434-3422 or write to the address above.

For information on using IDG Books Worldwide's books in the classroom or for ordering examination copies, please contact our Educational Sales department at 800-434-2086 or fax 317-572-4005.

For press review copies, author interviews, or other publicity information, please contact our Public Relations department at 650-653-7000 or fax 650-653-7500.

For authorization to photocopy items for corporate, personal, or educational use, please contact Copyright Clearance Center, 222 Rosewood Drive, Danvers, MA 01923, or fax 978-750-4470.

is a registered trademark under exclusive license to IDG Books Worldwide, Inc. from International Data Group, Inc.

About the Authors

Kathleen Allen, Ph.D., is the coauthor of *The Complete MBA For Dummies* and the author of *Entrepreneurship and Small Business Management,* 2nd Edition; *Launching New Ventures,* 2nd Edition; and *Growing and Managing an Entrepreneurial Business;* as well as several trade books. As a Professor of Entrepreneurship at the Greif Entrepreneurship Center of the Marshall School of Business at the University of Southern California, Allen has helped hundreds of entrepreneurs realize their dreams to start their first ventures. As the Director of the USC Center for Technology Commercialization, she is working with the Engineering School and the School of Medicine to develop the resources and infrastructure to commercialize technology developed at the university and provide an opportunity for students and faculty to work as teams to create new technology ventures. As an entrepreneur, Allen was involved in commercial real estate development for ten years — owning two businesses — and is currently cofounder and CFO of Gentech Corporation, a technology-based manufacturing company producing a line of patented, intelligent power source machines. She sits on the boards of directors of a medical technology venture and a NYSE company. Allen consults to Microsoft Corporation on various issues related to growing entrepreneurial ventures and their use of technology as a competitive advantage. She is regularly called upon to speak about technology and e-commerce issues in both large and small companies.

Jon Weisner acts as a liaison between the technical, creative, and business perspectives for the entertainment, technology, education, and medical industries. With more than ten years of experience in the technical field, he has worked in small, medium, and large business environments. Weisner's experience includes such areas as strategic planning, team management, project management, product/service design, conceptual development, desktop/ internet publishing, multimedia applications, system administration, remote access, implementation of ATM networks, WAN construction, digital libraries, and digital video distribution systems. Weisner consults to Microsoft Corporation and provides analysis on the implementation of Microsoft's products in small business environments. As an entrepreneur, Weisner is currently involved in an entertainment-based startup within the telecom industry. Weisner also consults to a number of small business ventures providing a knowledge base that increases efficiency and productivity through the use of technology. As an alumnus of the Lloyd Greif Center for Entrepreneurial Studies at the University of Southern California, Weisner has remained an active contributor to the Entrepreneur Program and is called upon regularly to lecture in its courses.

ABOUT IDG BOOKS WORLDWIDE

Welcome to the world of IDG Books Worldwide.

IDG Books Worldwide, Inc., is a subsidiary of International Data Group, the world's largest publisher of computer-related information and the leading global provider of information services on information technology. IDG was founded more than 30 years ago by Patrick J. McGovern and now employs more than 9,000 people worldwide. IDG publishes more than 290 computer publications in over 75 countries. More than 90 million people read one or more IDG publications each month.

Launched in 1990, IDG Books Worldwide is today the #1 publisher of best-selling computer books in the United States. We are proud to have received eight awards from the Computer Press Association in recognition of editorial excellence and three from Computer Currents' First Annual Readers' Choice Awards. Our best-selling ...*For Dummies*® series has more than 50 million copies in print with translations in 31 languages. IDG Books Worldwide, through a joint venture with IDG's Hi-Tech Beijing, became the first U.S. publisher to publish a computer book in the People's Republic of China. In record time, IDG Books Worldwide has become the first choice for millions of readers around the world who want to learn how to better manage their businesses.

Our mission is simple: Every one of our books is designed to bring extra value and skill-building instructions to the reader. Our books are written by experts who understand and care about our readers. The knowledge base of our editorial staff comes from years of experience in publishing, education, and journalism — experience we use to produce books to carry us into the new millennium. In short, we care about books, so we attract the best people. We devote special attention to details such as audience, interior design, use of icons, and illustrations. And because we use an efficient process of authoring, editing, and desktop publishing our books electronically, we can spend more time ensuring superior content and less time on the technicalities of making books.

You can count on our commitment to deliver high-quality books at competitive prices on topics you want to read about. At IDG Books Worldwide, we continue in the IDG tradition of delivering quality for more than 30 years. You'll find no better book on a subject than one from IDG Books Worldwide.

John Kilcullen
Chairman and CEO
IDG Books Worldwide, Inc.

*Eighth Annual
Computer Press
Awards ≥1992*

WINNER

*Ninth Annual
Computer Press
Awards ≥1993*

*Tenth Annual
Computer Press
Awards ≥1994*

WINNER

WINNER

*Eleventh Annual
Computer Press
Awards ≥1995*

IDG is the world's leading IT media, research and exposition company. Founded in 1964, IDG had 1997 revenues of $2.05 billion and has more than 9,000 employees worldwide. IDG offers the widest range of media options that reach IT buyers in 75 countries representing 95% of worldwide IT spending. IDG's diverse product and services portfolio spans six key areas including print publishing, online publishing, expositions and conferences, market research, education and training, and global marketing services. More than 90 million people read one or more of IDG's 290 magazines and newspapers, including IDG's leading global brands — Computerworld, PC World, Network World, Macworld and the Channel World family of publications. IDG Books Worldwide is one of the fastest-growing computer book publishers in the world, with more than 700 titles in 36 languages. The "...For Dummies®" series alone has more than 50 million copies in print. IDG offers online users the largest network of technology-specific Web sites around the world through IDG.net (http://www.idg.net), which comprises more than 225 targeted Web sites in 55 countries worldwide. International Data Corporation (IDC) is the world's largest provider of information technology data, analysis and consulting, with research centers in over 41 countries and more than 400 research analysts worldwide. IDG World Expo is a leading producer of more than 168 globally branded conferences and expositions in 35 countries including E3 (Electronic Entertainment Expo), Macworld Expo, ComNet, Windows World Expo, ICE (Internet Commerce Expo), Agenda, DEMO, and Spotlight. IDG's training subsidiary, ExecuTrain, is the world's largest computer training company, with more than 230 locations worldwide and 785 training courses. IDG Marketing Services helps industry-leading IT companies build international brand recognition by developing global integrated marketing programs via IDG's print, online and exposition products worldwide. Further information about the company can be found at www.idg.com.
1/26/00

Authors' Acknowledgments

We would like to give our sincere thanks and appreciation to our talented publishing team at IDG Books Worldwide, particularly Mark Butler, Suzanne Snyder, Norm Crampton, Donna Frederick, Pam Mourouzis, Megan Decraene, Heather Dismore, Carmen Krikorian, Marisa Pearman, and Jeff Goens. We would like to express our appreciation to our technical reviewer, Jeff Cloots, for his valuable contributions to the book, and to Mark Mosch of Aims2000 for being our role model of a great tech consultant. We also would like to thank our families who support us even when we work too much, and Starbucks Coffee — for the Frappuccinos that kept us going.

Publisher's Acknowledgments

We're proud of this book; please register your comments through our IDG Books Worldwide Online Registration Form located at `http://my2cents.dummies.com`.

Some of the people who helped bring this book to market include the following:

Acquisitions, Editorial, and Media Development

Project Editor: Suzanne Snyder

Senior Acquisitions Editor: Mark Butler

Copy Editors: Donna Frederick, Ben Nussbaum

Technical Editor: Jeff Cloots

Permissions Editor: Carmen Krikorian

Editorial Manager: Pamela Mourouzis

Editorial Assistant: Carol Strickland

Associate Media Development Specialist: Megan Decraene

Production

Project Coordinator: Maridee Ennis

Layout and Graphics: Jason Guy, Gabriele McCann, Tracy K. Oliver, Jill Piscitelli, Brent Savage, Jacque Schneider, Rashell Smith, Jeremey Unger

Proofreaders: Corey Bowen, John Greenough, Susan Moritz, Marianne Santy, Sossity R. Smith

Indexer: Sherry Massey

Special Help:
Norman Crampton

General and Administrative

IDG Books Worldwide, Inc.: John Kilcullen, CEO

IDG Books Technology Publishing Group: Richard Swadley, Senior Vice President and Publisher; Walter R. Bruce III, Vice President and Publisher; Joseph Wikert, Vice President and Publisher; Mary Bednarek, Vice President and Director, Product Development; Andy Cummings, Publishing Director, General User Group; Mary C. Corder, Editorial Director; Barry Pruett, Publishing Director

IDG Books Consumer Publishing Group: Roland Elgey, Senior Vice President and Publisher; Kathleen A. Welton, Vice President and Publisher; Kevin Thornton, Acquisitions Manager; Kristin A. Cocks, Editorial Director

IDG Books Internet Publishing Group: Brenda McLaughlin, Senior Vice President and Publisher; Sofia Marchant, Online Marketing Manager

IDG Books Production for Branded Press: Debbie Stailey, Director of Production; Cindy L. Phipps, Manager of Project Coordination, Production Proofreading, and Indexing; Tony Augsburger, Manager of Prepress, Reprints, and Systems; Shelley Lea, Supervisor of Graphics and Design; Debbie J. Gates, Production Systems Specialist; Steve Arany, Associate Automation Supervisor; Robert Springer, Supervisor of Proofreading; Trudy Coler, Page Layout Manager; Kathie Schutte, Senior Page Layout Supervisor; Janet Seib, Associate Page Layout Supervisor; Michael Sullivan, Production Supervisor

Packaging and Book Design: Patty Page, Manager, Promotions Marketing

◆

The publisher would like to give special thanks to Patrick J. McGovern, without whom this book would not have been possible.

◆

Contents at a Glance

Cartoons at a Glance

By Rich Tennant

"IT'S NOT THAT IT DOESN'T WORK AS A COMPUTER, IT JUST WORKS BETTER AS A PAPERWEIGHT."

page 7

"NO, SIR, THIS ISN'T A DATING SERVICE. THEY INTRODUCE PEOPLE THROUGH A COMPUTER, SO THEY CAN TALK TO EACH OTHER IN PERSON. WE INTRODUCE PEOPLE IN PERSON, SO THEY CAN TALK TO EACH OTHER THROUGH A COMPUTER."

page 221

INDUSTRY WATCHERS PREDICT THAT IN THE NEAR FUTURE MICROSOFT CORP. WILL DEVELOP APPLICATIONS THAT WILL BE COMPATIBLE WITH OS/2, WINDOWS AND KIRBY VACUUM CLEANERS.

page 117

"FOR US, IT WAS TOTAL INTEGRATION OR NOTHING. FOR INSTANCE- AT THIS TERMINAL ALONE I CAN GET DEPARTMENTAL DATA, PRINTER AND STORAGE RESOURCES, ESPN, HOME SHOPPING NETWORK AND THE MOVIE CHANNEL."

page 43

"TECHNICALLY HE'S A WIZARD, BUT AS A MANAGER HE LACKS PEOPLE SKILLS."

page 179

Fax: 978-546-7747
E-mail: richtennant@the5thwave.com
World Wide Web: www.the5thwave.com

Table of Contents

Introduction

*I*f you haven't begun using technology to any extent in your company, or if you haven't thought about technology as a competitive advantage for your business, it's time to do so. One of the most important strategic advantages your business can have today is a carefully crafted technology plan that supports your business goals.

Today, technology has reduced the transaction cost of collecting and exploiting information so that those who use new technology gain a significant advantage over those who merely sit and wait to see how it's all going to play out before they jump in. That's good news, and a wake-up call for small businesses. Because lots of small businesses out there still sit and wait, you have opportunities to gain a competitive advantage with new technology in a variety of ways.

In this book, you find out exactly what goes into a good technology plan and what the planning process entails. You come to understand that technology planning involves much more than going out and buying a computer or two. Don't be tempted to skip the business planning process; too many small business owners don't take the time to plan ahead, and it frequently costs them their businesses.

After you've completed the business goal-setting and strategizing exercises we recommend in Chapter 2, you've done a huge chunk — really the hardest part — of the groundwork for your technology plan. Then you get to apply what you've done to finding the best technology for your business. And don't forget the tech consultant. Finding and using a good consultant is critical to the success of your plan, and we help you do that, too.

About This Book

eBusiness Technology Kit For Dummies contains practical information, tips, and checklists that anyone who aspires to use technology in business can use to gain efficiency and create a competitive advantage. It doesn't matter whether you've ever owned a business or even have any business or technology experience. You can use this book to think about technology and how it can help your business become successful.

If you do own a business or work for a small, growing business, *eBusiness Technology Kit For Dummies* is a great reference tool to guide you in developing a technology strategy for your business that will help you gain a competitive advantage in the market.

This book is definitely grounded in the real world. It is based on research we conducted with small businesses and on our consulting practice, so there are no hypothetical situations here. We have pulled together the best information, the best tips, and the best strategies for making technology work for your business.

eBusiness Technology Kit For Dummies is a guide to everything you ever wanted to know about making technology work for you. Don't know where to get started? We'll help you. Don't know how to choose the right technology? We'll give you the information you need to analyze your business's information needs and processes so that you can talk intelligently to your tech consultant about your company's needs. Plus, we've included a CD-ROM with lots of resources and tools to put everything you read into action.

We think that this book, with its real-world examples, is going to inspire you to think of ways to use technology to improve and grow your business.

Foolish Assumptions

Before we began this book, we made some assumptions about you, the reader. (We know that's a dangerous thing to do.)

- We assume that you want to understand how to make technology work for you and your business.
- We also assume that you're ready to make an investment in your business's future.
- Finally, we assume that you want to find a great tech consultant whom you can count on to help you through the process.

Icons Used in This Book

We use little pictures, called icons, next to blocks of text throughout the book. They're designed to draw your attention to things we want you to note.

A good idea, trick, or shortcut that can save you time and money.

A piece of information that you shouldn't forget.

A tip that can help you avoid disasters.

Tech-heavy info that may make your head swim.

A reference to the CD provided with this book.

A real-life business example that you can learn from.

How This Book Is Organized

eBusiness Technology Kit For Dummies is organized into five parts, and each chapter within a part goes into detail on a specific topic. This organization makes it easier for you to find what you're looking for. We think that we cover everything you need to know to put together a winning tech strategy.

Part I: Getting Started

In this part, you discover the benefits of using technology to create a competitive advantage in your business. To get the most out of the technology you purchase, though, you need to have a plan that is based on your business goals and processes. Here you find out what makes a great technology strategy.

Part II: Creating a Technology Strategy

This part gets you started in the nuts and bolts of preparing a technology plan for your business. You begin by identifying how the processes of your business work and how information flows through your business. Then you find out how to match those business processes and your business goals to specific types of technology. After that, you look at how to close the gap between where your company is today and where you want to be in the future in terms of technology. Finally, this part deals with planning for the cost of technology and strategies for implementing the technology plan.

Part III: Using Technology to Grow

This part focuses on how to use technology in various areas of your business to help it grow. Those areas include winning and keeping good customers, creating a company culture, managing strategic partners, developing and marketing new products and services, and doing business on the Internet. You discover lots of helpful strategies and hints for using technology in creative ways.

Part IV: Dealing with Tech Consultants and Other Wild Things

One of the most important parts of your technology planning process is finding and keeping a great tech consultant. In this part, you explore the mind of the tech consultant and understand what's fair to ask for and expect from him or her. This part also gives you tips for finding and keeping a good consultant. In addition, it alerts you to problems you might face with your technology and gives you ways to solve them.

Part V: The Part of Tens

In this part, we give you some of our best tips for dealing with such things as technology mistakes that small business owners make, ways to make your tech consultant love you, and reasons to get a Web address. We finish this part with the best technology resources on the Web, and we include buzzwords you can use to test someone's tech IQ at the next party you go to.

Appendix A: About the CD

After reading the book, you will certainly understand everything you need to know to put together an effective and useful technology plan. But really getting the full benefit of what we talk about in the book takes more than reading; you have to do it. And that's basically what the companion CD is about — getting you to start doing what it takes to create a technology plan.

First, we provide you with templates of some of the tables and worksheets you find in the book. You can print them out and use them to gather the information you need for your tech plan. The Vendor Evaluation Matrix, which you can use to decide on your tech consultant and/or vendor, actually does the calculations for you when you enter your weights and rankings. Best of all, we include a template that walks you through the development of your Technology Strategy Plan by asking you questions and suggesting worksheets you should do to fill out a particular section of the plan. When you're done, you'll have a professional-looking tech plan that you can be proud of. Plus, you'll have the satisfaction of knowing that you and your tech consultant have been a team on this project, so its chances of success are that much greater.

We also include a video case study on a small business, showing how it integrated technology into its business environment. You can watch it right on your computer. It gives you a good sense of what it takes to design, implement, and maintain technology in your business. Just follow the step-by-step instructions that pop up in the window to start watching.

In addition, we thought you might want to see some great software and valuable services that you can use in your business. Here are two examples:

✔ **FrontPage 2000** (45-day trial version; Windows). The Microsoft FrontPage 2000 Web site creation and management program gives you everything you need to create and manage your Web site. This 45-day trial will enable you to create an attractive Web site even if you are a novice to the Internet. For more information, check out `www.microsoft.com`.

> ✔ **Internet Explorer** (Commercial version; Windows and Mac). Internet Explorer, from Microsoft, is one of the best-known Web browsers available. In addition to the browser, this package includes other Internet tools from Microsoft: Outlook Express, a mail and new reading program; Windows Media Player, a program that can display or play many types of audio and video files; and NetMeeting 3, a video conferencing program. For more information, check out `www.microsoft.com`.

Here are some more highlights from the CD:

> ✔ Case studies on small businesses illustrate how technology is integrated into business environments. These interviews, which we conducted, provide good examples of what it takes to design, implement, and maintain services that will be valuable to your business. They also demonstrate how certain technologies are used within different industries.

> ✔ On the Business Goals Worksheet, you can plot out your major goals and the strategies you will use to achieve them. With your business goals in mind, you're in a better position to look at your technology needs.

Appendix B: Tech Lingo Guide

The *Tech Lingo Guide,* on the CD and here in this appendix, is an index of commonly used key words and phrases that you may want to learn more about because they are common in the tech world. The intent of the guide is not to go into too much detail, but rather to give you a general understanding of what the terms mean.

How to Use This Book

If you want the most from this book, we suggest you start at the beginning and work your way to the end. You have a wealth of information to explore. If you have a fair amount of technical knowledge and not much time (what else is new?), you can skip from topic to topic depending on what interests you. The table of contents is organized to help you find what you need. Suppose you want to know more about e-commerce technology, for example. Just go to that chapter and the specific section you need, and you'll find exactly what you're looking for.

No matter how you approach the book, we're sure that you'll enjoy reading *eBusiness Technology Kit For Dummies.*

Part I
Getting Started

The 5th Wave
By Rich Tennant

"IT'S NOT THAT IT DOESN'T WORK AS A COMPUTER, IT JUST WORKS BETTER AS A PAPERWEIGHT."

In this part . . .

Face it: You have to start somewhere, and although preparing for creating a great technology strategy is not the most exciting thing you could be doing, it's essential to your success in using technology to give your business a competitive advantage. In this part, you take a good, long, look at your business, where it is, and where you want it to be. Business goals drive technology purchases — not the other way around — so when you finish this part, you should have a good sense of your business's future and the role that technology will play in it.

Chapter 1

Getting Your Business in Shape for a Digital World

In This Chapter

▶ Why you can't avoid technology

▶ Keeping up with technology: Is it possible? Is it necessary?

▶ What technology can do for your business

▶ The ultimate goal: the "Digital Nervous System"

*T*echnology — you can't get away from it. For better or worse, technology has taken over much of our lives. Newspapers, magazines, TV, and radio bombard everyone with the need to go faster, get on the Net, and join the technology revolution. But what exactly can technology mean to the success of your business in this new millennium?

In the 1980s, business focused on quality because the whole world wanted to catch up with the Japanese, who had used quality as a competitive advantage years before. In the 1990s, business became entrepreneurial, and even mega-businesses tried to look and act like small businesses. Today, businesses are focused on speed and speeding up business transactions, speeding up communication, speeding up production. Quality and flexibility are still important; they're just happening a whole lot faster.

Technology has changed the way we do our work, the actual work we do, and the reasons we do it. Statistics show that, on average, companies spend between 1.8 and 5 percent of their budgets on computing technology, trying to keep up with closing windows of opportunity, shortened product life cycles, and faster times to market.

For many businesses today, technology has even become the driving force. It is pushing businesses in directions they never dreamed of taking. The Internet is the clearest example of technology driving business strategy. In fact, its very presence has spawned thousands of new businesses that otherwise might not have been born.

In this chapter, we show you why you need to embrace technology and maximize its benefits for your business.

If you're not using technology to facilitate your company's goals, streamline your processes, and redefine your business, you probably won't be in business five years from now.

But you need to use technology wisely.

Adopting technology for technology's sake is never a good idea. Technology is an enabler that helps you take advantage of new possibilities for your business to be successful. Technology is the means to the end, not necessarily the end itself. The end is left up to you and the goals you have for your business that technology can help you achieve.

Taking Charge of Technology

The computer technology that has developed over the past 50 years continually reshapes and reconfigures the marketplace. For any business owner, steady change like this evokes a sense of unpredictability, which can be unnerving to say the least. To cope with the long-term consequences of rapid technological change, ask yourself:

- ✔ What opportunities do these changes make possible?
- ✔ How can my business take advantage of the opportunities that these changes bring?
- ✔ How will these opportunities change my business?
- ✔ How can my business manage the process of change?

To create value in your organization today, you want to create a smart company that's more than the sum of its tangible and intangible assets. Think of your business as a nerve center — practically a brain — that is highly tuned to its environment and can rapidly respond to any situation. In other words, think of your business as intelligent, not merely a machine that does the same thing over and over again. Your business is an intelligent system that grows, reacts, and reinvents in response to changing information.

Turning technology into knowledge

Perhaps the most important outcome of all the change technology has effected is not the hardware or software that you're all beginning to know and use, but the continuous flow of digital information that is now available. You can have access to text, sound, numbers, video, and graphics in a form that lets you send it and retrieve it from a variety of locations. You can even carry all your information around with you in the form of personal digital assistants (PDAs) such as the Palm Pilot and other handheld personal computers (PCs).

Your biggest dilemma is probably not how to find information but what to do with it once you find it, and how to deal with it in its frequently overwhelming proportions. In short, how is your business doing at managing information? To get an answer, ask yourself the following questions:

- ✔ Does most of the information in your office get distributed electronically or in paper form?
- ✔ Do you use technology to monitor the basic operations of your business?
- ✔ Do you use technology to run your production systems?
- ✔ Do you use technology to handle your accounting systems?

If you answered no to any of these questions, your work is cut out for you. This book will help.

If you answered yes to these questions, great! You're right in line with most businesses by using technology to automate your processes. Now you're ready to use technology to improve your business processes so that you can be more competitive in a digital world that will stay in the fast lane for the foreseeable future. You're ready to enter the highest level of information management: turning data into knowledge.

A study done by IBM, (James W. Cortada and Thomas S. Hargraves, *Into the Networked Age,* New York: Oxford University Press, 1999) identified four reasons for the increasing importance of knowledge:

- ✔ **Workers are no longer just doing tasks; they are providing solutions.** At a photocopying company like Kinko's, for example, workers don't just make copies anymore. They need to think about *how* they can use available technology to solve a customer's problem, whether by creating an image for the customer's company or finding the best way to present and package a report.

    Review your own business practices carefully to find ways to use technology to solve customer problems.

- ✔ **Many workers are free agents who bring their knowledge to an organization and then take it away.** More and more, businesses are essentially renting the knowledge of consultants. At the same time, top employee talent, increasingly, may leave your company if the employees get better offers somewhere else. The loss of their knowledge leaves you scrambling to reconstruct a system or process that no one else knows how to do.

Use technology to archive and systematize core knowledge in your organization so that when someone leaves, you can still do what you need to do.

✔ **Computers now gather information and make sense of it rather than just store information.** Using applications like databases, you can analyze the information you collect in ways that will help you and your employees turn that information into knowledge. You can then use that knowledge to help your business compete successfully.

Make sure that everyone in your business has access to the information they need to do the best that they can for the company. Using technology to facilitate the sharing of information will help all your employees to become knowledge partners in the business.

✔ **Traditional performance standards no longer work well in a knowledge economy because they reward workers for replication rather than innovation.** Rewarding speed and quantity produced was fine when everything was done by manual labor on an assembly line. Rewarding the same thing today may mean that you're rewarding the computer for a job well done, and ignoring the benefits that knowledge brings to your organization. Today, you want to reward knowledge outcomes, such as innovative ways of doing things or innovative products and services that help your customers and your business. Today, you need to measure and reward the intangibles that bring value to your organization.

Make sure that your reward system has caught up with technology.

Leveraging technology across your business

In a perceptive 1994 article in the *American Management Association Journal*, the authors write that businesses need to leverage technology in four distinct areas:

✔ Throughout the entire organization

✔ In collaborative work inside and outside the organization

✔ Through mass customization of products and services

✔ Through paperless offices

The following sections discuss these areas in more detail.

Sharing is good: Spread knowledge to every worker

The more your employees know about your operations and your customers, the more intelligent the entire organization becomes. Jim McElwain can attest to that fact. His company, Caldwell Architectural Services, of Marina del Rey, CA, installed a computer network that provides centralized file sharing for its growing business. Now everyone has immediate access to information on any of the many projects they have underway at any point in time. That shared knowledge has helped the company to make better decisions about the projects it targets and complete projects on time and under budget, which is a significant competitive advantage in the industry.

Use technology to make it possible for everyone in the organization to access the information they need to do their jobs better and to give constant feedback to management that initiates meaningful change.

Collaborating with the competition

Team efforts inside organizations are not a new phenomenon, and they are certainly helped by networked workstations that share common data files. But technology can help you initiate collaborative efforts beyond your own employees with customers, suppliers, distributors, and, yes, even competitors! At the same time that breathtaking advances in technology and communications have created vast opportunities for small businesses, a highly competitive, global marketplace demands that small businesses band together, even with their competition.

According to a 1997 article in Inc. magazine, Harry Brown bought a sickly company called Erie Bolt Corp more than ten years ago. Brown had a vision for how to give his ailing company — and the many others like it — a boost. He convinced his competitors that they could land bigger deals if they all joined forces. Though the other companies were very skeptical at first about sharing proprietary information, they found that when they focused on the particular skills each had instead of on the products they actually produced, they were able to combine these skills and maximize revenues, reduce costs, and increase quality. Technology makes it possible to coordinate such a collaborative effort more easily and effectively than was ever possible before. Today, Erie Bolt Corp is going strong as EBC Industries.

Take a look at your industry to see if there are ways you can network your customers, suppliers, and competitors to provide a win/win situation for everybody.

Mass customizing products and services

Does mass customization sound like a contradiction in terms? It's actually another great technique for leveraging technology. One of the real advantages that technology offers businesses is the ability to create products and services tailored to the needs of specific customers. Because it's easier to keep in touch with customers at an individual level, you can find out exactly what they want, when they want it, and how they want it.

Of course, mass customization requires that your company be flexible, and even here technology can help with things like flexible manufacturing systems, just-in-time inventory/supply systems (JIT), computer-aided design (CAD), and Internet distribution systems.

For example, Mary Naylor used technology to give the customers of her successful service company, Capitol Concierge, what they wanted. Capitol Concierge provides concierge services like errands, reservations, food deliveries, and shopping to people in large office buildings in Washington, D.C. By using an interactive database containing her customers' desires and preferences, and totally automating the system, she can increase individual sales to existing customers by triggering purchase orders at the point at which the customer typically purchases services.

Use technology to find out what your customers want, and then use technology to give them exactly that!

Does anyone really want a paperless office?

The concept of the paperless office has been around since at least the 1970s, but today, for the first time, we actually have the potential to create such a beast. The strange fact, however, is that today at least 95 percent of all information is still in paper form. What's more, experts predict that the amount of paper being consumed is doubling every four years! What's going on? We suspect that most people still like to print things that they need to study or edit. Some people just do it automatically and haven't changed their habits.

We contend that the paperless office can be achieved! One northern California real estate company decided to get rid of their paper. Were they surprised at the impact on their company! They set up systems to share information online, and now 38 agents do as much work as it would normally take 70 agents in less time and more effectively. Increasingly, the real estate industry is converting all their paper documents to electronic forms. Typically, only those documents that require signatures still appear in paper form, and even that may change in the near future.

You may not be able to get rid of paper entirely, but here are some easy ways to reduce the amount of paper floating around in your office:

- ✔ For standardized tasks, replace paper forms with electronic forms that access databases.
- ✔ Use e-mail instead of paper memos.
- ✔ Schedule meetings and appointments in a shared online calendar.

Keep employee records and other company information in private folders accessible through a company intranet (a private Internet).

Keeping Up with Technology: Can You? Should You?

Some people can't stand not having the latest version of an operating system or the latest upgrade of an application. But what's more, (and this gets scary), some business owners actually succumb to hardware envy — a technology disease that causes its victims to feel the need to demonstrate their technology prowess by comparing the power, speed, and storage capacity of their computers with their friends' computers. Don't play that game.

You have the choice of leading or following emerging technology trends. Early adopters of technology always pay more for it and also have to deal with the inevitable bugs that seem to proliferate in new versions of anything. Besides, most of the time new software only claims to run better but actually contains few new functions of great value. If you don't need any of the additional functions, or if your system is running fine, then don't upgrade until you need it. Also remember, it's standard practice in the software industry to release a new product before all the bugs are out. It's much cheaper to let early adopter customers find them and report them than to spend expensive computer programming time doing it in-house. Do you have time to be a software tester? We didn't think so.

The leading edge is close to the bleeding edge. Let the early adopters test it first, then if it really will make your business run better, go ahead and purchase it.

We contend that you don't necessarily have to "keep up" with technology, but you do have to *stay ahead* of your competitors and *stay in touch* with your customers. Technology can help you do both by reshaping how you do business.

Can technology really replace good old-fashioned human contact?

Susan Greco, Christopher Caggiano, and Marc Ballon tell this revealing story in a 1999 article in *Inc.* magazine: Jonathan Katz took pride in being an early adopter of technology. His 17-million-dollar company, Cinnabar — which creates scenery and special effects for commercials, movies,and theme parks — was always ready, willing,and able to purchase the newest innovations, from cell phones to e-mail, anything to keep in contact with customers who demanded such technologies.

So effective were Cinnabar employees at using communication technology that they often solved problems on a site from remote locations. In fact, technology became such a part of their culture that soon they found they had lost virtually all human contact with their customers and their partners.

In 1997, Cinnabar's business abruptly dropped off for no apparent reason; that is, until Katz realized that they had all become too dependent on technology for communication. In a moment of prophetic insight, Katz made his employees put away their cell phones, fax machines, and e-mail, and do the unthinkable — talk to the customers face-to-face. The result? In the last quarter of 1998, Cinnabar's business grew 50 percent. Sometimes, a good old-fashioned handshake is the most important thing you can do to compete.

In fact, we can tell you from personal experience with business clients that sometimes upgrading does more harm than good, if you have a stable system that is currently meeting your needs. A stable system that doesn't crash or freeze up on a regular basis is technology nirvana — you definitely don't want to mess with it.

On the other hand, at times even a stable system needs an upgrade. For example, we know of one company that attempted to upgrade its network operating system to insure that it would have no Y2k issues — a fairly straightforward task (or so it seemed at the time). As a result of the upgrade, they uncovered a whole host of aliens, gremlins, and other nasty problems that then had to be tracked down and resolved in order to put their network back into a stable condition. It took weeks to fix the mess that started with a simple upgrade!

So what's the bottom line?

The bottom line is that you don't have to keep up, but you do have to make yourself aware of what's out there and learn how it might help you improve your processes and take better care of your customers. Here are a few resources you can use to begin to educate yourself about what's new in the world of technology.

✔ *Wired* magazine keeps up with the latest things going on in technology. You can find it at your newsstand or check its Web site at `www.wired.com`.

✔ *TechWeb* is a portal for anyone interested in technology. It provides tech news, resources, an encyclopedia of tech terms, and much more. You can find it on the Web at `www.techweb.com`.

✔ *Inc Technology* is the technology version of the well-known *Inc.* magazine. It is geared to small to mid-sized businesses. *Inc.* also has a Web site at `www.inc.com`.

Getting beyond Word Processing and Calculations

Most small businesses still look at computers as tools to do word processing and calculations on spreadsheets. And when they claim to have a Web site, it's usually a static site that receives very little attention from its owner. That mindset may have been acceptable in the early 1990s, but it won't work today.

If you're only using technology to perform functions that were previously done with typewriters and calculators, you're handicapping your business. Consider some of the things that technology can do for your business:

✔ Technology enhances your chances for success in a rapidly changing marketplace by helping your business do everything better, faster, and more creatively.

✔ If your business has embraced technology as a fact of life and considers it as vital as the investment in plant and equipment, you have a competitive advantage against less tech-savvy businesses in your industry.

Today, people are empowered by information. The person who has the most information wins in an information economy. To empower your employees with information means making information available to them via access to the Internet and shared files and databases inside your company. Let's take your business operations as an example. Effective information technology helps you

✔ Understand how your business processes work because you will have to analyze them to design, incorporate, and implement the appropriate technology functions.

✔ Pull out information from a business process that should be shared with another business process. For example, sales data from the marketing process needs to be shared with the manufacturing process so that manufacturing doesn't produce more than can be sold.

> ✔ Give that information to the people who are actually doing the particular processes inside your business. For example, workers on the factory floor who have access to feedback from customers that marketing has collected will be able to identify problems in their processes and correct them.

For example, Bill Gates notes in his book *Business @ the Speed of Thought* that at Saturn Corporation, a dispatcher can view all the plant operations on one screen on a PC. The dispatcher instantly knows when something in the plant has failed and can immediately send out someone to take care of it. In all, the dispatcher is effectively monitoring 120,000 points of data that are analyzed every six seconds. That dispatcher has real power in his company. Moreover, workers can access reports on quality issues in their team's performance and make informed decisions about how to correct them. This is empowerment.

Creating a "Digital Nervous System"

We can't take credit for the term. Microsoft founder Bill Gates coined the handy phrase, *the Digital Nervous System,* in his book *Business @ the Speed of Thought* to refer to an internal communications mechanism that coordinates all the activities of your business.

According to Gates (and he should know!), every business is comprised of a bunch of interconnected processes. So, for example, your salespeople probably want to know from the people who handle inventory if something is in stock, back ordered, or not available. At the same time, those doing your manufacturing want to know from the marketing people which products are selling best so that the manufacturing process can focus on producing what is needed most.

Operating as a Digital Nervous System now makes this all possible. Until recently, businesses usually improved the efficiency of most systems independently, but lacked the ability to coordinate the various systems in a company so they could talk to each other. Businesses also need the ability to access data from various places and make some sense of it and, in other words, turn it into knowledge. According to Gates, the Digital Nervous System serves two purposes:

> ✔ It enhances an individual's ability to analyze things.
>
> ✔ It combines the multiple talents of many people to create a company intelligence and a unified force for action.

Obviously, technology is the key facilitator of the Digital Nervous System. Networking computers in your company is a way to share information company-wide. Using the Internet is a way to link with customers, suppliers, and others with your company as well. The Digital Nervous System is a tool that facilitates communication. Ideally, it resides in the background; you're really not aware of it just as you're not aware of electricity or the technology behind the telephone or your computer.

Applying the Digital Nervous System theory to your business

Here are some relatively simple things you can do to create a Digital Nervous System in your business:

- ✔ **Give everyone access to the information they need to do their jobs effectively.** It's surprising how often businesses provide more information to people outside the organization than they do inside the organization. For example, you may put together a comprehensive report on your business's activities and current financial status to provide to investors or to your banker. Yet employees who have a vested interest in the success of your business often don't have access to that same kind of information.

  Ideally, your employees — at a minimum your managers — should be able to access the latest data available on your business's operations. Now, practically speaking, there may be some information that should be kept private, but any information that may affect how an employee does his or her job certainly should be made available on the company network, the Digital Nervous System.

- ✔ **Pull information together that can help you make strategic decisions about your business.** Many business owners access information over the Internet and from internal databases to help them make company decisions. But how many know how to "massage" that data to predict things like growth potential? Make sure that you're not just gathering data, but that you are analyzing it in ways that give you more insight into your customers, your competitors, your financial health, and so forth.

  For example, you may gather information on how many customers you have in a certain zip code areas. You may also gather information on revenues generated by product sales. Now if you can correlate product sales to zip code areas, you can find those areas that produce the most sales, and then you can look at the demographics for those areas to deduce why and better target your marketing efforts.

Create a sales database and fill it with all the information you have related to sales of products and services, customers, and sales personnel. Then you can explore the data in every way possible and turn it into competitive knowledge.

✔ **Create a list of the information you need to run your business.** We help you do this in Chapter 4, but one way is to develop a list of questions that are critical to your business's performance. Then make sure that your technology is providing the information you need to answer those questions.

✔ **Make sure that the right people get the right information.** Information for information's sake is useless, for the most part. We all have too much information anyway. So make sure that your employees can get the information they need to make decisions that will benefit the company. If everyone is getting the information he or she needs and is distributing that analyzed information as knowledge to the appropriate people, the entire company benefits.

Final thoughts on the Digital Nervous System

The Digital Nervous System is not as complex or elaborate a concept as it may appear to be, and it certainly is not the sole province of large companies. The key to developing an effective system in your business is to think of it in very simple terms.

Think of your brain and all the activities of your body that it controls, from the steps you take to the thoughts you think. The core or brain of your company's Digital Nervous System is the server that contains the shared database of files and applications to which everyone in your company has access. Take a look at the Figure 1-1 to see what we mean.

Every computer is linked to every other computer as well as to the server. All the information on the server and all the new information generated by each user on the network is shared and can be accessible to everyone. This is the essence of a Digital Nervous System. Throughout this book, we show you ways to create a Digital Nervous System that works for your business. Just like almost everything else, it all starts with a plan, which we discuss in Chapter 3.

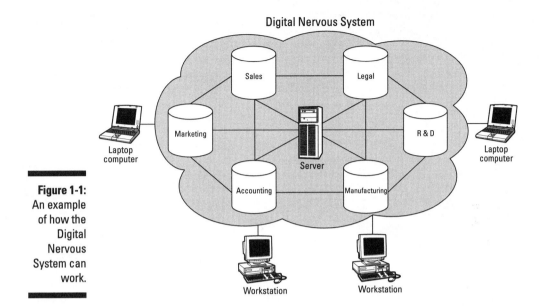

Figure 1-1:
An example of how the Digital Nervous System can work.

Chapter 2

Determining Your Company's Vision and Mission

In This Chapter
▶ Setting business goals and planning for technology
▶ Creating a vision for your company
▶ Establishing a mission
▶ Selecting strategies to achieve your mission

*Y*ou've probably heard the saying, "If you don't know where you're going, how will you know when you've arrived?" Well, this saying is true for business technology, too. If you don't have a business objective in mind, how do you know which technology can help you get there? Actually, if you don't have an objective in mind, it doesn't matter what technology you buy because you have no way to measure whether it's helped or hurt your business.

In this chapter, you discover why technology purchases don't usually drive your business decisions. Most often, your business decisions drive your technology purchases. Your decisions tell you what technology you need.

Anything worth doing well needs a good plan, or it won't reach its full potential. For your business, that plan needs to include how, why, when, and where you intend to develop your business. In this chapter you also find out how to develop the vision, mission, strategies, and tactics that will drive your business and will ultimately lead you to the right technologies.

Examining Your Business Goals and Plans First

Have you found yourself voicing one of the following concerns lately?

- ✔ "I need to find a way to automate routine tasks so that I can free up my employees to do more important things."
- ✔ "I need a way to stay in touch with my office when I'm on the road. The other day I left an important file at the office."
- ✔ "I need an inexpensive way to reach my customers on a regular basis so that I can get their feedback."
- ✔ "I'm tired of all these paper memos and calendars on my desk. I feel so disorganized; nothing is ever where I think it should be."
- ✔ "My business is growing fast. I want to expand to several locations, but I need to maintain the standard of quality we are known for in our current location."

These statements reflect real business issues — problems you need to solve, goals you want to achieve, challenges your business faces. Defining a problem that needs to be solved is certainly easier than creating a solution in search of a problem. Technology needs to bring a real solution to a real problem.

One reason that the planning process is so necessary today is that the marketplace is volatile. Some industries, such as high technology and e-commerce, are changing extremely fast. Business owners need to stay ahead of the game, but most can barely *keep up* with the rapid pace of change. Everything from production to marketing is mutating into something new. To prove the point, ask yourself these questions (and be honest!):

- ✔ When was the last time you did research in your industry to see what's going on?
- ✔ Which business periodicals and newspapers do you read daily?
- ✔ Do you belong to community organizations that enable you to network with other business owners?
- ✔ Do you read periodicals that cover technology for business?
- ✔ Do you know someone who can give you sound technology advice?
- ✔ Do you have a business mentor — someone you trust who understands your business and will give you objective, valuable advice?

How many of these activities are you doing? If you answered "all of them," you've hit the jackpot. You're doing the kinds of things necessary to get your nose out of your business and into the world so that you can see what's coming before it hits you.

If you're doing none or just a few of these things, here's a wake-up call. The world is at your doorstep, and someone with an Internet connection in New Delhi has just found a way to supply *your* customers with the same products you do at a lower price — all the way from India! You need to put your periscope up and scan the horizon. Even more competitors are on their way!

In the following sections, we look at two considerations that have a major impact on what happens to your business, and therefore an impact on the technology decisions you need to make: customers and competitors. Interwoven into each is a third consideration, technology itself.

Do you know enough about your customers?

Sometimes, a good-old fashioned handshake is the most important thing you can do to compete. When was the last time you actually talked with a real, live customer about his or her needs?

UPS, the package shipper, has been a pioneer in this relationship-building effort. They expect their drivers to not merely dump a package on the customer's doorstep, but to make an effort to talk a few minutes with the customer. Those few minutes every time that driver comes to your business start a relationship that can lead UPS to a better understanding of what you as a customer need, and that awareness makes the planning process that much easier for UPS.

Advertising alone doesn't sell your products and services. Customers are overwhelmed by advertising in all its forms: TV, radio, billboards, newspapers — even the phone book. You can hardly go to a restroom without finding an advertisement for something staring you in the face. Everyone is trying to plaster their brand on everything in sight. And who really pays attention? Do you? Your customers are your business, and what gets the customer's attention today is personalized service provided through the company's effort to build a relationship that goes beyond just selling things.

Technology enables businesses to build databases of customer information that employees can use in any form they wish to further meet a customer's needs. Consider Amazon.com, for example, where databases of information about a customer's prior purchases enable the company to suggest more products that fit the customer's preferences without the customer having to do much more than agree to receive e-mail.

Technology also provides the ability to construct interactive Web sites that give customers ready access to information about the products and services you sell, as well as provide a simple way for the customer to give feedback to the company or purchase the items. These Web sites are accessed at the customer's convenience, and can be tailored to meet each customer's individual needs.

Technology can help you make every contact with your customers a platform for offering new services and new products.

Your competition: Are you behind, ahead, or breaking even?

In the old days (say, five years ago), all you had to do to compete in the marketplace was find something unique about your product or service, lower your costs, or run your business more efficiently. Today, although you can certainly start to be competitive by doing one of these things, you can't sustain your competitiveness on one advantage alone.

In fact, your goal is not to keep up with the competition or even to do what they're doing. Your goal is to build an intelligent company that has superior execution and maneuverability. Sounds like a rather grand goal, doesn't it? Meeting this goal takes planning, strategies, and, naturally, technology.

Internet technology has been a lifesaver for busy business owners trying to keep up with market intelligence — the wealth of information about you, your competitors, and even your customers. Start with your competitors' Web sites. Also, check out a source called OneSource (www.onesource.com), on which you can find information about hundreds of industries and their major players.

Here's an additional list of great Web sites for industry or market information:

- ✔ **Standard & Poor's U.S. Regional Economic Service** (www.businessweek.com/smallbiz/resources/research/drireg.htm): Includes information on the economics of any region of the country

- ✔ **Standard Industrial Classification Index** (www.wave.net/upg/immigration/sicindex.html): A source for finding the Standard Industrial Classification Code (SIC) for your industry segment

- ✔ **Thomas Register** (www.thomasregister.com): A great guide to manufacturers

- ✔ **Securities and Exchange Commission** (www.sec.gov/): The primary source for information on public companies in your industry

- ✔ **IndustryLink** (www.industrylink.com): A good general source of industry information

- ✔ **Department of Commerce** (www.doc.gov): Great links to all sorts of sites from world trade to intellectual property

I have seen the enemy . . . and the enemy is us

So you've become successful. In fact, you've become so successful that you're the number one software company in the niche of financial management. All signs point to continued success, but all signs also point to the need for dramatic change. A 1999 article in *Nation's Business* describes how Intuit, the Silicon Valley–based company that produces such well-known products as Quicken and QuickBooks, has realized that the Internet has redefined customers' expectations. Intuit knows that if it doesn't adapt its business model to the e-commerce setting, it could quickly lose its enviable position in the market.

With more and more banks offering the ability to bank, invest, and do your taxes on the Internet for free, why would people invest in Intuit software? In 1998, 50 billion dollars in transactions were conducted on the Internet, the majority of which were business-to-business transactions. Intuit found itself with sales down and no vision or strategies for dealing with the Internet.

So what is Intuit doing now to proactively protect itself? Its employees are busy developing new content and services that electronically match consumers with financial service providers, whether those are banks, brokers, insurers, or lenders. They have a new vision for the company and a new mission:

To be the world's leading online financial supermarket.

If the enemy is bearing down on you, you can run away, stand and fight, or find a way to harness the energy of that rival and use it to your advantage. Intuit chose the latter strategy. Its Web site (www.quicken.com) has become a full-service financial hub. It's now looking for other partnerships to increase its strength on the Web. By using technology as its competitive advantage, Intuit is still going strong.

Creating a Vision

Great athletes can tell you that they envision every move they're going to make before they ever ski down that slope or play that championship game. World-class musicians can tell you that they hear every note perfectly before they ever pick up their instruments or begin to sing. Athletes and musicians envision their success before they achieve it. Vision is that distant star that keeps you moving forward in a constant effort to reach it. Of course, it's always just beyond your grasp, but the belief that you can reach it keeps you going.

Successful business owners are no different. They can see the ultimate success of their ventures long before those businesses are anything more than concepts on paper. Your business can be successful without a vision, but vision is essential if you want your company to endure and become the best in its industry.

Unfortunately, as a small business owner, you may often feel like your days are filled with little fires that you have to keep putting out. You're not able to take time off to think about where you're going. But if you decide where you want your business to be at some point in the future, you can make better decisions along the way to ensure that you get there. Equally important, if you don't know your ultimate vision for your company and you don't have a strategy for heading in that direction, you can't make effective decisions about which technology to employ or when to implement it.

Start with your core values

The vision you have for your business — to be the best in your industry or to be the next Hewlett-Packard — comes from your personal core values. Here are some examples of core values from real companies:

- ✔ We believe in total integrity.
- ✔ Our employees are our most important assets.
- ✔ We will treat everyone fairly and honestly.
- ✔ We will be state-of-the-art when it comes to technology.

You no doubt have core values of your own that affect the way you conduct business. Take a moment and list three of your core values:

1. _____

2. _____

3. _____

Now use an "endurance test" to see if what you listed really are your core values. A core value is something you would never change. Your business is known for these core values. They are sacred. Can you think of any scenario in which you might change one of the core values you listed? If you can, then that value is *not* a core value.

The great thing about identifying your core values is that doing so makes your decision-making easier. The values serve as guidelines; in other words, you won't make a decision to do something that goes against your core values.

After you define a vision — a picture of how you see yourself at some time in the future — based on your core values, you need to take stock of where you are now and what you need to do to make that vision a reality. That process involves defining a mission or major goal that is measurable and determining the strategies and tactics that will achieve the mission.

Figure 2-1 shows how this process comes together.

Figure 2-1:
Envisioning
the path to
your
business's
future.

State your mission (You don't need to be General Patton)

Whenever people talk about a mission for a company, they often slip into military metaphors. That's because a business mission is very similar to a mission that a military leader might define. The difference is that in a business situation, the mission reflects a company's culture rather than a military culture. And the strategies and tactics use people and equipment in an entirely different way.

For example, when Reebok was the king of the athletic footwear business, "Beat Reebok!" became the mantra at Nike, and it served to bring everyone together with a common purpose. Nike actually achieved its goal by becoming the leader in innovation in the athletic shoe industry. One reason was that everyone at Nike bought into the mission. They focused all the organization's energy on that goal — and that focus is what it takes.

A mission statement is a call to action for the company, so it needs to be powerful and ignite a fire under everyone to achieve it. It also needs to be realistic. Although you may not achieve your vision (because it's too lofty), you must achieve your mission.

A good guideline is to set a mission that your business can achieve within a reasonable period of time — not so far out that people lose their passion, and not so soon that the achievement is over too fast. One to three years seems optimal.

Your mission statement also needs to be measurable; that is, you want to be able to identify when you've achieved it.

Here are a couple of examples of mission statements that can be measured:

- We will grow our revenues by 50 percent in one year.
- We will be the number one distributor in our industry within three years.

Notice that each statement sets a time limit and identifies a measurable and major goal. Now you try. Write a one-sentence, measurable mission statement for your company, and then check it to see if you have included a *time for achievement* and a *way to measure success*.

_____

_____

_____

Create strategies and tactics

A strategy is a planned attack on the mission (there we go again with the military metaphors) that consists of the steps you need to take to achieve the mission. Take the following mission statement:

We will be the number one distributor in our industry within three years.

You can't achieve this lofty goal without effort and planning. First, you need to know the current number one distributor and approximately how much they're distributing. Then you need to know what you can do to match and exceed that company's current output. For example, you may determine that you need to

- Purchase 10 more trucks.
- Employ 15 additional drivers.
- Install a digital tracking system to make it easier to keep track of shipments from pickup to delivery.
- Link electronically with your warehouses, customers, and manufacturers in a type of private Internet called an *extranet* so that you can speed up your processes.

You may need to do many other things, too, but this list serves as a start. Notice that your business goal — to be number one in your industry — comes first; then comes your decision to install a digital tracking system and link electronically with key partners in order to achieve that goal. Technology is not the driver, but the enabler. The decision to invest in technology is a result of your business goal to become the number one distributor in your industry.

Tim McCollum's 1999 article, "End Your Internet Anxieties Now," in *Nation's Business* cites IPrint.com as an excellent example of a company that based a business decision on a recognized industry problem, then developed a plan to use technology to make its industry more efficient and effective.

IPrint.com examined the processes traditionally undertaken in the printing industry and decided that it could improve the situation. It had learned that up to 20 percent of orders sent to commercial printers had to be redone, mostly because of typographical errors due to transferring from a paper document to typeset. So the company's goal was to change the way that people buy printing services. Today, at the IPrint.com Web site, users can design and order customized business cards, stationery, and greeting cards, printed gift items, and other printed items. IPrint.com is then able to produce an order in a matter of days.

Iprint's plan was not to displace its competitors, but to get them to join the online trend, and to that end, it built a platform that accepted all types of printers. By using technology to solve a business problem — errors in transferring from paper to typeset — IPrint.com is succeeding against industry giants like Kinko's because it is a Web pioneer and doesn't have the baggage of brick-and-mortar companies with overhead that includes buildings and equipment.

The goals for your organization are a vital component of your success with technology because

- ✓ They give the entire organization guidelines and a focus for action.
- ✓ They motivate everyone to achieve them.
- ✓ They give the organization a way to measure achievement.

Develop strategies

Strategic goals are usually broad-based goals that deal with issues affecting the entire company. For example, if your mission is to grow your company to the next level, you may develop strategies for

- ✓ Raising capital for growth.
- ✓ Facilitating growth with your marketing plan.
- ✓ Creating a new product development plan.

When you have a mission for your company, coming up with strategies is not terribly difficult. But what if the marketplace has dictated that you need some new strategies just to stay alive?

More and more, changes in the marketplace are forcing small business owners to reinvent the way they do things and to create new strategies for achieving smaller goals as well as their companies' missions. As an example, a 1996 article by John Case in *Inc.* magazine describes how one company in the travel industry found a survival strategy when technology threatened to put it out of business:

For years, travel agents made their money through 10 percent commissions on airline tickets sold; in fact, nearly three fifths of their revenue totals came from airline tickets. That was until 1995, when Delta Airlines sent a shock-wave through the industry by beginning to sell tickets directly on the Internet, paying travel agents only $50 for a round-trip ticket. Quickly, the other carriers followed suit, and it looked like the small travel businesses would shortly face extinction.

As if the ticket challenge weren't enough, the very foundations of the travel agent business were collapsing. Travel agents are essentially information brokers; they get paid because they know what no one else knows. The problem is that the Internet makes everyone an information broker. Today, anyone can get on the Net and make airline reservations. As a result, everyone has gotten into the travel business, including companies like discount warehouse giant Costco.

Determined not to go down without a fight, entrepreneurial travel agents fought back with innovative strategies that turned the technology threatening to destroy them into a competitive advantage. For example, Aspen Travel was a boutique travel agency with a small market in isolated Jackson Hole, Wyoming. One day a film-production company from Los Angeles scheduled a shoot in Jackson Hole, and it was so pleased with the service it received that it used the Wyoming firm for other locations. Aspen's owners had the vision to see that they had found a niche in the market that could take them beyond their mountainous boundaries. Today, more than 85 percent of Aspen Travel's business comes from production companies referred to it by happy customers.

Aspen Travel has tripled in size, and technology has helped the business continue to operate from a remote location. Its strength is its ability to deal with the egos of directors and to handle unusual tasks like getting an AT&T phone booth to a location in Belize or transporting penguins to Moab, Utah. Aspen Travel continues to be an information broker, but the information is the hard-to-get kind, and the company has a talent for knowing what clients want before they ask for it — a serious competitive advantage.

Take a new tack on tactics

After you know how you want to achieve your business's mission — what strategies you want to use — you need to consider the details. The detailed steps you take when you implement your strategies are your tactics.

For example, if your company's mission is to be number one in your industry, and one of your strategies for getting there is to establish an e-commerce site, you may use the following tactics to execute your strategy:

- ✔ Hire a programmer and Web site designer
- ✔ Build a Web site
- ✔ Hire a marketing firm to help you develop an e-commerce marketing plan

Integrating Technology into Your Business Plan

Consider the example of a real company to see how you can tie together your mission, strategies, and tactics and use technology to succeed in a fast-changing world.

Described in "Deciding to Go Digital," by Keith H. Hammonds, in an early 2000 *Fast Company* issue, Diamond Technology Partners (www.diamtech.com) is a relatively young consulting firm (only five years old), but it now has 300 consultants and $82 million in revenues. How did it grow so fast in such a short time?

Diamond found a niche by joining business strategy with information technology to help companies identify e-commerce opportunities. Alliant Foodservice, Inc., is one of its clients. Alliant Foodservice is a brick-and-mortar distributor of food and supplies for restaurants, hotels, and hospitals, with lots of trucks, warehouses, and call centers. Diamond suggested that Alliant needed to reinvent itself by developing a vision and strategies for the next decade that would include putting its proprietary purchasing system on the Web.

In the meantime, two of Diamond's partners decided to learn everything they could about the restaurant industry so that they could better recognize new opportunities (this was a strategy). The partners spent six weeks waiting tables, cooking, and cleaning at the Rocky Cola Café in Los Angeles (the tactics to accomplish the strategy). What they learned was that the restaurant business isn't about food; it's about time — the owner's time — or lack of it. Most restaurant owners work 70–80 hours a week with no vacations. They have no time to plan menus or talk with customers.

Diamond believed that the way to more time was through the Internet. With Alliant online, restaurant owners could buy their food and supplies electronically from many distributors and buy more intelligently because they could easily compare distributors. Moreover, if restaurant owners joined forces online, they would have more clout to purchase at better prices. So they formed a new company, TheSauce.com, that is independent of Alliant but takes a cut of the purchasing transactions that Alliant generates through its Web site. It's a win/win situation all around.

Based on the information presented in this chapter, here are some steps you can take to prepare your business for developing a technology strategy:

1. **Write down your core values.**

2. **Picture where you see your business ten years from now — don't limit yourself.**

3. **Set a major one-year goal for the company that is guided by your vision.**

4. **List some strategies for achieving the goal.**

5. **Brainstorm some tactics that can help you achieve your strategies.**

6. **Identify technologies that support your strategy and tactics.**

Do these steps and you've accomplished the first critical step toward a technology plan that will work for your business.

Chapter 3

Understanding the Planning Process

In This Chapter
▶ Understanding the technology planning process
▶ Creating a good technology plan

*W*hy do you need a technology plan? In a word — *survival* — the very survival of your business. When we talk about a technology plan, we're not talking about a ponderous document that your tech consultant prepares one time in the life of your business, carves on stone tablets, and stores in a vault to protect it from change. We're talking about making technology planning a way of life in your business. If *you* don't create a flexible and dynamic technology plan for your business, someone else will — a competitor who renders your current technology obsolete and puts you out of business because you can't keep up.

Just like a business plan, a technology plan is a living document that constantly repositions your business to meet the demands of a globally competitive and technically savvy marketplace. In this chapter, you find out exactly what goes into a good technology plan and what the planning process entails.

Delineating Steps in the Planning Process

The technology planning process consists of four simple but vital steps, illustrated in Figure 3-1. These steps include creating the plan, screening and selecting vendors, implementing the plan, and monitoring its performance and maintenance. In the sections that follow, we discuss each step in more detail. Later in this chapter, we detail the components of a good technology plan.

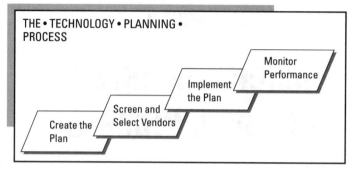

Figure 3-1:
Steps to the
technology
planning
process.

THE • TECHNOLOGY • PLANNING • PROCESS

Create the Plan → Screen and Select Vendors → Implement the Plan → Monitor Performance

Don't be tempted to skip the business planning process. Too many small business owners don't take the time to plan ahead, and it costs them their businesses.

Planning the plan

It takes a plan to make a plan. When you sit down to write a business letter, for example, you make sure that you have everything you need in place — information, letterhead for your company, a document file, and so forth. (We're assuming that you're not still doing business letters with pen and paper. If you are, then we're especially happy that you decided to read this book!)

Because your technology plan needs the input of key people in your business, decide who these key people will be early in the process and start delegating responsibilities for gathering the information required for the plan. It's as simple as that. (We believe in delegation whenever possible.)

Follow your vision

Where do you want technology to take your business? You already have the answer to this question if you read Chapter 2. Remember, you need a grand vision, something to keep your business moving forward, but you also need a mission — a goal that is close enough to achieve in a relatively shorter period of time — say, a year. With technology changing so fast, setting objectives too far out is a waste of time. By the time you're halfway down the road to achieving the objective, you discover that you now have to head in a completely different direction because something in your business environment has radically changed. And you need strategies to help you reach your mission and tactics to achieve those strategies.

If you don't have a business plan and you haven't read Chapter 2, stop right now and go back. This is important. You can't begin to plan what technology you need if you don't know where you want to take your business.

The planning process

The technology planning process begins with figuring out what you want your business to do so that you can communicate your mission to the technology consultant you will probably use to help you through the process. This means having some goals for your company that technology might facilitate. Leave the programming and hardware connection issues to the tech consultant and concentrate on your business processes.

Then you need to go through a process of identifying your information needs, micro-business processes, or activities that your business performs on a daily basis, and areas of your business that need improvement. At that point, you're ready to rank order your needs according to how much of an impact each will have on improving areas of your business. You find out how to do all these analyses in Chapters 4 and 5.

Once you know what your needs are, you can look at specific technologies to see how they might facilitate the achievement of your business goals. Then you're in a position to view the gap between where you are now and where you want to be in the future. That gap is where your tech strategy comes in, because it will help you define the steps you're going to take to reach your goal — in other words, to close the gap (look at Chapter 6 for ideas on how to close the gap). Part of looking at the gap is also figuring out how much the technology you need is going to cost. You will find out more about the cost of technology in Chapter 7.

Execution

A plan is nothing unless you can execute it. One of the key elements in creating the plan is selecting the person or persons to implement the plan. Surprisingly, you may not want to choose those who are most familiar with technology. To achieve an effective plan, you need to get the commitment and involvement of everyone in your organization. This plan is not something you can delegate to any one employee who happens to be technologically oriented. In fact, that may be the worst person to hand it off to. Many times, the computer nerd type is only interested in the inner workings of technology that you never see (and probably have no desire to see), whereas good technology plans are based on solving business problems and challenges.

A good technology plan is fundamental to a successful business. We can't be too emphatic on that point. Remember that you are not graded based on the weight or the number of pages in the plan. It's not quantity that matters but the quality of your technology research and your business plan that dictates a successful plan.

Screening and selecting vendors

If you spend the time and effort to construct a technology plan that reflects your company's goals, you can save an enormous amount of time — not to mention frustration — seeking, screening, and selecting the vendors to supply the hardware and software you require. Planning a technology budget that makes sense for your business is also helpful to your vendors in staging the purchase of the technology you will need over time. If you are dealing with a technology consultant, that person will be a tremendous help in finding good vendors from which to purchase your technology. If your consultant has helped you with the strategy and will implement it — but it is up to you to do the purchasing — we have some tips for you for dealing with vendors.

Chapter 7 has more tips on selecting vendors, but for now, you need to know that the process follows approximately these steps:

1. **Identify potential vendors.**

2. **Do a comparison across the various criteria you have identified as important to your business.**

3. **Narrow the field to about three or four vendors.**

4. **Invite those vendors to present their solutions.**

5. **Identify the strengths and weaknesses of each vendor and solution.**

6. **Select your vendor.**

Planning the implementation of the plan

Implementation is a critical stage in the technology planning process. As with creating the project, successful implementation takes the commitment of everyone. It also takes a plan with time lines, tasks, and assignments of responsibility for those tasks to the appropriate people, whether they're your own employees or independent contractors, as well as benchmarks to indicate how your plan is performing. Chapter 8 deals with the issue of implementing your plan in greater depth, including how to get everyone on board so the implementation goes smoothly and monitoring progress.

We cannot emphasize enough the importance of bringing everyone on board to plan the installation of new technology. Having a well-prepared technology plan that reflects your company's needs is all well and good. But if you can't execute that plan as effectively as you prepared it, it isn't worth much.

How one construction company decided to construct a plan

We can tell you with no uncertainty that technology planning and using a technology consultant can save you a lot of time, effort, and frustration.

One small Wisconsin construction company had implemented a well-known *peer-to-peer* computer network, which strings together several desktop computers (and often printers) via cable. The intent was for each user to be able to access information on another user's hard drive and for all users to share printers and other connected hardware resources. However, the network kept crashing.

Because no one had time to mess with the faulty network, the company returned to the old way of doing things — the proverbial "sneaker-net." One person would copy a file onto a diskette and run it over to the computer that was hooked up to the printer. When the owner wanted to look at some accounting information, he had to go over to his bookkeeper's computer screen and either read it there or have his bookkeeper print it out. Everyone was stressed out, but no one was sure how to solve the problem and still keep up with the daily work.

Once in a while, the universe smiles on a small business owner and sends in a knight on a white horse to save the day. This company's knight came in the form of Computer Business Solutions (CBS), which worked with the CEO to help identify what was needed to end up with the right system. Not only that, CBS held the owner's hand all the way through the process so that he never felt out of touch with what was happening.

CBS knew it was important to understand where the CEO wanted to take his business. CBS also wanted the CEO to understand his company's technology needs so that he would know why CBS was recommending a particular solution. Rather than simply submitting a grocery list of technology and its bottom-line price tag, CBS broke out all the parts and identified which were essential and which could be added later. The technology plan that CBS submitted was clean and simple. It had only three steps:

1. Upgrade the current operating system and give the bookkeeper a faster computer because she needed it most.

2. Replace the hodgepodge of different network cards in the various computers with a common brand to simplify system maintenance.

3. Reconfigure the network from a ring to a star configuration. Although a ring configuration is less expensive to implement, it is more vulnerable to crashes, which the company definitely wanted to avoid. (When computers are networked in a ring, if one computer goes down, they all go down; in a star configuration, all the devices are connected to a hub, so if one device fails, it doesn't bring down the whole system.)

A little planning went a long way. The company's new system was soon up and running with no problems, and the CEO found that the company could now handle up to 30 percent more customers. Thanks to the consultants at CBS, from now on, this construction company knows how to plan for its technology growth.

Monitoring performance and maintenance

You've spent a lot of time and effort getting to the installation point, and now the system you designed is in place. You may figure that's all there is. Unfortunately, there's more. You want to know whether you made the right decisions — if this new technology is really doing what you planned for it to do — so you need to monitor your company's performance after installation and compare it against the benchmarks you set up in your plan.

Of course, training everyone on the new technology and getting them up to speed on their normal tasks always takes time. In fact, we can pretty much guarantee that it will take more time than you think. We discuss training and the implementation of your plan in detail in Chapter 8.

Once you're up and running, you can't forget about ongoing maintenance. Complex technology systems have distinct personalities. Some systems hum along happily for long periods of time, rarely encountering glitches or problems. Other systems seem to have been born with gremlins inside, designed to annoy you at every turn. If you include in your technology plan a strategy for dealing with problems when they arise, you can at least reduce some of the stress associated with things like your server crashing just when your team is putting the final touches on a major customer's project.

Planning for growth in your systems is also a must. Improper planning has been known to create some of the problems referred to in the previous paragraph. As your business scales up, your system must move with it. You need to understand the mid- and long-term perspective of your business so that you can plan for the technology that's needed to support it. To try to upgrade from what you originally chose as a less expensive option now may turn into the most expensive route later.

Putting the Right Elements into Your Technology Plan

A good technology plan is a pretty simple document. It tells you where you are today, where you want to be, how you're going to get from here to there, and what you're going to use to get there. And you don't have to think of it in any more complex terms than that. In this section, we'll outline what you'll find in a good technology plan: goals, the current status of your business, technology appropriate to your business, implementation, and follow-up.

Start with your goals

The first part of the technology plan identifies your goals for your business in terms of where you want your business to be at some point in the future. You may have one overriding major goal like *we want to be number one in our niche within two years.* Then, because businesses move forward on small wins, you want to set some smaller goals that can be achieved more quickly and give everyone a sense that they're moving forward. These goals might revolve around such things as how to reach your customers better, how to reduce your overhead costs, and how to operate more efficiently and effectively.

Be sure to review Chapter 2 for more information about setting goals for your company.

Map out your business

The second part of your plan looks at where you are today. It's a snapshot of your business and your industry, and where you fit in the picture. (This analysis, by the way, can result in a rude awakening for business owners who have been too busy running their businesses on a day-to-day basis to step back and objectively assess their status.) Here are the basic questions your plan needs to answer:

- What does your business look like?
- What kinds of information are processed in your business?
- How does information travel through your business?
- What's standard in your industry? What are your competitors doing?

Chapter 4 shows you some great ways to study your business from an information and process standpoint. If you do all the suggested tasks (and we make them easy and fun!), you will understand the nature of your business and how it operates better than you ever have before. And the job of choosing technology that's right for your business will become much easier.

Scout the technology

This part of your technology plan is made up of two parts:

- How big is the gap between where my business is now and where I want it to be?
- What technology will help me do what I need to do?

Again, no rocket science here. Chapter 5 can help you match technology to your information needs, not the other way around. You don't want more technology than you realistically need. Then again, you do want to stretch a bit in terms of getting the latest technology so that you have room to grow and not have to update so quickly. It's amazing how fast you can outgrow your technology if you haven't planned for growth.

After you create your wish list, come back to earth and look at the difference between what you currently have and what you want to acquire. How to do that is the subject of Chapter 6.

Implement the plan

The last part of your technology plan discusses your implementation strategy and how you intend to monitor the effectiveness of the plan over time. It will include the names of the people in charge of the implementation and what their specific tasks are, the particular tasks to be accomplished, and the time line for accomplishing the tasks.

Technology is nothing without you. You have nothing to fear from technology. You are more intelligent than any technology that has been created because you tell the technology what to do.

Part II

Creating a Technology Strategy

The 5th Wave   By Rich Tennant

"FOR US, IT WAS TOTAL INTEGRATION OR NOTHING. FOR INSTANCE-
AT THIS TERMINAL ALONE I CAN GET DEPARTMENTAL DATA,
PRINTER AND STORAGE RESOURCES, ESPN, HOME SHOPPING
NETWORK _AND_ THE MOVIE CHANNEL."

In this part . . .

You've done the preparation from a goal perspective, and now it's time to get down to the nuts and bolts of doing a technology plan. In this part, you look at your business processes and how information flows through your business. This self-assessment puts you in a good position to identify the types of technology that may work best in your business environment. You also consider where you are in terms of technology and where you want to be, and then figure out a way to close the gap. That means that you consider the cost of technology.

Chapter 4

Understanding Your Business's Operations

*1*f someone were to ask you the following question, what would your response be?

What kinds of information do you use in your business?

No, it's not a trick question, or a question that only a technically savvy person can answer. It is, however, one of the fundamental questions business owners need to ask themselves before they talk to a tech consultant about investing in technology.

Your response to this question can assist you in deciding on the specific pieces of technology that can help you, your employees, and your business increase productivity and efficiency and build a competitive advantage.

In this chapter, we help you figure out what kinds of information you use in your business. If you can communicate more clearly about how your business operates and what kinds of information flow through your business, you're on your way to creating your tech strategy. Believe it or not, it's a challenge for most owners to define what actually occurs on a daily basis in their business. They're so wrapped up in their own particular tasks that they rarely think about the operations as a whole. You need to look at the whole picture in order to find the best tech strategy for your business.

This chapter helps you identify how information gives life to your organization as it flows through it. You'll find out how to describe your information processes in such a way that they can be matched with the technology that is appropriate for your specific business — technology that will help your business, not hurt it.

Exploring Different Solutions for Different Companies

No two companies are exactly the same or have the same technological needs, even if they're the same size, are in the same industry, and have the same customers. Whether it's the way they deal with clients or customers, the way they manufacture a product, or the way they perform a service, each business has its own company culture — its own way of doing things. Here are a couple of examples.

Engineering Firm #1

Engineering Firm #1 is a full-service design and construction company with clientele from the industrial, aerospace, airline, and port facilities industries. This company reports that its jobs are comprised of approximately 25 percent job design, 50 percent contract documents, 5 percent securing building department approval, and 20 percent field work. At any given time, it has about 15 projects in the works.

Although the company does subcontract work, it bases the majority of its team members in one main office. This allows architects, project managers, and others to work together physically. It also permits project information to move from one desk to the next. The company culture demands that technology should focus on increasing productivity and efficiency by making information easier to find and share.

Engineering Firm #2

Engineering Firm #2 is in the same industry as Firm #1 but caters to different markets. It is also a full-service design, engineering, and construction management firm that targets commercial, industrial, institutional, and government customers. It bases its competitive strategy on being the single point of contact and responsibility for customers on very complex real estate projects. This company employs architects, engineers, project managers, and other staff at one primary site and two satellite offices.

Some of the important services Firm #2's teams offer include cost estimating and scheduling, as well as generating and submitting project proposals to secure contracts — an activity that takes the collaboration of every team member regardless of his or her location. The company's culture stresses consistency and efficiency in order to insure that projects remain within budget and are completed on time, while at the same time meeting the highest quality standards.

Different businesses, different technology solutions

Because Firm #1 has most of its people located in one office, its ability to have impromptu meetings or move hard copies of project information from one person to the next is reasonably quick. Information transmission rates have been enhanced by using e-mail, project-scheduling software, and file sharing over a local area network. (Read more about LANs in Chapter 17.)

On the other hand, Firm #2 has people located at multiple, remote sites so they use a combination of phone, fax, and courier services to share information quickly. Remote-access services let employees connect to a central source of information at the business, and improve the access, ease, and speed of information sharing for this firm.

You can see, from the two examples of Firm #1 and Firm #2 — two companies that are similar in many respects, yet different in others — why we say over and over that there is no one technology solution for every business, because no two businesses are alike.

Discovering Your Company's Information Flow

It's vital that you have a complete knowledge of the types of information that make your business run — including all the invoices, documents, messages, and other forms you use in your daily operations. The information that you gather or generate in your business supports the goals that you set for your business (refer to Chapter 2 for a further discussion of goal setting).

This section gives you an overview of the kinds of questions we, as information management consultants, would ask you if we were sitting in your office trying to understand the types of information your company uses and how they move from place to place. The approach that we've found most effective is to ask you to describe a day in the life of your business.

A day in the life of your business

Think about what you and your employees do on a daily basis. Picture, for example, what happens when you arrive at work in the morning. What is the first thing you do? The second thing? (And so on throughout the day.) In short, you should identify

- ✔ What work is being done?
- ✔ Who is doing the work?
- ✔ What information is generated?
- ✔ Who gets that information next?
- ✔ What activities does certain information trigger in your operations?

To help you understand more clearly, here's an example we've summarized from one of our clients so that you feel like you're walking through his day:

The first thing I do when I walk into the office in the morning is check my voice mail. I take hand notes, writing down phone numbers and other comments my customers have left me in their messages. I then walk over to the fax machine and look for any faxes that may have come in. I look on my calendar, which is pinned up on the wall, to see what's in store for today and I wonder if I remembered to tell everybody about an important client coming in tomorrow at 11:00 a.m. So I walk back into the office and put a sticky up on everyone's computer monitor to remind him or her. Next on the list is to write and distribute a memo to everyone regarding a faxed request sent overnight by a customer. Yadda, yadda, yadda . . .

Now, do the same thing with your company. Get everyone to describe his or her typical workday. We have found that this exercise can be a real eye-opening experience because, by doing so, you gain a complete understanding of how the business works. Up to this point, you may have been so involved in your own tasks that you never understood how the things you do integrate with the tasks and activities everyone else is doing. After you complete the day in the life of your business, you'll probably find that each task has types of information and persons or groups associated with it. You can then sort these tasks by function so you can better understand what happens where.

Figure 4-1 is an example of how you can chart the functions of your business.

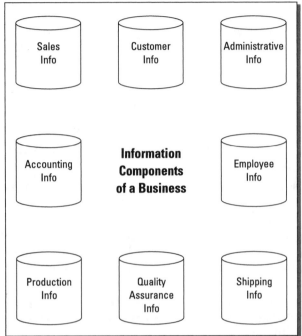

Figure 4-1:
A sample illustration of information components in business.

We like to think of various functions in a business as containers into which you put information. In Figure 4-1, you see some examples of the functional containers that you find in a typical business. The information in each container takes a variety of forms: invoices, inventory sheets, purchase orders, project tracking charts, and so forth. There is information that has relationships and dependencies with several functions, and which moves from container to container. Some containers may add or modify information to these forms while others are simply dependent on reviewing them.

Feel free to relabel, add, or remove any of these containers to better reflect your business environment.

In fact, on the CD you'll find a template you can use to look at your own business. After you identify the information that exists in your business, the next step is to understand how that information needs to get from place to place for it to be useful.

A day in the life of a manufacturing company

Now look at Figure 4-2, which depicts a typical workday's operation in a manufacturing business, starting with a customer who places an order.

1. **The company's marketing efforts make the customer aware of its products and services. The customer calls with a request to purchase product that triggers the salesperson to generate a quote.**

2. **The salesperson faxes the quote back to the customer.**

3. **To commit to the purchase, the customer faxes in a purchase order based on the quote.**

4. **The salesperson confirms the order with the customer via e-mail and hand delivers a copy of the purchase order to manufacturing and another copy to accounting.**

5. **The manufacturing plant produces the product and, after it's completed, sends it to shipping. Manufacturing also hand delivers a completion notice to sales and accounting, which triggers them to send an invoice to the customer for payment.**

6. **The sales person writes a personalized thank-you letter for the opportunity to do business with the customer, and carries it to shipping to include with the delivery.**

7. **Shipping calls accounting to confirm that it's okay to ship the product, and so on.**

Here are some of the pieces of information that you find in this single example:

- ✔ E-mail
- ✔ Fax
- ✔ Invoice
- ✔ Letter
- ✔ Memo
- ✔ Plant Production Order form
- ✔ Purchase Order form
- ✔ Quote & Order form

From Figure 4-2, you can see that a manufacturing company's information components are different from those depicted in Figure 4-1.

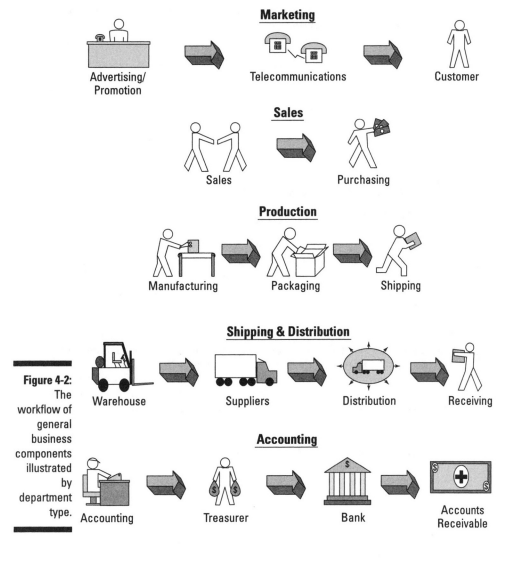

Figure 4-2:
The workflow of general business components illustrated by department type.

Finding the Source of Information

After you identify the information, you need to figure out who generates it. Using our example from Figure 4-2, this is what you get:

✔ The sales department generates quote, order, purchase, and billing data using template forms that compile various pieces of information. These forms link together and actually create a process that needs organizing, streamlining, and managing (for example: product assembly, delivery tracking, and so on).

> ✔ Correspondence with the customer/client/vendor is usually comprised of faxed or e-mailed documents, memos, or formal letters.
>
> ✔ This company conducts internal communications among people or entire departments through face-to-face contact or telephone.

Once you know *who* is generating specific types of information, it will be easier to begin to look at how these various sources interrelate — how one affects the other. That's a critical step to converting information into company intelligence.

Turning your information into business intelligence

Keep in mind that every person who generates information contributes his or her own part to the whole intelligence of your business. Every business is really a system, and every part of that system interacts with every other part. Everyone relies on a common body of information, although much of the information isn't critical to every group.

This common information can be something as simple as the particular product a customer orders. Every group in your business does something different in relation to what a customer orders. The sales group collects and verifies this information and makes it available to the rest of the business. The production group uses this information as a reference to know which products to make. Accounting uses the same information to generate billing, and so on.

Look at Figure 4-3 to see what we mean.

In a very simple way, this illustration depicts shared knowledge. The outside circle represents the business in its entirety. The three circles within the outside circle are groups that have specific objectives within the company (for example, sales, accounting, and production). There is no magic number of circles in the center — you can use as many as necessary, depending on the core functions of your business. Some of the groups don't need most of the information that other groups generate, as you can see by the figure. The very center of the diagram — the section in which all three circles overlap — represents the shared information that all three groups use to perform their responsibilities.

Although shared information has always existed in businesses, it's not uncommon to see three business functions using completely different technologies that don't allow them to share information. When that happens, information is not only not shared, it's duplicated. And that's a waste of time and money.

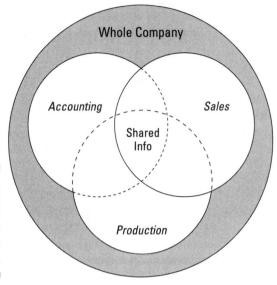

Whole Company

Accounting   *Sales*

Shared
Info

Production

Figure 4-3:
Identifying
information
shared by
business
groups.

Here are some of the problems you face with systems that can't share information:

 ✔ When it's time to update information, someone has to take the information and duplicate it on each computer to update the files. This is a time-consuming process that is prone to errors.

 ✔ You can't always count on timely or accurate distribution of all the information. And much of the time, it may actually be lost.

 ✔ Some of this information can be vital to the management of project or service timelines. Leaving any area of the business out of the loop during this process can create serious problems.

 ✔ Duplicating processes, such as distributing information, is simply a waste of time.

As you can see, identifying information common to the different functions and groups in your business is very important.

Identifying and organizing information

Here is a summary of suggestions for identifying and organizing the information in your business:

1. Gather and organize your information.

   Collect a complete set of documents that your office commonly uses.

   Lay all of your company paperwork (templates, letterhead, and so on) out on a table.

   Arrange the documents in the order that those in your office use them throughout daily operations.

Organize the documents by function (for example, marketing, sales, production, accounting, and so on). Make copies of forms that your company uses in multiple functions. If sales, production, accounting, and shipping all use the order form, make sure that each function has one.

Identify links between your documents and highlight any redundancy or commonality.

2. Match people's responsibilities with specific documents and identify how they use the information.

Looking at Your Business from a Tech Consultant's Perspective

At this point, it's a good idea to step back and look at your business one more time from another perspective — that of a tech consultant, the person who focuses on the various types of technology you will use in your business. Understanding the kinds of questions the tech may ask about your business and its information flow better prepares you to deal with him or her. (Of course, we devote an entire chapter to the fine art of working with techs. See Chapter 15 for more information.) To help you, we've provided some of the key questions you might be asked by your tech consultant.

Questions about your business's use of technology

We include a summary of some typical tech questions in this section. It's a version of what you can find on the CD included with this book.

- When you think of the computers in your office, which functions do you see them performing?

- How do you store your information (file cabinets/electronically)?

✔ Are you satisfied with the technology you have now?

✔ Are you aware of any available technology that could make your business run more efficiently?

✔ How do you deal with correspondence? (handwritten letters, typed letters, e-mail, and so on).

✔ Do you use any software applications to help you keep up with your customers and their needs?

✔ Do you keep logs of your telephone conversations?

✔ Do you record customer preferences/info so that you can recall past information from previous orders or conversations?

✔ Do you track customer status and correspondence?

✔ How do you use e-mail?

✔ How often do you use e-mail?

✔ Do you share information with other companies/vendors/contractors on a regular basis?

✔ What kinds of files do you have around the office? (letterhead, memos, order forms, invoices, and so on).

✔ Which files do you store electronically?

✔ Who needs access to which files?

✔ Are there security issues with certain files?

✔ Do your employees need to share the same information?

✔ Do you use a database for storing/retrieving information?

✔ Do you back up this information? How?

✔ Do you have an Internet service provider (ISP)?

✔ Do you have your own Web page?

✔ Are your machines networked?

✔ What are some of the most time consuming and difficult tasks within your office environment?

✔ Of these tasks, which would be the most important to try to improve?

✔ When you're out of the office, do you find yourself needing information that's in your office?

✔ Would having access to your files from outside the office be beneficial to you?

Matching your business to one of these scenarios

As consultants, we have had the honor, joy, and frustration of being inside hundreds of businesses of all types, from upscale attorney offices to small manufacturers in the less desirable parts of town. We see these businesses as they really are, not all dressed up for public viewing. We see them with all their problems and frustrations.

Here are two business environments that are in need of some help from a technology perspective. Maybe you will see your business in one of them. If so, reading this section may convince you that you need a technology plan.

Confusion reigns in this real estate company

When you walk through the doorway of this company, the quiet reception area hides the confusion and disarray found within the interior of the office. This company deals with significant amounts of paperwork: orders, schedules, bills, site plans, and so on. There appears to be no identifiable system for managing anything, except for file cabinets with paper files and stacks of papers to be filed on desktops — a common technique with small businesses.

The realtors — working within a real estate company that manages properties — often visit their properties to take care of maintenance issues. Right now they have no centralized method for tracking any of the maintenance requests, so confusion often reigns and, consequently, some tasks are not completed while others get done more than once!

When someone calls the office to ask about the status of a job, there is no central place that anyone can get that information quickly. This is a real problem because answering requests quickly is something for which this company wants to be known.

The way that communication occurs in the office is through the traditional *sneakernet* (running a floppy disk from one computer to another). One day while we were talking with Bob, the company's owner, Janet, the receptionist, dashed in and slapped a Post-it note on Bob's computer monitor. Of course, how she found space among all the other rainbow-colored Post-its decorating the monitor was beyond us. Post-it notes are great, but wouldn't another way of conveying information be easier?

We asked Bob if there was some hidden organization in all that mess. He replied that if Janet has something really important for him to see, she puts it on his chair so he has to pick it up to sit down. Otherwise, he periodically looks at the Post-its to see if there is anything important. This system may work some of the time, but Bob doesn't realize how much time he spends trying to keep track of all those random pieces of paper.

Diving beneath the surface of a law firm

When you step out of the elevator and into the beautiful lobby area of this law firm you experience a sense of professionalism, tradition, productivity, and success. Under the surface, however, it's a different story. The firm's operations include all the traditional administrative tasks that come with having multiple lawyers operating out of one main office. This far-from-paperless office deals with everything from searching through and tracking evidence and logging phone conversations and meetings, to dealing with all the paperwork the courts require — and that's just the beginning.

The company essentially does everything by hand, with very little help from computers that are too old to do anything but frustrate the users. Stored in filing cabinets and paperwork that travels from desk to desk, information fills the office. Each attorney has his or her own space allocated for case information, but that information is not easily accessible to other members of the firm. Tracking one another's schedules requires referencing a calendar distributed on paper once a week. If anyone makes a change to the calendar, there is no convenient way to let everyone know.

One of the most significant problems, similar to the preceding real estate example, is that there is no centralized place for people to look for up-to-date information. The company doesn't spend its time, money, and human resources nearly as effectively as it could. Bottom line, the company has been successfully (in its own estimation) operating like this for years. The firm's members argue that there's no need to change. We suggest that the company needs to be proactive about improving the way it does things. If not, it will be playing catch up when it finally notices that its competitors, who have adopted technology, have left it behind in the dust.

Selling the Plan to Employees: What's in It for Them?

Any time you expect employees to change the way they do something, change a pattern of behavior, or change the work environment, you're going to encounter resistance unless you can successfully show them what's in it for them. It would be nice to think that philanthropically minded employees will make major changes in their work patterns just for the good of the company, but unfortunately for most employees, that's not enough incentive. Just as you expect new hires to demonstrate the benefit they can provide to your company, you have to explain to your employees why these changes will be good for them in the long run.

One of the quickest ways to get their acceptance is to ask employees what would make their job easier, more effective, and more enjoyable. Chances are, something they list can be provided by the new technology you are proposing for the company.

For example, suppose one of your employees complains that she has a difficult time scheduling nonroutine sales meetings. It takes a long time to go to each salesperson and find out when he or she is available, then go back to the calendar and figure out a time and day that satisfies everyone and doesn't conflict with something else that's going on in another part of the company. If you can show this employee that the new system will provide the ability to have a common calendar for the company where everyone can enter critical appointments, meetings, and dates when they're out of town, she can probably see quite easily how much time she'll save by not having to contact everyone. She'll simply log onto the central calendar and find an open date.

That's just one example of a benefit that may encourage an employee to enthusiastically agree to exploring a new technology.

Another great way to get employees to enthusiastically accept your technology plan is to include them in the planning process at every stage so that their concerns are addressed as you consider types of technology and put together an execution strategy.

Incentives are a good way to get employees excited about familiarizing themselves with the new technology. Prior to the installation, have your employees rank their most critical tasks. That can become the order they use to decide where to focus their efforts first with the new technology. Have them set goals for themselves, and then provide them with some incentives to reach those goals. How about an after-hours pizza and beer party when a major goal has been achieved?

Chapter 5

Making Technology Work with Your Business Information

*A*ny technology consultant can come into your business and install several computers, give you an Internet connection, and tell you that you now have a top-of-the line network. However, before the design and installation, did that technology consultant ever ask you what problems your business was facing?

Technology is here to support you and your business. To leverage all the help different technologies can provide, you must identify the specific problems your business operations face. Look at where your business processes and technology solutions can meet and complement each other. Specific tools exist for specific jobs.

The media and the marketplace present you with the perception that your business will automatically benefit if you spend a lot of money and install a bunch of computers. To us, that's flying blind — a bit like buying a hammer when you really need a drill to get the job done right.

This chapter helps you understand how to match a business process with a technology solution and how to deduce your specific company's needs.

Matching Information Systems with Business Goals

No matter what type of business you have, you share common goals with other businesses. All businesses want:

- ✔ Fast, reliable, easily available communication so that people in your company can talk with each other and share information.

- ✔ Fast, reliable, easily available communication with customers and suppliers so you can meet their needs and they can meet yours.

- ✔ Efficient administration of office tasks — daily support tasks like correspondence, filing, and organizing.

- ✔ Rich, detailed customer profiles that let your company provide better customer service and build individual customer relationships.

- ✔ Sharing of information and knowledge throughout the organization. Centralizing information, such as contacts, scheduling, and files, helps your company build its competitive intelligence.

The following section contains a real example that describes how one company matched its business goals to its technology.

Metal Fabricators

Metal Fabricators is a medium-size mill distributor that offers a full-line service center and is a retailer of industrial type metals. Referred to as the "7-Eleven" of metal distributors, Metal Fabricators has about 30 employees who respond to their customers' needs by processing orders for same or next-day delivery. They order any items not in stock and transfer them within 24 hours among any one of their three locations. They deliver two-thirds of their product by truck and walk-in customers pick up the rest.

Over the years, the company has installed various systems to increase efficiency and effectiveness for its employees. Here are a few of problems the company identified and the specific technology solutions they employed in order to resolve them.

Problem #1

The company receives a majority of its sales by phone, and 80 percent of the customers need to receive their orders by next-day delivery. Traditionally, customers called their sales representatives, who completed blank order forms by hand. Each salesperson walked a written order to the accounting department where they generated a quote/work order and entered it into the accounting system.

Each salesperson then faxed quotes and orders to the customer for approval. They printed and walked the work order to the mill where they assembled and then shipped the order. The process was cumbersome and prone to error, and made it difficult to achieve the company's next-day goal.

Solution: Metal Fabricators' problem screamed for a shared database. With the help of a technology consultant, the company developed a database that they placed on the central server. The shared database lets the sales department do away with handwritten orders and put the information directly into an electronic form that everybody can see — anytime and anywhere.

The database alleviates the need for carrying forms from one desk to the next. Instead, the salesperson can call the accounting department and let them know that there is a new request for a quote/work order. The accounting person can then click a few times on his computer to bring up all the information he needs in order to create a quote/work order in the same database that's immediately available. The salesperson can fax the quote from her computer to the customer. The amount of time and frustration this company saves by doing things the new way is significant. Next-day delivery is a reality.

Problem #2

Often salespeople receive calls from customers requesting copies of test reports on metals that they are purchasing. Steel producers, who analyze the composition of the metals that they ship, generate these reports. Formerly, the company scanned the reports and stored them on a computer designated to hold this information.

Anytime someone needed to reference these reports, they had to submit a request — a lengthy process. Someone then had to go to the machine containing the request and print a report. This report then went back to the salesperson who faxed it to the customer.

Solution: The company put a public folder on a network server. Now, everyone who has access to the public folder can see the scanned reports. The salespeople can get reports to customers quickly because they can access them from any computer connected to the network. In fact, often before the customer can hang up the phone, the salesperson retrieves the report and tells the customer that the report is on its way. The amount of time and energy the company saves increases their efficiency and lets them give far better customer service.

Problem #3

Metal Fabricators receives daily market rates on the metals they sell by phone and fax. In the past, they figured these rates for customers by using a calculator to determine the sales price. They distributed copies of the rate sheet daily to keep the sales crew up-to-date on prices to quote.

Solution: Now, Internet connections give salespeople easy access to Web sites that show daily market rates of metals. They enter the rates into a shared database that automatically calculates the appropriate selling price for that day.

As you can see from the previous examples, after you clearly identify a problem, it's much easier to find a solution that can really help. Some businesses, however, fail to integrate all their systems, which leaves tremendous gaps in their business processes. These gaps result in duplication of effort, as well as errors and delays.

The more specifically you can identify a problem, the better. You'll then be able to reap the benefits of your technology investment. And, more importantly, you actually solve the problem.

Executive Suites

For decades now, hardware and software companies worldwide have been working on products and services that can make life within your business more efficient and productive. For a business that operates with little or no technology, the basic functions found in a network system can provide a positive boost to operations and make a company more competitive in a digital marketplace. In some cases, simply understanding what technology is available may open doors to business opportunities that you may never have considered possible. Such is the case with the next example. Here is a business that has existed for many years but is now on the brink of being reinvented based upon a wise investment in technology.

Executive Suites is a property management company that offers centrally located executive office suites for start-up, small, and virtual-type businesses. The company supplies turnkey solutions to a variety of clients, from high-tech companies to advertising companies, psychotherapists, and translation firms. In addition to providing space, Executive Suites has traditionally offered services such as centralized reception, secretarial, shipping, and other concierge type services. They assure the professionals choosing to lease space that they can meet any of their business needs (photocopying, transcription, notary, and so on).

Problems

Early in 1999, the founder/president, Sandra Jones, realized that her company was facing a major challenge in managing all of its ordering, scheduling, and billing information. A significant portion of the problem stemmed from the fact that the company had two separate locations that shared resources. Some of the issues included:

✔ Communication between employees was through phone conversations and faxes — a practice which was inefficient and often prone to error.

✔ Computers in the two offices were not networked, so they couldn't "talk" to each other. This meant that everyone had to rely on a sneakernet type system.

✔ The company's third party accounting and property management packages ran independently, on separate computers that couldn't talk to each other. If you wanted to take data from the accounting package and include it in a word processing file that you were creating, the two often weren't compatible.

✔ When the main office assigned tasks such as showing office space or taking care of maintenance requests, someone in the office had to try to reach the appropriate person in the field by phone. This task usually resulted in lengthy phone tag episodes, delaying completion of the assignments.

✔ There was no centralized way to log and track the status of tasks at the various buildings the company managed, so mix-ups occurred on a regular basis.

✔ Communication within the office was poor, which reduced productivity and efficiency.

✔ Internal messages and tasks were scattered around the office. They were often lost, misinterpreted, or forgotten.

✔ It was difficult to meet the company's goal of satisfying customer requests as soon as possible because there was no common database in which to post problems. Therefore, when a customer called in to check on the status of an issue, it took a long time to find the information.

✔ Employees traveled from one office location to another to take care of paperwork because they had no shared database and no way to access information remotely.

Solutions

In June 1999, Jones sought help from a technology consultant who understood the problems she was trying to solve. The consultant oversaw the installation of a network and server, several new workstations, and a Microsoft Office productivity suite. The network linked all the workstations, provided remote access to link the two offices as well as e-mail, secure Internet access, and Web site hosting. This new technology was able to resolve the internal communications issues that had plagued Executive Suites. Here is how some of those issues have been resolved.

✔ Public network folders allow employees to access common information immediately from their own desktops. Previously, when they needed this information, they put the customer on hold and then went to another room to check the filing cabinets.

✔ With a shared database, employees can access all client account information immediately and fax or e-mail the information from their desktops.

✔ E-mail has increased communication flow internally as well as the communication flow to the sites they manage.

✔ The office now has remote access services connecting the two office locations so that employees can share information regardless of where they are.

✔ A T-1 connection lets the company provide secure, high-speed Internet access to its clients, employees, and tenants. It gives Executive Suites a significant competitive advantage in its marketplace.

✔ With the T-1 connection, the company can use Windows NT Server's Internet Information Server component to host its Web site, which produces significant sales results for the company. The company has secured several clients off the strength of the company's Web-based virtual tour of office space.

✔ Previously incompatible third-party software for accounting and property management now integrates with office productivity software.

Within just six months of installation, Jones saw a 30 to 40 percent increase in efficiency in the two offices. The company is filling vacancies at a much faster rate than previously, and communication is streamlined. Jones now wonders how she ever ran her business the old way.

Many types of technology products are currently available to help you achieve your business goals, and these products are changing daily. Because each company has its own specific requirements and its own personality, we don't want to suggest that the following products are necessarily the right ones for you. That is something you should discuss with your technology consultant. Use the following lists of products and the previous case-study examples as guidelines for that discussion.

Two categories of technology exist that provide basic services: hardware and software. Hardware is simply the physical machines you use — computers, printers, scanners, and modems, just to name a few. Software is the way you actually interact with those machines. Software applications let you use the potential of the hardware to get things done. For example, a word processing application allows you to use all the components of the computer to write, edit, print, and save letters.

In the following sections, you will see some familiar terms that you may be intimately involved with already. Chances are you will know a good percentage of the items mentioned. Nonetheless, this is a good opportunity for you to come up to speed on those devices or applications that you may not be familiar with.

Technologies that make businesses feel better

Prescription medications treat specific symptoms. A doctor must first understand what the symptoms are and then make an educated decision on what medication may help to alleviate the problem or create a good balance so that the problem is no longer an issue. The same holds true for technology in a business. View problematic business processes as symptoms and then look to technology for the medication to alleviate the pain. If you're successful in matching the two, you will either alleviate your problem or create a good balance.

Hardware

The following list contains a brief description of a variety of hardware components that are commonly used by small businesses to increase productivity and efficiency. The list also includes some hardware that you may need in your business later if not immediately. A good idea when shopping is to visit your local computer store and physically see and touch what it is you might buy. You may be lucky and even find someone who knows what they are talking about and can help you understand how a piece of hardware or software works and how you might be able to integrate it with everything you already have. Don't feel obligated to buy immediately. Do some comparison shopping by looking through catalogs or going on the Internet to places like *Computer Shopper* (www.zdnet.com/computershopper/) and CNET (www.cnet.com) where you will find a wider selection available.

- ✔ **Backup devices:** Floppy drives and tape drives have been around for some time now. Writeable CD drives, Zip Drives, and Mirrored drives are most commonly used today. Writeable CD drives are similar to floppy disk drives. Insert a blank CD and then copy files to it just as you would to a blank floppy disk. Zip disks are just as easy to use. A mirrored drive is the ultimate backup device because it is an exact replica of a basic hard drive. Anytime you add or change something on your computer or server, the mirror performs the same task. If your regular drive should fail, you can use the mirror to bring your computer/server back up.

- ✔ **Desktop computers:** The traditional full-size computer is a desktop PC that sits on your desk with a monitor and keyboard.

- ✔ **Laptop computers:** Portable computers, or laptops, are convenient for traveling or multi-venue businesses.

- ✔ **Modems:** Modems let your desktop, laptop, or server call other computers over regular telephone lines to share information.

- ✔ **Network hubs:** All of your computers attach to a network hub via a network cable. A network hub links computers together so that they can share files and other resources.

- ✔ **Network printers:** Network printers are the same as regular printers except they have a built-in NIC (see the following bullet) that lets them attach to the network. That way, computers on the network can share them. These printers can be more expensive, but if you think of the alternative of buying more than one, the cost starts to make sense.

- ✔ **NICs:** Network interface cards install into your computer to let your computer or laptop attach to a network hub.

- ✔ **Scanners:** Businesses are using scanners to archive letters and bills that they receive. Depending on your business, you may want to take photos of products, scan them into a digital format and post them on your Web site or e-mail them directly to customers.

- ✔ **Servers:** Think of a server as a normal computer on steroids. It has all the same basic pieces that make it work, but is built to be stronger because it performs a serious job with a lot of responsibility. The server is the central storage place for all the files and programs that reside on the network.

Software applications

In any computer store, catalog, or online outlet, you can find a variety of software to meet any need your business might have. Here are some of the major categories of business software to give you a start.

- ✔ **Contact manager:** The contact manager provides a common place to store all the contact information on other business, your employees, family, and friends.

- ✔ **Database:** Databases let you enter information once and then create different screen layouts to work with that information. You can perform searches, and manage and manipulate information in the database.

- ✔ **Spreadsheet:** Spreadsheets let you create financial statements quickly and easily. They also make it possible to do "what if" scenarios without having to re-enter all the information.

- ✔ **Word processing:** Word processing software is probably the most commonly used program in any business because from it you can generate letters, invoices, and advertising — just to name a few functions.

- ✔ **Desktop publishing:** Today's desktop publishing software lets you bring all the prepress activities you might do to promote your business in-house.

- ✔ **Web creation:** Software designed to walk you through the process of setting up a Web site can put you in the Internet business in no time.

- ✔ **Desktop faxing:** A modem or network connection lets you send a fax from your desktop computer.

✔ **E-mail:** Electronic mail is trendy to say the least. It has become one of the best ways to communicate inside and outside the walls of your business.

✔ **Internet browser:** An Internet browser is a graphical user interface (GUI) that lets you view Web pages on the Internet or on a company Intranet.

✔ **Intranet:** An intranet provides your business a private Internet and a way of navigating information in the same way you navigate Web sites.

✔ **Scheduler:** Calendar-based applications like schedulers help you plan your days, weeks, and months. Schedulers also keep track of daily tasks that you have assigned to yourself or others.

✔ **Antivirus:** With more and more viruses infecting computers via the Internet, you must include antivirus software in your plans.

✔ **Utilities:** You need to do lots of little tasks to maintain top performance on your computer and get rid of files that may be clogging the system. Utilities software can help you do that.

Determining Whether You Need Customized Software

After you know which types of technology and applications you need to reach your business goals, you need to decide whether to use off-the-shelf products or have someone build a custom application for your business. Boxed software in a computer store or on-line is an example of an off-the-shelf product. In contrast, custom applications are programs that a designer/programmer specifically creates to meet the unique needs of your business.

It's important that you understand the critical differences between the two types of programs. To do that, you should be aware of the most significant criteria to consider when choosing between off-the-shelf and custom applications. They are

✔ **Ease of use:** Will it be easy enough to use that people can actually enjoy its benefits? (If the software is too difficult to implement, your employees won't get the benefit and it will be a waste of time and money.)

✔ **Cost:** Can the business afford to invest in this software, and what is the return on investment? In other words, how long will it take to recoup the cost of the software investment?

✔ **Time:** How long will it take to get this solution up and running so that it can start to help your business?

Off-the-shelf applications

Off-the-shelf applications come prepackaged with solutions that most average businesses need. If your needs are simple and you have some flexibility, you may want to find an off-the-shelf product. For example, if you need something to help organize all the phone numbers, addresses, and other information on people your company deals with, you can likely find contact management software that is right for you among the many available on the shelf.

A visit to your local computer store may convince you that there are almost too many options available! It helps, therefore, to have read up about the various types of contact managers before you visit the store. Expert evaluations of software in popular computer magazines can help you narrow the field before you face the mind-boggling array of choices at the retail outlet. Of course, your technology consultant will definitely have some opinions as well.

In terms of the three decision criteria discussed earlier, here's how off-the-shelf applications stack up:

- ✓ **Ease of use:** Because developers build these products for the masses, a major focus is on how user-friendly the products are. To judge that for yourself, go to a computer outlet or Internet site that lets you "test drive" the software. You should be able to understand and use the fundamental components almost immediately — that is, if you are somewhat familiar with computer technology.

- ✓ **Cost:** Off-the-shelf applications normally cost less than custom applications because they sell in high volume and developers design them to be do-it-yourself type products.

- ✓ **Time:** Chances are you'll be up and running a lot faster with an off-the-shelf application than with one of your own creation.

Customized applications

If you can't find what you need in an off-the-shelf product, you may want to consider hiring a programmer to design and develop an application specific to your business. You need to make sure that the new application shares a common platform with your current software so that they can talk to each other. Here's how custom applications stack up against the decision criteria we give you earlier in the chapter.

- ✓ **Ease of use:** With custom applications, ease of use can vary depending on who builds them and how. There are no guarantees like there are with some off-the-shelf products. That is why you should thoroughly discuss your needs — including ease of use — with the designer of your program. Let the expert know how you like to use applications, so that he or she can consider those issues when programming your customized application.

✔ **Cost:** Customized applications are normally more costly because of the amount of time that developers need to design and program them. Also critical to mention here is the maintenance of a custom application. Normally once a custom application is up and running, it works. However, if you need to make any modifications — due to growth, for an example — you'll have to call in the programmers again. Most off-the-shelf products are designed to mold to your needs out of the box.

✔ **Time:** Some customized packages may take a long time to work through before they ever get to the level of functionality that you originally envisioned, if they get there at all. Always plan on at least twice as much time as originally planned to get a customized program in place.

Some technical consultants may try to convince you that you need a custom system built (more money and business for them, of course) when, chances are, you don't. You're going to have to be the judge of this and use your instincts. Make sure that you fully understand what the outcome, in terms of the three-decision criteria, is going to be from each scenario a consultant presents.

The story of Market Insights (see the sidebar "It takes more than technology," later in this chapter) is a clear example of the technology consultant having the technical skills to put a large system together, but not having the business skills to understand how to integrate the technology with the business processes. Market Insights may have been able to do quite well with an off-the-shelf product that would have had an equal or greater impact than what was actually realized, would have cost less than the aggregate of all the mistakes made, and would have been up and running more quickly.

On the other hand, there are cases in which wonderful custom applications were developed that have had an enormous impact on the companies that commissioned them in addition to a large return on investment.

If you decide to use a consultant to guide your decision-making about customized applications, you should ask to look at some applications he or she has developed for other clients. This will show you the quality of his work. Also, ask to speak to a few of his or her clients as references. You may want to ask the following questions:

✔ Did you have a good experience working with this solutions provider?

✔ How is the application solution they built for you running?

✔ Have they provided good support for problems that arise?

✔ Is the application easy to use?

✔ How often do you use the application in your company now?

✔ Does everyone use it, or only a few people?

✔ Has the application increased your efficiency in the area intended?

It takes more than technology

Market Insights is a data analysis company that focuses on the health-care industry. It compiles and analyzes huge quantities of data of interest to people in that industry and then sells its analyses to hospitals and health-care consultants. It is, by all accounts, a great example of an information-age company.

In the August 5, 1999 edition of *Inc.* magazine, Deborah Asbrand reported that Market Insights executives knew in 1997 that, to remain competitive, they had to look to technology to help them gather and study the growing amounts of data now available over the Internet. They consulted a technology expert to get some advice. His solution lay in an expensive data warehouse — to the tune of hundreds of thousands of dollars. This idea troubled Rick Louis and Anthony Milano, Market Insight's founders, because their relatively small, self-funded company had made a profit every year since its inception, and investing in this level of technology would negatively affect their positive financial position in the short term.

Louis and Milano agreed, however, that the company needed an Internet presence to grow. With a data warehouse, their customers could access certain data for themselves over the Internet for a subscription fee. That way, the company could focus on more in-depth, customized reports. The new technology would add value to the company and give it more options for the future. Although the decision was a difficult one, they decided to forge ahead, relying on the advice of their technology consultant.

What they didn't know was that the gap between getting up and running with off-the-shelf technology and doing it with a custom application is enormous. But they found out. Two years and $1 million later, their new technology had yet to provide a return on investment. Louis blamed it on his and Milano's inexperience.

They made their first mistake by not putting in writing the details of the project or their agreement with the technology consultant who drove the project and who joined the company as the chief technology officer (CTO). Moreover, no defined schedule or progress deliverables existed, and no one knew who was responsible for what. On top of that, the CTO kept raising the bar on the software, operating system, and hardware. Before the project had even begun, they had spent $580,000 on software licenses, the data warehouse software, and a dual-processor Digital AlphaServer 4100 running UNIX.

Their next mistake lay in underestimating their worker needs for the project, and — because of the enormous investment in hardware and software — not having enough cash to hire the people they needed. Slated to take a month to complete, the project actually took more than nine months. To top it off, when the partners couldn't decide on the amount of the equity stake to give their CTO, he left. By the end of 1998, they were getting nowhere fast.

With nothing operating the way it was supposed to, the partners were forced to access a line of credit to hire programmers and turn the project around. Today, Market Insights uses portions of the data warehouse, but the special software developed for it still doesn't do what it was supposed to.

In retrospect, Louis and Milano regret not planning and more carefully considering the type of technology that would work best for what they were trying to achieve. The complex UNIX system was a much more powerful tool than they really needed to satisfy both their business goals and their customers. Sometimes the lure of technology can blind a business owner to the easiest, most cost-effective solution to help achieve the business's goals.

Finding the right mix for your business

Choosing technology comes down to this: What can help you do the things you need to do? We suggest looking for off-the-shelf solutions first. They can be the least expensive and fastest way to support the processes you have in your business. Most of these applications let you customize some aspects, such as how your desktop looks when the application is running, so you can feel like the application is your own.

If a product has some features you need but not others, try using a combination of off-the-shelf products and see if you can mix and match them to meet your needs. The disadvantage with a combination is that there is usually no easy way for information to flow between two programs from different manufacturers. We're not saying you can't do it in some cases, but it can get messy.

Databases are usually the number one software application that businesses seek to help them log, manage, and process information. A database can hold all sorts of information including text, sound, and pictures. Companies use databases for everything from contact management to inventory, accounting, phone logs, and much more.

- ✔ FileMaker Pro by Claris Corporation is one of the easiest database packages you can buy. It comes with a number of templates for home and business so you can get going right away. It also allows you to teach yourself how to build a database from scratch. If you want to figure out how databases work, this program is probably the easiest.

- ✔ Another popular and very powerful application is Access by Microsoft. The templates included with Access are also user-friendly, but understanding how to build and change things in this database takes more effort.

Databases are also one of the most commonly customized applications in any business. Because every business is different when it comes to the types of information that each wants to store and retrieve, no generic database is going to meet, completely, that business's needs. You may want to ask your technology consultant to design a template for your database that reflects your business and the information it uses. This is an example of taking an off-the-shelf product and customizing it. Most database applications provide plenty of options for customization.

The bottom line is that you should first identify your business processes and the problems you're having with them. Then match the appropriate technology to those problems so that you end up with technology that actually solves those problems.

Chapter 6

The Technology Gap: Getting from Here to There

. . . .

In This Chapter

▶ Measuring your technology gap

▶ Choosing among technology options

. . . .

*W*hen you look into the distance and envision where you want your company to be, do you see a line stretching from here to there for what seems like forever? Does the task of reaching "there" seem almost insurmountable? What kind of technology can move your company to that level? How will you acquire all the technology you need to put you where you want to be?

Many a business owner has felt overwhelmed by *the gap* — the distance between where your company's technology is today and where you want it to be in the future. At that point, many give up and go back to running the business the way it has always been run. They never reach their goals, not because they don't set any, but because they don't know how to close the gap.

This chapter looks at the gap between where your business is now, in terms of technology, and where you want it to be. We give you ways to get yourself and your business off the starting blocks and racing toward that future you envision.

Determining the Size of Your Technology Gap

One of the most difficult tasks when you start to consider the gap between where you are today and where you want to be in the future is figuring out how long it will take to get there. If you're starting from virtually zero in terms of technology (like most smaller businesses), you probably see the enormous amount of time, money, and effort it will take.

Broaden your vision: Technology flowers on the frontier

According to a 1999 story by Leigh Buchanan in *Inc. Technology* magazine and the founders' own rendition on their Web site (www.prairiefrontier.com), at least one little company has been able to grow from a grassroots operation into a technological wonder. Deep in the heart of Minnesota sits an Internet company that specializes in native wildflowers and prairie grasses. The company is the result of a devastating tornado that destroyed the woods on Deb Edlhuber's family farm. Sometimes in the midst of devastation, there are signs of hope. With sun now hitting the previously dark forest floor, a carpet of wildflowers of every type suddenly emerged and covered all of the obliterated landscape. Edlhuber and her husband, amazed by the miracle of new life, began photographing every species of wildflower they could find. Wanting to preserve this natural beauty and share it with others, the Edlhubers also began propagating seeds. In 1995 they started supplying seeds to garden centers.

Buchanan reports that Deb Edlhuber's exuberance over this new hobby led her to begin a quest for more information about wildflowers and prairie grasses. She bought her first PC in 1996, connected through AOL to the Internet, and she was off and running. Before long, she had acquired a wealth of information. She felt compelled to share not only her wildflower seeds but also all the knowledge she had gained from studying them with other enthusiasts. Edlhuber had a vision of becoming the center of the universe for everything related to wildflowers. What started as a part-time occupation was quickly becoming a full-time business. But how would she get from her small town in Minnesota to the world?

In 1997, with no training other than what she had learned on the Internet, and with nothing more than a scanner and some programming she had found online, Deb Edlhuber built Prairie Frontier. But almost as soon as her company went on the Internet, things snowballed. Here's a chronology of what happened, according to Buchanan:

✔ She signed up with LinkExchange, a tool for small companies wanting to swap banner ads so that she could reach more people more quickly.

✔ She posted photographs of her catalog of wildflowers and prairie grasses to attract customers to the site.

✔ She added games, wildflower-themed puzzles, and a slide show depicting how to create your own prairie.

✔ She started discussion forums, which became enormously popular with wildflower enthusiasts.

✔ She then added a shopping cart to streamline the purchasing process.

✔ To diversify, she added a series of free musical greeting cards that visitors can send by e-mail. This was a form of electronic advertising.

✔ She acquired multiple domain names such as `Wildflowerseeds.com` and `Gardencountry.com`, which she intends to turn into an auction site.

✔ The future? She's trying to figure out how to sell merchandise besides her seeds.

Edlhuber now has thousands of visitors to her site on a regular basis. She had a big vision that she is well on her way to achieving. She planned a series of little technology steps, each one building on the previous one, and she kept her costs minimal. Her site is not the most professional one you can find on the Web, but her customers tell her that they like it just the way it is. After all, these are people who love prairies and wildflowers!

You, too, should have a far-reaching vision for your company — the bigger the better. After all, with technology being what it is, the sky's the limit. So now that you've got your big vision, come back to earth for a minute and figure out how big of a gap you're facing. Start by thinking about where you are right now.

Begin with your goals

Chapter 2 explains the importance of having a mission, goals, strategies, and tactics. After you decide on a mission, you can use it to find a way to get from here to there. Remind yourself right now of your vision — where you see your business in, say, five to ten years. Write that here:

My Vision:

_____

_____

_____

Now write your mission for the coming year — that big, audacious goal that you want your company to achieve.

My Mission:

_____

_____

_____

What is it going to take in terms of technology to help you achieve that mission? If you need help figuring this out, Chapters 4 and 5 cover this topic.

My Technology Needs:

_____

_____

_____

_____

_____

_____

_____

_____

_____

_____

_____

_____

Now you're ready for the hard work: Start by rating your current technology.

Rate your current technology

You may think that rating your current technology is a waste of time because what little of it there is probably isn't worth anything. But don't forget Deb Edlhuber, the wildflower guru, who started with a simple computer, a scanner, and an Internet connection and ended with a blooming Internet company. You don't need much to form a foundation, and additional technology can be added as you need it.

Table 6-1 provides an example of one company's report card on its technology architecture. We define the specific technology architecture in Chapters 4 and 5. As with your school report card, A means up and working well. Anything below a C means trouble. F means *don't have.*

Table 6-1		Technology Report Card	
Client/Server	F	Disaster recovery	F
Connectivity	F	Security	B
Integration	D	Maintenance	C
Data integrity	C	Real time	D
Relational	D	Bar coding	F

You can't start much lower than this company. Obviously, it's a long way from being where it wants to be, so the technology gap is large. In terms of hardware, it needs to add a client/server network, Internet connectivity, integrating systems, relational databases, a disaster recovery strategy, and the ability to do things in real time. Where is your company now relative to where you need it to be?

Don't worry if you don't know what client/server networks, Internet connectivity, integrating systems, and relational databases are now. They're defined in Appendix B and on your CD in the Tech Lingo Guide, and we talk about them later in the book.

You've defined your technology gap. Now, you need to take a look at your operational gap.

Grade your operations

Chapters 4 and 5 help you examine how your organization works and how technology can improve those operations. Now you need to grade each process that you identified in your information flow assessment against a benchmark of where you think you should be. Table 6-2 presents a portion of one company's operations report card.

Table 6-2	Operations Report Card
Strengths	*Weaknesses*
Our current systems are reliable and enable us to run the business quite well.	We can collect a lot of data, but we don't have effective methods for analysis.
Our data entry processes seem to be accurate.	Our systems are not user-friendly, so employees need a lot of training and resist learning the systems.
We can gather a lot of sales information and store it.	We can't always get the exact measures we want from the current system without having to do a lot of extra manual work.
	We can't easily track orders from generation through delivery.
	We don't have the ability to communicate on a worldwide basis or to access company files from remote locations.

One thing we can say about the current system of this company is the advantage of familiarity — they understand their current system (you can see that from the number of weaknesses they list). Many times, companies hang onto outdated or clunky systems just because they're comfortable and familiar. Jumping into something new is always a challenge, and most small business owners have enough challenges in their day-to-day operations. Still, our example company could have gone on for pages about the weaknesses in its current system.

From the abbreviated report card in Table 6-2, we believe that the current system might be meeting about one-third of the company's needs, whereas a more effectively designed system should meet nearly all of a company's needs.

You can find an interactive version of the operations report card for your company on the CD in the Tech Evaluation Package.

Weighing Your Options

Believe it or not, you really can discover options for systems and applications that could satisfy all, or nearly all, of your business needs. We discuss these systems in the next section. But first, now that you know the size of your technology/operational gap, you need to consider four fundamental alternatives to addressing that gap:

 ✔ Sticking with what you have

 ✔ Upgrading

 ✔ Buying a new system from scratch

 ✔ Using someone else's technology

We discuss these strategies in detail in the sections that follow.

The old bubblegum strategy: Sticking with what you have

If you determine that you need new technology to reach your company's goals, why would you decide to stick with what you have? Every business decision involves costs and benefits associated with those costs. You need to determine whether the benefits justify the costs. For example, in Table 6-2, the company's current system is reliable and basically does what the workers need it to do to run their business. However, they apparently also need to do some analyses that their current system can't support. Under what scenario should they decide to keep the current system at the expense of not being able to easily do their analyses? Well, if those analyses are done infrequently and the cost of a new system or upgrade is substantial, the company may conclude that continuing to do things the old way may be the best solution, at least for a short period of time.

The alternative of sticking with what you have is probably the least attractive for most businesses because it does not recognize that in the long run, your growing business needs to take advantage of the power and versatility of new applications. Remember, these new applications will probably satisfy 98 percent of your needs and over the long term will save you time and money. Also, the more time that goes by without implementing new technologies, the further back you slide on the ever steeper learning curve. Attempting to catch up later will only become more difficult.

The never-ending ladder strategy: Upgrading

Upgrading involves purchasing new hardware components and new releases of software applications to bring your current system up-to-date. Hardware upgrades usually involve such things as a faster processor, additional RAM, a faster modem, a bigger hard drive, and sometimes even a new motherboard. You're probably already familiar with software upgrades.

For most businesses, however, upgrading constantly is not necessary. Often, the new releases add bells and whistles that you may never use. In some cases, though, the upgrade is worth it, particularly when the software manufacturer has corrected problems in previous versions and is not offering a patch that you can download for free from the Internet. It is also worth it when an operating system upgrade means better functionality and a more stable system, as was the case in the move from Windows 3.1 to Windows 95. (The upgrade from Windows 95 to 98 was less dramatic and on existing systems often caused problems that never before existed. In that case, it was better to wait until you needed to purchase a new workstation that had Windows 98 preloaded instead of upgrading a stable Windows 95 machine and taking the risk.)

Keep in mind that at some point you might be forced to upgrade as new technologies replace old. New operating systems and new revisions of software applications are built both for present and future hardware, so it's possible that the next software upgrade you want or need will require that you purchase new hardware that is faster and more capable of handling the requirements of the software. So it might be beneficial to consider an upgrade strategy.

The most important tip we can give you about upgrading software is to watch for free, downloadable upgrades and patches to fix bugs in the software you have. All software companies have Web sites with areas (usually called *support*) that are devoted to these issues. Also, do some homework before you decide to upgrade. The popular computer-related magazines run lots of articles evaluating upgrades and suggesting to business owners whether they should upgrade, how the upgrade should be done, and how to check that you did a good job on the upgrade.

The scorched earth strategy: Doing something entirely new

Perhaps you've been using the first system you bought several years ago for your business. We've actually seen 486 machines with Windows 3.1 or lower still being used as the workhorses in some small businesses. When you're that far behind the technology curve, upgrading will be costly, maybe impossible, and certainly a waste of money. Generally, businesses stick with outdated technology for four reasons:

- ✔ **Money:** They can't afford to upgrade or replace.
- ✔ **Habit:** They like what they have and don't want to reinvent the wheel.
- ✔ **Custom design:** They have industry-specific software that is too expensive to upgrade to a newer operating system.
- ✔ **Waste not, want not:** They feel that every computer they have is an asset and they need to use it somehow.

If you fall into this description, it's time to bring your business into the new millennium, technologically speaking. Yes, replacing your existing system is the costliest alternative of the four, in both time and money, but you're making an investment in technology for the future of your business. Newer systems can be more easily upgraded, and the latest won't need upgrading for a while. If you make this choice, you can put your company on par with the most successful businesses in your industry — the ones that have already discovered technology as a competitive advantage they can't afford *not* to have.

The borrowed cup of sugar strategy: Using other people's technology

Who said you have to put out money to have access to technology that your business can't afford but needs? For basic business applications, most small businesses can find a way to purchase what they need. But some businesses require more expensive technology that's difficult and costly to maintain. Examples include

- CAD/CAM (computer-assisted design and manufacturing technology)
- EDI (electronic data interchange, a way for companies to talk with each other and do their ordering and purchasing)
- High-speed T-1 Internet connections (used to transfer more information more quickly to and from the Internet)

All these technologies are now the norm in mid-sized companies. To deal with or compete against these companies, smaller companies need the same capabilities. Fortunately, a win/win solution has emerged. Many larger companies now see an advantage in providing their technology to smaller companies at much-reduced rates in exchange for entry into new niche markets and an increased customer base.

Some entrepreneurs have found very creative ways to access technology that they need, but can't afford, by forging partnerships with larger companies. Pabulum (www.pabulum.com/vre.htm) is an Internet-based virtual real-estate development company and advertising agency that develops blocks of cyberspace in the same way a brick-and-mortar strip mall gets developed. In 1997, when Jeremy Davey started his business, he knew he would need a large number of computers with state-of-the-art scanners and design software. But more importantly, he would need a high-speed, full-time connection to the Internet, namely a T-1 line. The problem was that he had little money.

He found the building of his dreams in San Francisco. To get the master lease for the 20,000-square-foot building — so that he could rent out the space for enough to pay his company's space — he told the owner that he would get the entire building connected to a T-1 line, which would mean that the landlord could charge premium rents. In San Francisco, these types of buildings are in high demand. This began a series of deals with a wireless communications company building a network in San Francisco that needed sites for its transmitters. The story is an elaborate journey through the maze of wheeling and dealing with much larger companies when you essentially have nothing to deal with. (You can read this interesting story on Pabulum's Web site, which will link you to a 1998 *Inc. Technology* magazine article about the company).

Businesses like Davey's that partner for access to technology (and figure some things out the hard way), provide great tips:

- Know exactly what you want out of a technology partnership before you weave a tangled web.

- Make sure that your partners are financially solvent and have the technology you need.

- Show your potential partner how the partnership can benefit his or her business as much as yours.

- Allow enough time for negotiations if you're going after partnerships with larger companies. They tend to take more negotiation time than partnerships with small companies or individuals.

Deciding Which Option Is Best

The best way to choose among the four basic options is to compare each across a variety of variables. In Table 6-3, we have put the most important variables into a matrix so that you can do your comparison right here. Look at each variable and decide which alternative best fits your company's situation, then put a check in the appropriate column. There are no right or wrong answers. Every business has unique needs. Be honest in your evaluation so that you get the best solution.

Table 6-3	Considering Your Options			
Variable	*Keep the Status Quo*	*Upgrade the System*	*Go with a New System*	*Find a Partner*
Costs of hardware and servers: Do you require more than one server? Do you need a development server? Do you need additional peripherals for things like bar coding, archiving, and backup?	❏	❏	❏	❏

Variable	Keep the Status Quo	Upgrade the System	Go with a New System	Find a Partner
Software: Do you have unique software requirements? Do you need licenses for upgrade software that enables new hardware?	❑	❑	❑	❑
Consulting or contracting: Do you need consultants for conversion programming, new applications, networks, business processes, or project management?	❑	❑	❑	❑
Training: Do you require additional technical training?	❑	❑	❑	❑
Travel: Will you need to travel to deal with remote users?	❑	❑	❑	❑
Supporting Software Packages: Do you need additional software packages for utilities and other support areas?	❑	❑	❑	❑
Network and PC Costs: Which hardware upgrades are necessary? Figure $25,000 per user for a project that includes software, hardware, consulting, and network.	❑	❑	❑	❑
Time: How much time will it take to install and train on the new system? What is the latest you can begin? Don't underestimate here, because it always takes longer than you think.	❑	❑	❑	❑

(continued)

Table 6-3 *(continued)*

Variable	Keep the Status Quo	Upgrade the System	Go with a New System	Find a Partner
User Resources: How many human resources are necessary? Will these people be part-time or full-time? (Remember, you will need some full-time people.)	❑	❑	❑	❑
Benchmark Information: Why are your estimates correct? Are there examples from other companies in your industry?	❑	❑	❑	❑
Advantages and disadvantages of this option.	❑	❑	❑	❑

Considering Return on Investment: Does It Really Matter?

Technology companies and small businesses alike are concerned with what they're getting for their investments. *Return on investment* (ROI) is simply a way to look at the cost versus the benefit of any investment in technology. Some companies use a net present value of future earnings, while others use an internal rate of return. Which you choose really doesn't matter. What's important is to understand that you're getting a positive return for your investment in technology. Whether it be in higher revenues or lowered costs, the return should be greater than the value of your investment.

In general, ROI is based on several factors:

✔ **The impact on sales:** Usually, your investment in newer technology affects sales because your connections with customers become more effective. All the aspects of customers' transactions with the company are now more accurate, and the response time is quicker for things like orders, shipping, credit card processing, and bar coding. Such efficiency makes customers happier.

✔ **Materials savings:** A new system that includes remote connectivity usually produces reduced purchase costs because suppliers now have access to forecasts and specs from outside the office. Productivity often goes up because you have more streamlined access to suppliers.

✔ **Improvements in manufacturing resources:** The new system can produce more efficiently because you can do more without adding more resources, especially costly labor.

✔ **Improvement in the management of assets:** The new system can improve tracking of inventory returns and diminish the need to purchase new assets.

✔ **Improvement in ability to track quality:** You can track consistency of quality in products and services and their compliance with government regulations much more easily.

Only you can determine what is the important ROI for your company. After all, you are the one who ultimately has to determine whether this investment will have a significantly positive impact on the company, enough to make its undertaking worthwhile.

Getting Everyone on Board

Ultimately, you have to convince everyone in the company that this new technology is going to make a significant difference in the company's performance. You need everyone's cooperation in the implementation of your technology strategy because it will affect the entire organization. But, naturally, that cooperation is not always easy to accomplish.

In general, we find that employees resist change. In many smaller businesses, you may be dealing with a generation of workers who were not raised on computers. So it's important that you recognize their deep-seated fear of the unknown and find ways to introduce technology in a friendly environment with no pressure and no stress. You can do so by providing several things to the people you have to convince:

✔ Present your findings about your current technology status versus where you think the company should be in terms of information technology.

✔ Explain the basis on which you believe you need to make this technology investment. Will the current systems not be able to handle the demands of your company's growth? Do you really want to continue to put money into old systems — is that a good use of your resources? What are your competitors doing?

✔ Demonstrate the scope of the technology effort and the impact on the business.

✔ Describe timing and effort required to develop the new system, and compare to other goals currently important to the business and its employees.

Ultimately, you need to point out how this new technology investment can help the company achieve its business goals. This is, after all, the most important outcome.

Chapter 7

Planning for the Cost of Technology

· ·

· ·

*Y*ou have a choice: You can constantly buy the latest and greatest technology, install it in your business, and hope that it solves all your problems. Or you can plan for technology, acquire exactly what you need when you need it, and be certain it will solve your business problems affordably. Now, which scenario do you choose?

In this book, we come down on the side of planning — not obsessive, drawn-out planning that never gets finished, but clear, concise, and targeted plans that make sense for your business. In this chapter, you find out how to plan for the cost of technology so that you don't get any unwelcome surprises.

You Mean We Have to Pay for It?

Cash-strapped smaller businesses are always looking for ways to get the equipment they need on relatively limited resources. If your business fits this profile, you're not alone. When you calculate that a new computer has about a three-year life span before it ends up in your technology museum (Confession: One of your authors still has the original Commodore Vic20 in a closet somewhere and the other still has an Atari 1200xl), you realize that you're faced with purchasing new equipment and figuring out how to get rid of the old stuff every 36 months.

Now, the reality is that some businesses use their computers primarily for word-processing tasks, so they may have a bit more life in them than the standard three years.

If you're using your technology to gain a competitive advantage in your market, replacing it regularly is going to become a part of your business life, whether you like it or not. You should be aware that there are also personnel costs associated with technology. Whether you have a technical consultant in-house or you outsource your needs to a technology consulting firm, you're going to be paying for support.

Unfortunately, too many small businesses pour thousands of dollars into computer technology and information systems that don't even begin to solve their business problems or enable them to achieve their business goals. Businesses leaders make this mistake for several reasons:

- They rely too heavily on people whose only goal is to sell them products and services.
- They don't take the time to learn about what technology other businesses in their industry are using.
- They think that technology has to cost a lot of money to be up-to-date and useful.

In this section, we offer some alternatives to shelling out big chunks of cash: leasing, outsourcing to the Net, and working with partners.

Pete's wicked LAN

In a 1995 article in *Inc.* magazine, "LAN of Opportunity," Brian McWilliams tells how an investment in computer technology helped one small company get big. In 1990, Pete's Brewing Co. of Palo Alto, California, was a three-person operation that lived off credit cards (it was founded in 1986 by home brewer Pete Slosberg). But it did have a computer network — of sorts. Actually, the network was a PC mounted on a rolling cart, and it was passed among the three entrepreneurs as needed. Typically, the person who handled orders for Pete's Wicked Ale got it first, and then it was rolled down to the next person — a precursor to the "sneakernet," so common in smaller businesses today.

But by 1992, Pete's Brewing was beginning an exponential growth path, and the computer-on-the-cart just couldn't hack it anymore. Slosberg hired a tech consultant who asked how fast the

business was projected to grow (fortunately, he found one who was interested first and foremost in understanding the business). The consultant learned that for this virtual brewing company (at that time, it brewed under contract in St. Paul, Minnesota), the ability to manage information and exponential growth was critical. That consultant ultimately saved the company thousands of dollars because he saw that what the company needed was a network that could be expanded each year as company growth more than doubled.

McWilliams concludes that between 1992 and 1995, Pete's Brewing spent more than $400,000 on technology, but the return for its investment was a company that had the fastest growth in its market segment, with over $33 million in sales. The company is among the top five craft brewers today.

Leasing the latest

"What? Throw money away on rent?" you say. Perhaps for you, leasing invokes images of polyester-clad car salesmen, or maybe you remember the old leases in which you could get stuck for a big payment at the end. Until fairly recently, most businesses owned their physical assets and tools.

Well, those days are over. Does it surprise you to know that by 2002, one out of every four personal computers will probably be leased? That's what market research firms like IDC/Link and the Gartner Group are projecting. This increasingly popular financing strategy has taken hold with large and small businesses alike for several reasons:

- ✔ Leasing provides flexibility. You can change or modify computer systems quickly as you grow your business.
- ✔ You avoid having to come up with a large sum of money every 36 months to replace old equipment.
- ✔ You keep your cash to use for growth.
- ✔ You can deduct the cost of a lease to reduce your taxable income.
- ✔ When it's time to get rid of an old computer, you simply ship it back to the manufacturer or lessor.

Maybe you need to revisit the idea of a lease and take a closer look.

Choosing the best leasing deal

Everyone has gotten into the leasing business, from retail outlets like Gateway PCs to manufacturers like Dell and all those independent leasing companies. Here are some examples of the kinds of leasing deals you find in the market today:

- ✔ **The three-year market option:** In this plan, you lease the computer for three years, and then you have the option to buy it at the end of the lease for its market value at that time.
- ✔ **The 10 percent option:** With this variation on a standard lease, your option-to-buy price is set at 10 percent of the original retail value. That way, you know exactly what it will cost you to purchase the computer at the end of the lease.
- ✔ **Everything but the kitchen sink:** Today, small companies can enjoy the benefits that only the biggest companies could take advantage of previously. For example, IBM Credit provides a 36-month lease that includes such things as installation, six months of technical support, and the option to upgrade after two years — all for a fixed fee. You can even add to your options things like system monitoring and maintenance for a fixed price. Fixed pricing is important in a world where the costs of maintaining a system can be as much as one-third of the original price of the machine.

If you run the numbers on a lease, you will quickly see that you may spend more than the retail price. But that's not the final number because the IRS provides larger tax breaks for leasing by allowing you to deduct the fees every year. If you buy the computer instead, you have to depreciate it according to a much stricter formula. And when you consider that many businesses have to finance the purchase of their computer equipment with a loan on which they pay interest, the difference between leasing and buying suddenly becomes a moot point.

And now the downside

If we made it sound as if leasing is absolutely the way to go, hold on. You have some negatives to consider as well:

- **The rising sticker price:** Watch out for lessors who raise the sticker price and lower the future value (called the *residual*). This practice can increase your monthly payments.

  If you know for certain that you're not going to buy at the end of the lease, then what you want is the honest sticker price and the highest residual you can get. That means your monthly payments will be lower, and you'll pay less for the lease over its term.

- **The cost of financing:** Find out the annualized cost of the lease and compare it to what a loan to purchase would cost. The general rule is that if your lease rate is less than 1 percent higher than the borrowing rate, leasing is a better way to go from a financing perspective.

- **Breaking the lease:** Never go into a lease thinking that you can always get out early. Think of leasing companies like the Godfather. You try to break the lease; they'll give you a deal you can't refuse. You will have to pay the remaining lease installments, and they will demand a huge financial penalty. The only way around this with some lessors is to agree to upgrade. Remember, they're in this to make money off you in whatever way they can.

The bottom line is, if your company doesn't have to have state-of-the-art technology all the time, purchasing is probably better. If it does need the latest equipment to function optimally, take a careful look at leasing. Also consider using a hybrid approach: Lease cutting-edge technology for those in the company who need it, and purchase the rest.

Outsourcing to the Net

Entrepreneurs have long used outsourcing as a way to gain capabilities that they don't have in-house. They essentially purchase or trade capabilities with a company that specializes in what they need. With the advent of the Internet, outsourcing has become big business.

One of the biggest growth areas on the Internet is business-to-business trans-actions and support. Internet companies are sprouting up everywhere to offer specialized services, products, and support to small and mid-sized com-panies that want to focus on what they do best or that don't have the tech-nology resources to do some of the things they need. Because these Net applications and their associated information are accessible through a Web browser, all your company needs is computers that are capable of connecting to the Internet and you can use these outsourced functions as easily as if they were running on your own server. Yet you don't have the cost and main-tenance of setting up the server technology to run the applications. No more concerns about compatibility and software upgrades. Everything's available with the click of a mouse button.

These outsourcing sites are doing everything for business, from travel arrangements to data storage and debt collection. But the two areas that have received the most attention are human resources management and informa-tion technology. Today, your business can put together a virtual HR depart-ment that rivals anything you could do in-house — if you could even afford to do it — and you don't have to hire any more employees to make it happen.

Imagine the plight of one telecom company, which began as a business in 1997 and by 1999 had 750 employees and more than $4 million in sales. Not only that, but it was adding 100 people a month to sales offices located around the country. Although having a human resources person in each office was physically impossible — not to mention cost-prohibitive — all new employees needed access to information about all the benefit programs that the company provided.

Help arrived in the form of a young Internet company that develops digital versions of a company's HR functions and runs them on its Web site. For one-quarter of the cost of a dedicated benefits administrator, the rapidly growing telecom company can service 300 employees a month at the Web site. Employees can do everything from calculating the impact of a health plan on their paycheck to watching a multimedia slide show explaining the benefits available to them.

You can achieve similar efficiency in information technology. Instead of spending thousands of dollars on data archiving and storage space in your office, you can outsource this capability to a "server farm" or data ware-house, just as you do when you rent a storage facility to store all that old office furniture you just know you're going to use sometime in the future.

The Net can even help your company have an intranet — an in-house version of a Web site on the Internet. One example of such a company is HotOffice (www. hotoffice.com/home), which, through a subscription service, can give your company a private Intranet where your employees can log onto the company's site and find their personal desktops with all the familiar icons for e-mail, calendars, directories, and so forth. There's even a Document Center, where your company's files reside and a Communication Center for bulletin-board discussions and virtual meetings. Companies like HotOffice are providing smaller businesses with technology infrastructure they can't otherwise afford.

Outsourcing to the Net has worked for many companies because they are willing to look at new alternatives. Still, Net outsourcing is a very new area of Internet technology, so any potential buyer should beware and do some homework before leaping into this kind of partnership.

Here are some issues to look out for:

✔ **Investigate any company thoroughly.** Ask to speak with some of its customers so that you have a more objective opinion about what to expect and what not to expect. Also speak to other companies in the industry — competitors, vendors — to get their opinions about the company.

✔ **Inquire about the site's ability to handle traffic.** In any contract you create with an Internet company to outsource services, be sure that the hardware will be maintained. Your main concerns should be that your site is fast and accessible to those surfing the Internet. Here are some things to ask your host about:

   • **Redundant connections:** If a company is going to host your Web site, it obviously has a connection to the Internet. A "redundant" connection is a second, or backup, connection in case something goes wrong with the first. Having a redundant connection lowers your risk tremendously of having the site go down and not be available.

   • **UPS devices:** Uninterruptable Power Supplies are rechargeable batteries that connect to your computer. If the power goes out, the UPS device will keep your computers running until the power comes back on. This capability reduces potential problems from computers being shut down improperly and causing damage that could take time and money to fix.

   • **Scheduled maintenance:** We're not suggesting that you will understand or want to know all the technical things that will be done to the server on which your site is being hosted. However, it is important to know that the tech consultant has a plan for how to keep everything running in good order. For example, if the tech consultant needs to do work on the server that is hosting your site, make sure that your site is temporarily moved to another server so it remains up and running.

✔ **Find out whether the company provides protection from hackers.** With regard to security, the level required depends on how sensitive your information is. For most information, a password is sufficient; but for highly sensitive information, you need more secure layers of encryption. Interestingly, in our experience people tend to hold Internet companies to a higher standard of security than they have for their actual paper documents in their own offices.

✔ **Don't expect to run your entire information systems operation off the Internet.** The technology is not quite there yet; the Internet will have to reach new speeds and higher levels of reliability before it can go that far. Companies are developing new ways to remove the traditional headaches that small businesses owners have had implementing technology solutions. Most of these companies have a set of core strengths and a few special things they do to try to differentiate themselves from others. The following sites will help you review hosting service companies that might suit your needs:

- www.webhosters.com
- www.tophosts.com
- www.hostsearch.com

You can also type "hosting services" in any search engine. If you don't search often on the Internet, here are a few suggestions for search engines:

- www.excite.com
- www.yahoo.com
- www.altavista.com

Outsourcing to another company

If you want to grow your business without adding resources or turning to the Internet, consider outsourcing to companies that have what you need, particularly if those resources involve *technology-intensive functions,* a fancy term for expensive hardware and software.

The reason that these outsourcing partnerships work so well is that they're a win/win proposition for companies big and small. A large company gets to leverage its technology to a variety of markets, while a smaller company gets the benefit of the technology without making an enormous capital investment.

If your company has any of the following needs, it may be a candidate for out-sourcing to another company:

- ✔ You have technology needs that go way beyond your ability to invest in them.

- ✔ You need to take advantage of economies of scale (as volume goes up, costs come down) quickly to survive in the market.

- ✔ You need to drive down costs, so outsourcing expensive functions is important. Every industry has companies that regularly handle the special needs of companies that outsource. Talking to other business owners in your industry and contacting trade associations can help you find reputable companies to use.

How outsourcing can work

One small company with a big vision partnered with a technologically savvy company to make its dream come true. The Smith brothers had seen enough of crime; in fact, they had lost two close friends to a random shooting. So they decided to go into the self-defense business and look for an alternative to pepper spray and mace. Working with the inventor of the taser device, they came up with the air taser, which transmits an electronic pulse that zaps the nervous system and incapacitates the target for several minutes.

To keep this weapon out of the hands of criminals, the Smiths needed a computerized registration system that would track every store and every customer who purchased one. Of course, tying the registration system into their warehouse and shipping system would be nice, too.

To get some advice on how to go about creating all this, the Smiths visited a local direct sales and marketing company, Insight, which specialized in micro-computer products and services. That's when they learned how complex their plan really was. They would have to

- ✔ Track code numbers for every part, as well as the contents of every kit they shipped.

- ✔ Register the serial numbers and bar codes of every item shipped.

Insight estimated that this tracking technology plus warehouse space, fork-lifts, and labor would run about $200,000 in the first year and $100,000 a year thereafter. Of course, none of this included management or maintenance.

Unwilling and unable to spend so much money, the brothers designed a part-nership deal in which Insight would handle their fulfillment functions (packing and shipping) in exchange for a percentage of each sale. So, in the end, the only technology the Smith brothers had to buy was three networked Pentium PCs, which had remote connection to Insight's computers. They then had read-only access to the database of registrations and tracking information maintained by Insight.

Handing this technology function over to an experienced partner gave the new Air Taser company the ability to focus all of its energy and resources on sales and products. They have had a successful relationship for several years now and have no plans to bring the fulfillment function in-house. The company is now known as TASER International (www.airtaser.com), with facilities in the United States and Mexico and sales in more than 60 countries around the world. The company has firmly established itself as the leading manufacturer of high-quality, nonlethal protection systems.

What you need to do to have a successful partnership

A successful partnership with a vendor to whom you are outsourcing some of your needs doesn't happen by accident. It takes work. Here are some steps you can take to make sure that your partnership is successful:

- ✔ **Have a written contract that spells out the essentials.** A contract can save you many headaches down the road if things don't go as planned.

- ✔ **With your partner, find a simple pricing strategy that can handle changes over time.** Be sure to include criteria such as reducing the price by so much when the volume reaches a certain level.

- ✔ **Carefully define what is being provided and by whom.** If a problem arises and someone has to pay for it, who is that someone?

- ✔ **Agree on quality and performance standards.**

- ✔ **Have one person in each organization be the key contact or liaison for the company.** This system makes communication much easier.

- ✔ **Always spell out in advance a way to end the relationship.** Just like a prenuptial agreement, such a clause details who gets what and who is responsible for what if the partnership fails.

Shall We Dance? Picking Your Vendor Partners

After you have agreement from everyone in your company that the time has come to invest in new technology, the real work begins. If you hire a technology consultant, you'll get lots of help on types of hardware and software to consider and also the consultant's opinions on the best vendors. (We talk about developing your relationship with a technology consultant in Chapter 15.) If you choose your tech consultant well, then your worries may be over, but you may still want to read this chapter so that you know when you've found a great consultant.

For now, assume that you're ready to choose the vendors and suppliers of your outsourced functions, companies whom you hope will help you with your technology transformation. (To simplify things, we'll refer to both vendors and other suppliers of functions and services as "vendors.") You begin by sending out requests for quotes (RFQs) to a variety of reputable vendors in your area.

Preparing Requests for Quotes (RFQs)

A Request for quote (RFQ) is sometimes called a Request for proposal (RFP) or a Request for information (RFI). Whatever your name of choice, the RFQ is really a device that helps you choose a vendor. It's a way of screening vendors to narrow the field because you want to interview only three or four at the most.

In general, the RFQ gives the vendor information about your company and what your requirements are.

You can find a sample template that you can use to build your own RFQ on the CD that comes with this book.

The following is a listing of the major components of an RFQ:

- ✔ General guidelines for how the vendor should respond to the RFQ
- ✔ General information about the company, including a description, the status of its information systems environment, and its business goals
- ✔ The computing architecture requirements for your business
- ✔ Any other information that would be important for the vendor to know
- ✔ A nondisclosure agreement to ensure that information provided is accurate and will be kept confidential
- ✔ A questionnaire for the vendor, designed to find out what you need to know about the vendor's company
- ✔ A request for cost estimates on the various components of your proposed computing architecture

In preparing the RFQ, remember that you don't want to overwhelm the vendor with pages and pages of requests for information. Make sure that you are as clear and concise as possible. This first round is a way to narrow the search. The vendors know that's what you're doing. They don't want to devote hours of time to an RFQ when they haven't yet made the first cut.

Also recognize that vendors will resist giving you estimates at this point; and where they do give them, they will tend to 'lowball the estimate to give themselves a better chance to get the bid. (That approach, of course, assumes that you're going to settle on the lowest bid — which we hope you don't!)

Let vendors know that you want an honest estimate of what they can offer and how much they expect the cost of the system to grow. This kind of information can help you sell the project to everyone on your end and demonstrates that you are not focused only on cost.

After you receive all the vendors' responses, you can compare them on several levels.

Narrowing the field

Your first task is to narrow down the field of vendors to about three, whom you then ask for a formal presentation detailing why you should choose that company to handle your business's technology transformation. This is the hard part because you may never have met any of these people; you're just going on the strength of the vendor's response to the RFQ (and hopefully some recommendations from business colleagues).

One of the easiest ways to evaluate the vendor responses is to set up a table that allows you to compare all the vendors across the different questions that you asked in your RFQ vendor questionnaire. Table 7-1 is a portion of one such matrix, located on the CD just to give you an idea of how you could do this. You can, of course, add any additional subheads you might need for your business.

Table 7-1	Vendor Evaluation Matrix		
Criteria	*Vendor 1*	*Vendor 2*	*Vendor 3*
Customers			
How many customer jobs are currently in production?			
How many are on maintenance?			
Training			
Offers training in-house			
Uses outside vendor			

(continued)

Table 7-1 *(continued)*

Criteria	Vendor 1	Vendor 2	Vendor 3
Costs			
Costs			
Software			
Hardware			
Installation			
Maintenance and Support			
24-hour availability			
Cost — support			
Cost — annual maintenance			

You can do a more elaborate comparison by weighing the various criteria according to how important they are to your business and its goals. For example, what is your number one priority from a vendor? Is it maintenance and support? Cost? Training? Using the four major categories in Table 7-1, you can weight the factors.

Here's a step-by-step plan for using rankings and weights to find out which is the best vendor for your purposes:

1. **Rank the criteria according to which are the most important to your company.**

   Using the preceding example and just the major headings for simplicity's sake (you would also rank the subheadings when you do it), you may end up with something like this:

   • Maintenance and support

   • Costs

   • Training

   • Number and type of customers

2. **Weigh the criteria based on this ranking.**

   Use numbers from 8 to 10, with 10 being the most important. These weights will be your multipliers. Here's how you might rank the four categories in the example:

- Maintenance and support   10
- Costs   10
- Training   9
- Number and type of customers   8

3. Rate each vendor against the criteria on a scale of 1 to 5.

Assume that a 5 means the vendor is superior, a 3 means average, and a 1 signals a weak vendor.

4. To calculate the results, multiply the criteria weight times the vendor weight for each criteria.

Then total the scores across all the vendors and voilà — you have just figured out which vendors are the best! Table 7-2 shows how the sample matrix might look when completed.

Table 7-2		Rating Vendors		
Criteria	*Weight*	*Vendor 1*	*Vendor 2*	*Vendor 3*
Maintenance and support	10 ×	5 = 50	3 = 30	2 = 20
Costs	10 ×	3 = 30	1 = 10	5 = 50
Training	9 ×	5 = 45	5 = 45	3 = 27
Size of company	8 ×	5 = 40	3 = 24	1 = 8
Total Score		**165**	**109**	**105**

From the results in this example, it appears that Vendor 1 is the best. If you were rating ten vendors, it would be easy to shrink that number to three or four by using this technique. Other potential categories that can be added to this table are

- **Growth potential:** Is the company able to provide the services that might be needed in the future to help grow the company?

- **Scope of work:** What is the range of services the company provides?

- **Guarantees:** What guarantees does the company provide on its work?

- **On-call technicians:** If there is a problem, how easy will it be to get someone out to your site?

- **Customer testimonials:** Will the company provide customer references?

The show must go on

After you decide which vendors you may want to work with, invite the final three or four to give a presentation so that you can determine whether what they claim on their RFQ responses matches what they say in their presentations.

Make sure that you prepare for the interview presentations by doing the following:

- ✔ Consider a plan for what you want to see and how you want to see it. Make sure that the vendor focuses on those things that are relevant to your business. Remember, you are test-driving an application that you may ultimately choose to use in your business; to say that this is an important decision is quite an understatement.

- ✔ Compile information from your business that you would like to see used in the vendor demonstration.

- ✔ Make sure to identify your key requirements for your business no matter which software application you ultimately choose.

- ✔ Plan in advance for a way to measure each vendor's effectiveness. If you don't have objective criteria in place prior to the interview, you may be comparing apples to oranges.

- ✔ Plan an agenda so that you control the meeting with the vendor, not the other way around. It's a good idea to get your agenda to the vendors in advance so that they have the opportunity to come prepared to meet your needs.

- ✔ Allow the vendors to visit your company prior to the actual demonstration to learn more about your business processes and environment. Doing so is only fair if you want them to present a realistic solution to your challenges.

And the winner is . . .

After you've seen the presentations of the vendors you're considering, compile a list of strengths and weaknesses for each vendor. You can also decide on the best software for your company by identifying the applications that the vendors recommended the most often. In addition, you can compare more detailed cost estimates based on what the vendors said. We're not going to give you any actual costs here because they change all the time, and they're also a function of what you're trying to accomplish, how elaborate your system needs are, and which secondary costs (upgrades, maintenance, and so on) apply to your system.

Here are some of the items for which you want to know costs:

- ✔ Hardware: servers, workstations, desktops, network components, and so on

- ✔ Operating system software and tools

- ✔ Business application software, including database software and any custom interfaces tailored for you

- ✔ Additional "bolt-on" software packages or customized software to ensure that all of your business's operations are fully covered

- ✔ Training, training, training, and more training

- ✔ Consulting

- ✔ Network maintenance

- ✔ Upgrades (hardware and software: how often)

- ✔ Travel

If you complete this process, you'll feel much more confident about the choice you finally make. We're also sure that you will end up spending less money and getting more for the money that you do spend.

Chapter 8

Implementing Your Tech Plan

● ●

In This Chapter

▶ Executing your plan efficiently

▶ Getting everyone involved

▶ Keeping track of progress

▶ Minimizing risks

● ●

*F*or most business owners, reaching the implementation stage with their technology plans becomes a complex dichotomy of euphoria and anxiety. The euphoria comes from realizing that you are about to do something that will empower your business to achieve the goals that you've set. What a feeling of power! The anxiety comes from throwing your business into a whole new environment, a new way of doing things, with new technology that you don't understand, but that your employees will have to figure out quickly. What a feeling of powerlessness!

If you're really a high roller and into masochism, you have decided to install all this new technology yourself. Congratulations, you may now advance to Chapter 14 and read about what it takes to be a technology consultant. Or, we can make it easy and just list all the reasons why you don't want to do it yourself. Here are some of them:

✔ You will be deemed the network guru, and everyone will come to you for every problem they encounter until the day you either leave the business or die, whichever comes first.

✔ You will automatically increase the number of possible network problems tenfold.

✔ You will become addicted to Jolt Cola, Twinkies, and anything else that will keep you awake long enough to deal with all the problems.

Just because the power comes on when you flip the switch doesn't mean that the system is running okay. Just take our word for it: *You don't want to do this yourself.* Hire or at least talk to a technological consultant for this part.

By now, you have probably figured out that to succeed in this digital world, your company must be willing to change and willing to discover new ways to do things. Your company is already a learning organization (one that is continually looking for new and better ways to do things) to some extent, or it wouldn't have gotten as far as it has. However, in a digital world, exploring new technology is not just a sometime thing; it's a way of life. Your technology plan is based on some basic goals you have for your business and is designed to take you in stages to reach those goals. But, as a learning organization, your company needs to bear in mind that technology may change before you actually reach your business goals. That's the nature of the digital world.

Even huge companies like Microsoft face these same disruptive changes that small companies do. Your authors have experienced this first-hand. By the time we completed a pilot study on a project for Microsoft — a matter of mere months — Microsoft had perceived a shift in the marketplace that sent us off in a new direction entirely. So even the best-laid plans of professionals have to be flexible enough to change when the environment says to change.

Although plans are important — and we highly recommend them — don't become obsessive about them. In a marketplace that doesn't wait for you to complete a long, drawn-out planning and implementation process, you need to be flexible enough to experiment. In this chapter, you discover some effective techniques for quickly implementing your technology plan.

Executing a Great Strategy

Any strategy is useless until you make it happen. That process is called *execution* — an interesting choice of words when you consider that most technology plans actually kill themselves because of poor execution. We also hate to use the world *plan* when talking about implementing a technology strategy because it sounds so formal, structured, and final. And when you operate in a digital world, that simply isn't possible. So, when we refer to a plan, we're not talking about pages and pages of strategies, tactics, and action steps. You can probably do a great *execution plan* in two pages by making sure it answers these three questions:

✔ Who is responsible for what?

✔ What action steps do you need to complete the implementation?

✔ How can you minimize disruption to business operations during the implementation?

In the following sections, we explore these issues in more detail.

Knowing who does what

In Chapter 6, we talk about the importance of having a project manager as the key person in charge of directing the implementation. That way, at least one person knows everything that's going on and how it all fits together. Someone has to lead this orchestra or everyone will do his or her own thing, and — chances are — you won't be happy with the result.

Here are some of the things that need to be coordinated during the implementation:

- ✔ Ordering hardware and software.
- ✔ Backing up important files prior to installation.
- ✔ Testing your backups by using them to restore files to make sure they work. You can do all the backups you want, but if they don't work, they're useless. This is your chance to make sure that you're covered in case something goes wrong.
- ✔ Planning for an installation period that will permit minimal disruption of business operations.
- ✔ Making sure all hardware and software are on site and ready to go before installation.
- ✔ Working with the technology consultant who is managing the installation (assuming you took our advice seriously about not doing it yourself).
- ✔ Having your consultant connect and test as much of the new equipment as possible at his or her office before bringing it to yours. When you're working with new equipment, this isn't generally a problem.
- ✔ Checking that everything agreed upon was actually installed and is working properly.
- ✔ Having a checklist where you and the consultant initial each task that is complete.
- ✔ Making sure the system is debugged before putting the business online.
- ✔ Coordinating training for all those who will be using the system.
- ✔ Providing for continuing maintenance of the system. And don't do all the continuing maintenance yourself, either.

This job is obviously more than one person should handle. You probably want to outsource most of the installation and the ongoing maintenance unless your business has reached a size that can justify having an in-house technology person. You probably also want to outsource training.

With all these different activities and people to coordinate, it's important to know ahead of time who will take charge of what. The project manager's job is to choreograph the installation process so that the right people do what they're supposed to do when they're supposed to do it. This job may sound easy, but as soon as you realize that your installation is not the only job your technical people are dealing with, you understand why sometimes scheduling the installation doesn't go as smoothly as you had hoped. We get into that a bit more later in this chapter.

Adding action steps makes things happen

If you want action, include action steps in your implementation strategy. Action steps are the specific activities that you or someone else has to do to get the outcomes you want. If you want to make training part of your implementation strategy (and we hope you do!), what steps do you have to take to make that happen? "Well," you say, "our implementation strategy says that we will have training." Great, but are you planning to wave a magic wand and make it appear? Here is an example of some action steps that will make training a reality:

1. **Identify those applications for which your organization may need training.**

2. **Investigate training companies.**

   You can ask your technology consultant for a recommendation.

3. **Interview the training companies to make sure that they can supply what you need at either your site or theirs.**

   Training people on the machines they use every day is often more beneficial.

4. **Set up a schedule for training that begins immediately after the installation is complete.**

5. **Oversee the training to make sure that you are receiving what you contracted for.**

6. **Plan for follow-up training if necessary.**

To finish, add deadlines for completion of each step and the names of the people who will be responsible for seeing that each action step happens. Table 8-1 shows a sample Action Step Grid for the training portion of your implementation plan.

Table 8-1	Sample Action Steps to Complete the Training Component	
Action Step	*Deadline*	*Responsible Person*
Identify those applications for which your organization may need training.	March 5	Office Manager, Technology Manager, and key employees
Investigate training companies.	March 12	Office Manager and Technology Manager
Interview the training companies.	March 19	Office Manager and Technology Manager
Schedule the training.	March 26	Office Manager
Oversee the training.	April 1–5	Office Manager and Technology Manager
Schedule follow-up.	April 10	Office Manager

If someone is accountable for these action steps and deadlines for assigned completion, you are more likely to implement your technology strategy in a timely fashion.

Minimizing disruption

One of the biggest challenges in the execution of your technology strategy is doing it without disrupting the operations of your business and negatively affecting your customers and your employees. Depending on how extensive a technology makeover you are undertaking, you may be able to complete the installation and testing over a long weekend if your technology partners are agreeable and you've stocked enough caffeine-type drinks. On the other hand, if you're facing a major overhaul, a weekend may not be enough. In that case, you may want to do nondisruptive work — cables, wire, hubs, and so forth — during normal hours and save things like network hook-up and migration of existing files and programs to the new system for after-business hours.

As we discuss in Chapter 15, where we talk about how to deal with technology consultants, you want to make sure that you're working with a technology person who understands how businesses operate and who has some communication skills. On more than one occasion, we've seen a tech consultant walk into a business during normal business hours and, with no warning, shut down the company's network operating system and effectively put the business "out of business" for a time. No business should have to go out of business to implement its technology strategy. Careful planning and scheduling, as well as a business-savvy technology consultant, should minimize disruption.

Have your technology consultant outline for you which installation activities will disrupt your business operations and which will not. Then work with him or her to find a schedule that will produce minimum disruption.

Timing your training (It doesn't happen overnight)

Even if the installation goes smoothly, you still face the issue of getting people comfortable with the new system; that comfort level only comes from spending time using the system and training, training, and more training. Of course, every employee won't attain a thorough working knowledge of new technology in one sitting. Recognize that training is going to take time, probably more than you think. Most business owners we've dealt with have suggested a couple days at the beginning and then another session about 90 days later. That way everyone has time to work with the system and come up with some questions that can be answered at the last training session.

Make sure that the people dealing with the most critical operations and processes are trained first.

Generally, those critical processes are related to the customer, such as orders, billing, and so forth. It may be a good idea to warn your customers that you're upgrading the technology in your company to serve them better and ask for their patience during the process.

It's always a good tactic to prepare customers for the worst, but then give them an unexpected, positive experience. They'll remember that!

Getting Everyone to Join You

When taking care of planning, scheduling, and controlling the implementation process, be careful not to leave out perhaps the one piece that could destroy all your efforts — your employees.

Just as it's important to have everyone buy into the vision and mission for your company, everyone also has to buy into the implementation strategy for your technology makeover. You can't simply announce one day that this is what's going to happen and everyone had better adjust. Doing so will set up resistance that you won't be able to overcome, and your wonderful technology strategy will fall apart. This section suggests some steps you can take to ensure that everyone in your organization agrees this is the best decision you ever made.

Getting ready for the kickoff

Before the installation begins, get everyone who will be affected (and that's probably everyone!), including the technology people that you've hired for this process, together for a kickoff meeting to make sure you're all on the same team with the same expectations. Set aside a good amount of time for this meeting — a half day or full day, depending on the extent of the technology makeover. And don't forget the food: There's something about starting a project this important that makes everyone hungry.

Getting off to a positive start — checking the details and making sure everyone is on board and going in the same direction — is the best way to ensure a successful implementation.

The kickoff meeting can accomplish several purposes. You want to

- Review the objectives for the technology plan to make sure that everyone understands why you're doing this and what you intend to accomplish.
- Review the responsibilities of each person who will be managing the installation process.
- Run through how the various functions of the organization will work together to make this happen.
- Agree on the deadlines for all action steps.
- Review the potential obstacles.
- Agree on what to do if the installation gets sidetracked for some unexpected reason. Always have a backup plan.
- Set the mood for the installation by creating an atmosphere of excitement, enthusiasm, and fun. You want to generate some spirit for the project and what it means to the future of your company.

Let's be honest: No installation of technology is fun and games. It's an experience you just want to get through as quickly and painlessly as possible. So kick it off with a positive spirit that you hope will last for the duration of the installation.

Recognizing project team stages

Project teams go through several common stages as they come together and get to know each other's work style:

1. **Triggering the start-up:** The kickoff meeting is certainly part of the first stage, where the team comes together, perhaps for the first time, to clarify tasks, roles, and responsibilities. At this point, you probably have more unknowns than knowns, but the important goal is to get everyone thinking about what they need to do to make this happen.

2. **Running around in circles:** Until you actually get into the installation, you really don't know for sure how everyone is going to work with each other and whether everything is going to work the way you planned. In the beginning, everyone runs around like chickens with their heads cut off. They have so much to do and, yes, they have an action plan, but the tendency is to forget the plan and do everything at once. This is also the stage where you find out who is going to carry their share of the load and who is not.

3. **Getting on track:** Soon everyone begins to find ways to work with each other as a team. At this stage, they have greater understanding of what lies ahead, so the level of commitment to see the project to its completion increases.

4. **Moving full speed ahead:** In the final stage, the team gets organized and moves quickly toward its goal. They are able to work together to overcome any challenges. Everyone is excited about his or her progress and accomplishments.

Although the ideal would be to have a team that operates in the fourth stage for the longest period of time, the reality is that during a lengthy project, a team may go through the four stages several times.

Encountering a major obstacle that the team disagrees about often triggers going back to start-up. If the team is prepared in advance for this eventuality, they will spend less time in the early stages than they did the first time around and, instead, move quickly to the fourth stage.

Selling the plan to employees: What's in it for them?

Any time you expect employees to change the way they do something, change a pattern of behavior, or change the work environment, you're going to encounter resistance unless you can successfully show them what's in it for them. It would be nice to think that philanthropically minded employees will make major changes in their work patterns just for the good of the company, but, unfortunately, for most employees, that's not enough incentive. Just as you expect new hires to demonstrate the benefit they can provide to your company, you have to explain to your employees why these changes will be good for them in the long run.

One of the quickest ways to get their acceptance is to ask employees what would make their job easier, more effective, and more enjoyable. Chances are, something they list can be provided by the new technology you are proposing for the company. If not, you had better go back and read Chapter 4.

For example, suppose one of your employees complains that she has a difficult time scheduling nonroutine sales meetings. It takes a long time to go to each salesperson and find out when he or she is available, then go back to the calendar and figure out a time and day that satisfies everyone and doesn't conflict with something else that's going on in another part of the company. If you can show this employee that the new system will provide the ability to have a common calendar for the company where everyone can enter critical appointments, meetings, and dates when they're out of town, she can probably see quite easily how much time she'll save by not having to contact everyone. She'll simply log onto the central calendar and find an open date.

That's just one example of a benefit that may encourage an employee to agree enthusiastically to explore a new technology.

Another great way to get employees to enthusiastically accept your technology plan is to include them in the planning process at every stage so that their concerns are addressed as you consider types of technology and put together an execution strategy.

Taking it nice and easy gets you there

We must emphasize again that implementing major technological change in your company cannot be a surprise. It has to be staged; you have to warm people up to the idea. If done effectively, by the time you reach the actual installation of the technology, employees will be excited to dig in and find out about all the new applications. Well, most of them will be. The die-hard resisters will likely become interested only when they see their co-workers enjoying the benefits of the new technology. Keep in mind that you are providing training to your employees that is extremely valuable, and the skill sets they pick up can increase their value to the company.

Post-installation letdown often occurs shortly after the installation is completed and employees have had a chance to test their wings with their regular tasks. When employees think that, using the new technology, they can simply jump in and do their routine tasks at the same speed and effectiveness that they've always done them, they often face immediate discouragement. Routines are hard things to break. When things on your workstation aren't where you remembered and when you have to look in new places to find what you need, it can be frustrating. All this is especially difficult to adjust to when you're still facing the deadlines and work pressures you had before the installation. You need to prepare employees for the time it will take to explore the new environment so that they're not surprised. After they begin to feel comfortable, their understanding of the technology becomes exponential. Incentives are a good way to motivate them to keep finding out more.

Prior to the installation, have your employees rank their most critical tasks. That can become the order they use to decide where to focus their efforts first with the new technology. Have them set goals for themselves, and then you provide some incentives for them to reach those goals. How about a pizza and beer party when a major goal has been achieved?

Some employees may deal with the newness better than others may. Be sure to reward employees who, in their spare time, help other employees catch up. And when your customers congratulate you on how well the system makes your company run, be sure to let your employees know about it. This is a team effort.

Tracking Your Progress

One of the dangers you face, both during and after the installation, is to neglect to assign someone to track what happens and monitor how the organization responds to the new technology. It's as if everyone expects things to just happen the way they're supposed to without any tweaking or debugging or any of the other arcane things that technology experts do with the networks they install. Of course, you'll hear the cry loudly and clearly if someone is having trouble with the system, but how will you know whether or not you are on your way to achieving those goals you set when you started this process in the first place?

Just as you needed an action plan to make sure that you implemented your technology strategy, you need an action plan for tracking your progress during and after implementation over several months to a year.

Who's watching what?

The best way to track your progress is to get those people who are using the technology to give feedback on the effectiveness of the new processes you have put in place. Now might be a good time to read Chapter 5, where you identify your goals for the business, the business processes that are critical to achieving those goals, and the technology most appropriate to facilitating the processes. The people who are performing the tasks in those critical processes are in the best position to help you decide how to measure progress.

Measure your "sticking points"

If your company is going to do business with much larger companies, having a technology plan in plan can pay off in a company that is efficient, flexible, and fast. One example is a company that produces remedies for a variety of skins rashes that are sold through large discount drugstore chains. One reason the company has been so successful in dealing with these discounters is that it has an ongoing, detailed technology plan. Although the company first installed PCs in 1983 and added new ones consistently as it grew, it never bothered to upgrade the old machines. The result was a patchwork quilt of custom software and old computers. By contrast, the company's manufacturing operations were very exacting. Employees actually logged how long it took a product to go through each step of the production process. If they found that a labeling machine, for example, began to stick, they knew it was time to replace it. This was their "sticking point strategy."

But, in 1996 the company realized that the same practices that made its manufacturing process so successful could be applied to its information systems. Employees started keeping track of how much time they spent on computer activities and projected those hours out to a year's time. What the company found out was astounding. On average, an employee spent:

✔ 105 hours per year running to printers

✔ 52 hours converting files from one operating system to another

✔ 75 hours in unnecessary document management

✔ 40,000 dollars in labor per year

The company lost no time in looking at new technology to stop the bleeding. For a basic investment of $20,000 (half of what they were losing in labor time), they set up a Windows NT network that not only solved productivity problems, but had the added benefit of allowing their salespeople to dial in from remote locations. Now they regularly upgrade and add new components they can justify.

For example, suppose one of the critical tasks in your business is tracking orders from the point at which they're taken from the customer through production to shipping, delivery, and billing. Right now you transfer paper from function to function through several different people. These people also write the same information over and over again, each time incurring the risk that a number or some other piece of information will be entered incorrectly, causing an error that may not be discovered for some time. What can you track to see how the new system can improve the process? Here are a few ideas:

✔ The average time it takes for an order to go from original entry to billing.

✔ The average time it takes for each leg of the journey, traveling from department to department.

✔ The number of errors encountered in an order.

✔ How many people have to deal with the order.

These are measurable events that can be tracked; you can readily see if you're improving or not. Of course, when the system (in this case, probably a network with a shared database) is new, you will most likely experience poorer performance initially as people become accustomed to new ways of doing things. But then you should see dramatic improvement that can be measured.

What if you get off track?

When you deal with technology, anything is possible, and we're not necessarily talking about things you can achieve. Anything that can go wrong is also possible. Given the complexity of most technology and the number of people you may involve in your implementation strategy, something undoubtedly will send your well-crafted plan off its track. What do you do when that happens?

The first thing you need to do is regroup, send out for pizza and drinks, and gather all the relevant people together for a brainstorming session. (The pizza and drinks will insure that everyone starts thinking outside the box.) Recognize that any problem that throws the plan off-track is only a momentary setback that can be solved if everyone doesn't panic.

Here's a technique that's often used in product development situations, but can also work quite well to solve unexpected problems with your new technology. Its acronym is PDCA, for plan, do, check, and act.

1. **Plan.**

   You know that things did not go according to plan. That's why you're having this meeting in the first place. Define exactly what went wrong and why. Then brainstorm some ways to correct the problem and choose one.

2. **Do.**

   Apply your technique for solving the problem.

3. **Check.**

   Monitor the results to see if the new procedure or technique actually solved the problem.

4. **Act.**

   Make it a permanent part of the system if it worked. If it didn't, it's back to the drawing boards, and bring in more help.

This procedure is certainly a simple, intuitive one, but it's amazing how often teams skip one aspect or another and take longer than necessary to solve a problem.

Kathleen relates the following story: One company that I work with was very good at the planning process but when it came to "do," "check," and "act," they faltered. They had great difficulty devising a way to get from where they were to where they wanted to be. I got the key decision makers together to discuss the problem and had them list on a white board all of the things that went wrong with their business planning process — why none of the goals they had set were actually achieved.

Because I was trying to get them to change some long-standing habits, we chose one goal to focus on first to learn the PDCA process. The goal was to implement a centralized database of company information that was accessible by everyone. The company had the appropriate tech people and plenty of resources to implement such a technology, but it hadn't happened because the tech people were more interested in purchasing and installing the latest technology and the business people knew what they wanted but were too intimidated by the tech people to stand up to them.

We brainstormed some ways to correct the problem. In brainstorming, the suggestions go from the ridiculous to the sublime, but that's good. Out of big pot of dozens of ideas came one that everyone wanted to try. We decided to relocate a couple of key business and technology decisionmakers in the company to work with the tech consultants and we pulled a couple of tech consultants to do a tour of duty in the various business functions of the company. We hoped by this to achieve a better understanding of the two cultures and ultimately get the centralized database function the company needed so badly.

From our group of brainstormers, we got four volunteers for the "do" phase and put them to work in their new cultures. The goal of the tech consultants was to understand how the business functions from a business person's point of view. The business peoples' goal was to understand the environment of the technology person.

After a month, we brought the planning team back together to assess the results (check). The business people came back to report that they were working closely with the tech consultants on designing the new database, and the tech consultants came back enthusiastic about their new understanding of business processes. The plan had essentially worked and with some minor tweaking, it was decided that this mixing of cultures should become a regular part of the company's environment (act). Of course, the PDCA process also become part of the new company culture.

Managing Your Risk

Any time you take on a major project, such as a technology transformation of your business, you have to account for the potential of failure of something. It's Murphy's Law (in essence, whatever can go wrong, will). And when you're talking about complex technological systems, a lot of things can go wrong. So you need to plan — not for failure, but for recovery should something go wrong. You need to know in advance where the likely problems will come in executing your technology strategy.

Here are a few reasons why technology strategies fail (you can add your own unique experiences to the mix):

- ✔ **Not communicating well.** Communication is number one on almost every list. Everyone in your company and everyone you're dealing with from the outside needs to be kept apprised of the progress of the implementation at each stage so there are no surprises (or minimal surprises).

- ✔ **Not putting someone in charge of project management.** Someone in your organization (yes, it may have to be you) needs to be the chief liaison between the vendors, the consultants, and the business. There needs to be one good source that anyone can turn to who knows everything that's going on. In other words, you need a target.

- ✔ **Not allowing enough time for completion.** Let's face it; this project is not going to happen as quickly as you would like. It's not the nature of the beast. So allow more time than you think you'll need and then add some more. Believe us when we say that it's worth it not to push, but rather to allow as much time as necessary to do the job right the first time around.

- ✔ **Not considering the disruption to the business.** Careful planning *before* you start installing new technology into your business environment will minimize disruption. With any luck, you'll be able to do some of the transformation outside of your normal business hours — in the evening or on a weekend. Installing a new network during business hours is not too bad. However, any migration of data or other change should be done in the evening or on the weekend, though it may be more expensive. If evenings or weekends are not possible, then make sure you have a clear schedule that everyone understands and stick to it.

- ✔ **Not planning for enough training and testing.** You've spent a good sum of money on this new technology. It's wise to spend a little more to ensure that people can use it correctly and to its fullest capability. You also want to run several tests to make certain that it's doing what it's supposed to do before you sign off on the project and begin conducting business in the new environment.

Introducing new technology into a business that's been running on manual systems or minimal technology is a risky proposition, but not nearly as risky as not doing it.

Part III

Using Technology to Grow

The 5th Wave   By Rich Tennant

INDUSTRY WATCHERS PREDICT THAT IN THE NEAR FUTURE MONDOSOFT CORP. WILL DEVELOP APPLICATIONS THAT WILL BE COMPATIBLE WITH OS/2, WINDOWS AND KIRBY VACUUM CLEANERS.

In this part . . .

*I*t's important to know how you're going to use technology to create that competitive advantage for your business. In this part, you see how you can use technology to grow your business, bring you closer to customers and strategic partners, and develop new products and services both offline and online. This part gives you a lot of great strategies for using technology in creative ways.

Chapter 9

Using Technology to Win New Customers and Keep Old Ones

. . . .

In This Chapter

▶ Determining your customers' expectations

▶ Identifying and researching target markets

▶ Building customer relationships

▶ Collecting to survive

. . . .

*W*e can safely say that technology plays a major role in all the changes that are going on in business today. So it's not surprising that marketing — all the activities related to moving your products and services from the producer to the customer — has also been affected. In the "old days" (really only a few short years ago), marketers gathered potential customers together in a room to conduct a focus group. On a board, they posted some of the questions they wanted answered:

✔ What do you look for when purchasing a product of this type?

✔ If you could change one thing about this product, what would it be?

The focus group would write its answers and the company would use that information in its marketing strategy.

Here's the same scenario today. Marketing sends an e-mail to all the functional groups in the company — production, finance, design, and so on — and asks them to post potential focus group questions to the shared workgroup file designated for this purpose: an electronic bulletin board of sorts. As the questions pour in from the various areas of the business, marketing people edit and sort them online and continue to get responses until they achieve a questionnaire that satisfies everyone. They post this questionnaire on their Web site, asking customers to fill it out in exchange for some incentive. In addition to customers at large, marketing can target specific groups of customers in various geographic areas. These digital focus groups regularly supply feedback on the company's products.

The marketing world has certainly changed.

Technology has had major impacts on marketing and customer relationships that every business owner should be aware of. The following is a list of those impacts:

✔ Computer networks and online services have given rise to a concept called *mass customization* and the newest buzzword, *mass personalization*. Mass customization means giving your customers what they want, when they want it, and in the way they want it. Mass personalization is one-to-one marketing with individual customers so that the customer doesn't feel lost in the crowd. In addition, technology has made it easier to achieve those long-term relationships with customers that you want.

✔ Technology has succeeded in leveling the playing field a bit for small companies competing against much larger companies. E-mail, teleconferencing, networked databases, and — without a doubt — the Internet have all contributed to the new power that small businesses enjoy in the marketplace. Today you can set up your e-commerce site right next to Xerox on the Web and look just as big and important.

✔ Technology has changed the way you organize and structure your business. You can now effectively decentralize your business using computer networks and the Internet, which means that you can virtually run your business from anywhere.

✔ Technology has increased the amount of business competition. As soon as you introduce your new and unique product or service, your competitors quickly imitate you. Now customers face a huge selection of identical products. The challenge becomes how to differentiate your products and services from all the rest. The correlated opportunity is that those same customers need information to decide which product to buy. And it's your company's job to give them that information.

✔ Technology has also contributed new tools for marketing. Here are just a few of these tools:

   • **E-mail** lets you communicate quickly and easily with customers, strategic partners, suppliers, and others all over the world. This reduces your travel costs and saves time.

   • **Teleconferencing** lets your business hold sales conferences when the participants are located in cities around the globe without ever having to fly to a common site.

   • **Commerical online databases** put marketing information and customer demographics in the hands of anyone who wants to learn more about the markets they're targeting.

   • **Databases** are now centrally located on company networks that gives everyone who needs customer information the ability to access it easily and quickly.

Finding Out What Customers Expect

Because technology has had such a big impact on the way companies conduct business, customers' expectations have risen. They now regularly look for e-mail addresses and Web site URLs, and are surprised if your company doesn't provide them. Because of the speed of e-mail and fax, customers expect to receive responses to their requests and complaints much faster. The pace of business has definitely moved into Internet time.

Customers also want to feel in control of their business dealings. With companies like Fedex giving customers the ability to track their shipments, and companies like Dell Computer Corporation giving customers the capacity to configure their own computers, purchase them, and track their production progress online, customers feel greatly empowered. Society perceives this kind of customer control as a right — which means that for a business to differentiate itself from its competitors, it must do something more to provide customer empowerment. In the not-too-distant future, if your business doesn't have the ability to conduct at least a portion of its transactions on the Internet, it's going to be left behind because customers will expect it as a matter of course.

Changing with the times

Does your company have to change what it's currently doing to become a digital marketer? Absolutely not! If you listen to your customers regularly and often, they will tell you if you need to change the way you're dealing with them. You'll hear from them if they need a personal touch, or whether for some things e-mail or a Web site works fine.

For example, if your customers want the ability to contact your company 24 hours a day, 7 days a week, find out if they want to talk to someone who will listen to them and assure them that things will be taken care of, or if they are satisfied leaving their thoughts on a voice mail or a Web site. Why hire a person to sit at a phone for hours if your customers are just as happy leaving the company a message. After all, many customers just want to know that there's a place where they can express their feelings on a particular issue. They don't need to have a conversation about it.

For some customers, the only time they have to shop for things or search for information is late at night after normal business hours. These people don't expect to find a human being at a desk ready to take their call at 3 a.m. But they may want the ability to buy your products during those hours.

Customer preferences are never static. They change with the times. That's why it's important for you to plan for the expansion of the technology you currently have or the technology you may purchase. You need to make sure that you're in a position to add technology as it becomes available so that you can offer your customers the latest options for interacting with your business.

Becoming an information company

Many small and growing businesses are finding that they have to redefine themselves because of the power and pervasiveness of the Internet. In fact, many product companies find that they're in the information management business as much as they are in the product business.

If you are using technology to deliver products and services to your customers, you may actually find that technology is becoming your core product. What we mean by this is, suppose you're in the transportation business — you have a trucking company that delivers shipments from local manufacturers to other parts of the country. You certainly don't need technology to do that, but you do need lots of information to do it well. At the minimum, you need to have the following:

- Shipping and insurance documents from the manufacturer
- Invoices to bill the manufacturer
- COD documents if the purchaser is to pay upon delivery
- Insurance and transit documents on your trucks and the people who drive them
- Tracking documents to monitor the progress of the shipment

We didn't list all the potential information you may need just to deal with one shipment. In fact, we haven't even dealt with the issue of organizing the many shipments that one truck carries so that people can offload the right packages at the right time. Wouldn't it be important to your customers to know the status of their shipment?

So are you in the trucking business or the information business? Acquiring or developing technology that helps you manage this information more efficiently and effectively, and makes it easier for your customer to work with you puts you in the information business.

Today, the information you have and can deliver to your customers is what differentiates your business from your competitor's. The ability to have real-time information on schedules, availability, and status is what makes your company stand out and what brings customers to your business.

Identifying and Researching Target Markets

One thing that the Internet and database technologies do is make it easier for businesses to find a target market for their products or services and reach the customers in that market. Once they find those customers, technology helps businesses talk to those customers and learn more about their specific needs. That makes it possible for companies to improve their product and service offerings. But technology can do more. It can help you build a database of information about your customers so you can begin to build those important long-term relationships. It can also let your customers learn more about your company and develop a sense of loyalty that makes them come to you first whenever they need something.

Identifying target customers' needs

Database marketing has long been the province of major corporations that tracked customer information in order to better plan their marketing campaigns. But today, that same power is in the hands of small business owners who can achieve the same kinds of success as big companies.

For example, suppose you own an independent bookstore serving your community (let's further suppose that Borders and Barnes & Noble have not yet discovered your community). One way to begin to identify who your target customers are and what they typically buy is to issue customers a Frequent Buyer Card. To get the card, the customer has to provide some basic information such as:

- Name
- Address
- Phone number
- Types of books preferred

You store this information in your business's database. Every time a customer purchases a book, you enter information about the title, author, and purchase date into the database. Before long, you can go back to your database and segregate the names of those who like books on travel, fiction, nonfiction, and so forth.

The following is a list of additional information you may want to include in your customer information file:

- The customer's most recent purchase.
- Frequency of purchase.
- Average amount spent per purchase and over the previous six months.
- For a business customer: Who is the principal contact in the business?
- For consumers: What is the composition of the household?

✔ Date of first purchase and all subsequent purchases.

✔ Location of purchase.

✔ Returns and reasons for return.

✔ Promotions sent to customer and when.

✔ Complaints from the customer and how they were resolved.

✔ Customer's image of the company versus competitors.

✔ Comments from dialoguing with the customer.

Deducing the buying patterns of your customers may lead you to suggest to them certain new books. You may even trigger multiple sales to customers who only normally buy one book at a time, by sending them an offer to get a second book at a discount.

Using database marketing techniques

The idea behind database marketing is to sell more products to your current customers instead of trying to get new customers. Certainly, both goals are important, but it is far less costly in marketing terms to sell more to your current customers than it is to reach new customers.

Here are some database marketing techniques you can use to identify your customers' needs and reach out to attract new customers by using technology:

✔ **Use the Internet to access proprietary online databases in the trade areas relevant to your business.** You can find out what others are saying about your customers. What are their current buying patterns? What trends are emerging? What are your competitors doing to satisfy their customers? What needs are not being served? Serving those unmet needs may let your business move beyond its current position.

✔ **Put up a Web site to promote your business and its products and services to customers who may not live in your community, but may want to take advantage of the unique offerings you have.**

✔ **Review newsgroup listings on the Internet.** Newsgroups are similar to listings in a newspaper on virtually any subject. Every topic has its own area where people assemble to voice their opinions, ask questions, and make suggestions. It's possible for you to spy on your target market and see what they are telling each other that they need and want from a product or service similar to yours. You can also start to spread the word that your company offers products or services that may meet the needs of those in certain groups by using a signature line on your newsgroup postings that contains the name of your business and what you do. But remember that you can't use blatant advertising on these forums.

Giving Your Customer a Chance to Know Your Business

Brand recognition is as important today as it ever was, maybe even more so. But today, it's not just about product branding, it's about company branding. You want customers to seek you out because they associate superior products, services, and customer relations with your company. That way, when you introduce new products and services, customers are more likely to seek you out.

To achieve that brand recognition and loyalty, you need to be able to communicate your company's beliefs and information to the customer in multiple ways. You need to celebrate every small win with your customers. How do you do that? Why, with technology, of course!

Turning customers into cheerleaders

Get your customers who love what you do to talk about it on your Web site, in brochures, in your advertising, and anywhere you can. You're trying to create what Tom Peters calls in his 1999 study, *Reinventing Work: The Project 50*, a "noisy-but-organized cheerleading section" for your company.

To make this happen, you have to organize the process of gathering and analyzing customer input. Here are some things you can do to create a system that produces cheerleaders:

- **Put a page on your Web site that lets customers tell about their experiences with your products.** What they say is automatically e-mailed to you (or better yet, entered into an electronic database). That way you can sort the best and use them in the testimonial section of your Web site.

- **Regularly e-mail a newsletter to your customers.** Include timely information that is useful to your readers. More importantly, let your readers contribute their stories and helpful hints. This is also a good way to gather more information from your customers about their needs.

- **Start an electronic idea box where your customers can suggest new products and services for your company.** A wonderfully innovative company in Pennsylvania with the unlikely name of New Pig Corporation does just that. New Pig provides products that help companies deal with industrial waste. They solicit ideas for new products from their customers and award prizes for implemented ideas. The company enters new ideas into the Pigalog, which is their idea database, then sorts and distributes the list to people inside the company who can think about how to implement them. You can find New Pig at www.newpig.com.

> ✔ **Give your customers a toll-free number** where they can leave an idea, thought, or suggestion that you can immediately transfer to a database. With that database you can access, sort, use, and share the information with everyone in the company.

The bottom line is to make your customers feel they are an important part of your company. Choose technology that helps you do that, and the process of gathering and analyzing customer input is a snap!

Making your customers your partners

Who better to test your new product/service ideas than a group of customers who really believe in your business? These customers don't have to be located right near the business to become your product development partners. In fact, it's probably wiser to find customers who love your business but who live in out-of-the way places where you can conduct testing away from the penetrating eye of the press. After all, it's okay to fail or to have problems — it's part of the process — but it's much easier to do it in private with loyal customers than out in public where you chance damaging your market reputation.

Using customers as beta sites saves you the embarrassment of putting out a product that has mistakes or gives customers problems when they use it.

Think of the term *beta* as a synonym for test or prototype. When someone mentions a "beta site" to you, he or she is most likely referring to a test site. If someone refers to a "beta tester," think of someone who is testing prototype software that is not ready for the masses to use just yet.

When Microsoft Corporation introduced Windows 95, they had 300,000 beta site testers — approximately one billion dollars worth of free advice! Learn from the big boys and do your own version of the beta site test.

The following are more tips for turning customers into partners:

> ✔ **Link your customer beta testers to your company via your Web site.** Put a secured page on your Web site that you can only access with a password. Your customers will feel like they're entering a private club with VIP privileges. On the site, give them insider information, special deals, and their own personal "digital desktop" in the company where they can store the information they need to do the testing they conduct. You can also provide electronic evaluation forms so they can input their responses directly into your database.

> ✔ **Conduct focus groups online using a hosting service like** www. e-groups.com. Customers log into their designated group on the site and leave their evaluations and questions. This works well when you want your customers to interact, when visual contact is not important, and when they are separated geographically from each other.

A more expensive alternative is videoconferencing. Most small businesses cannot afford this type of technology, but a variety of companies like Kinkos provide videoconferencing capability to small businesses on a rental basis. Just have your customers go to the designated Kinkos site at the appropriate time and voilá, you have a virtual focus group!

✔ **Let your beta site testers loose to create some buzz for your fully tested and approved product.** Who better to chant the praises for your new product than the people who were there when it was just a primitive working prototype? They are the real believers, so now it's time to give them some airtime. Make them stars on your Web site; put their testimonials in your brochures and other promotional materials. If every one of your customer beta testers tells nine other people about this new product, you have a good product launch. Keep the testimonials coming.

Building Customer Relationships

Your company's goal should be to build trusting, satisfying, and long-term relationships with your customers that produce shared customer and company goals. This is particularly important in the global marketplace that technology has brought to your doorstep. Buyers from other countries are much slower to make purchase decisions and don't typically buy until they feel comfortable that they can trust you.

The advantage that technology gives you in this new environment is the power to transmit information about your company to customers around the world, easily and quickly via the Internet, e-mail, and fax. The ability of customers to get their questions answered builds trust that is necessary to solicit loyalty from them.

Rewarding your best customers

Sometimes, business owners spend so much time searching for new customers that they forget to take care of the ones they have. This constant search for more "hits" is becoming increasingly prevalent, given the prominence of e-commerce companies. Customers are nameless, faceless, and voiceless — just another hit on the screen.

Would it surprise you to know that most companies lose 25 percent of their customers annually? If you assume that it costs five times as much to acquire a new customer as to maintain an existing one, that's a lot of wasted money, especially for a small, growing company that can't afford to waste anything. In fact, studies have shown the following:

- Almost 65 percent of an average company's business comes from current, satisfied customers.

- A company that, each day for one year, loses one customer who generally spends $50 a week will suffer a sales decline of $1 million the next year.

- As few as 24 percent of your customers account for 95 percent of your revenues.

Retaining your current customers should be the primary focus of any growing business. The following are some tips that you can use:

- Sort your customer database on frequency and amount of purchases to constantly track the patterns of your best and worst customers.

- Establish a VIP or frequent user program that rewards repeat purchases.

- Program your database to trigger important dates relative to your best customers, such as birthdays, holidays, time to repurchase, or sales notifications.

CASE STUDY

Bring the vineyard to the customer

In an effort to promote the sales of California wines, Peter Granoff and Robert Olson founded Virtual Vineyards in 1994, a Web site dedicated to marketing and selling their products exclusively on the Internet. The business concept was not particularly unique, except when you consider that it was in 1994 that the first graphical user interface for the Internet — Mosaic — became available. That was also the year that Netscape — the offspring of Mosaic — was first given free to users who wanted to experience this new world.

So, Virtual Vineyards became one of the charter members of what, over the next three years, would become the burgeoning e-commerce marketplace. By 1995, the company had reached $1 million in revenues by taking commissions from contractors on each sale.

For their customers, the benefit was the ability to find an enormous variety of fine wines and unparalleled information. Granoff and Olson knew that to keep their customers coming back, they had to cater to their needs and create value

at every turn. On their Web site, customers could get their questions answered, create personalized wine labels, and search for rare wines. Because they chose the Internet as their base of operations, Granoff and Olson also had an immediate global marketplace at their fingertips. In fact, international customers, eager to sample new wines, are a significant part of their business.

One of the important lessons that Granoff and Olson learned is that the value of a Web site is not measured by the number of visitors alone. That's only part of it. The maximum value is attained by the following:

- Providing information that customers can't get anywhere else.

- Building an online community of wine lovers.

- Customizing the site to meet customers' changing needs.

You can find Virtual Vineyards under its new domain name: www.wine.com.

Giving your customers a forum for when things go wrong

Of course, every business likes to get compliments and positive input from its customers — who wouldn't? But when you connect to your customers, you have to be willing to listen to everything they tell you. And that means taking some bad with the good. It's an essential part of your ongoing customer relationships.

Sometimes, customers find faults. This does not mean that they will immediately switch their loyalty to another company. Far from it. If you work with the customer to correct the problem, he or she has a vested interest in staying with your company because it listens to its customers. On the other hand, if you don't deal effectively with a customer complaint, you may quickly find that the grapevine effect (which expands exponentially as a result of the power of the Internet) can destroy your company's good reputation.

You need to think of complaints as an opportunity to improve your company's operations, products, and services. With that in mind, the following list shows ways to encourage feedback, even when it's a complaint.

- **Make it easy to complain.** One way to make it easy to complain is to provide an 800 number. Pizza Hut does this. When a customer calls in to complain, he or she talks to a trained representative (Pizza Hut outsources this to a professional company) who then sends the complaint electronically to the appropriate manager. The system requires the manager to contact the customer and resolve the issue within 48 hours.

- **Provide bulletin board services on Web site to allow customers to post their complaints.** Be aware, though, that this solution can work almost too well. It's very easy to complain anonymously. Groups of customers with axes to grind have been known to spam a company in an attempt to destroy their market share. To avoid creating a negative momentum that can start with a few complaints posted in plain view on your site, arrange for the postings to be immediately e-mailed to your company and not remain in public view on your site.

- **Provide satisfaction surveys at important points of contact with the customer.** This is a good way to discover problems quickly and eradicate them before they grow out of proportion.

Weeding out your worst customers

While you're making sure that your best customers are happy, you should also consider getting rid of your worst customers. That may sound harsh, but the reality is that it's costing you a lot of money, time, and effort to try to turn these "bad" customers into good ones. Sometimes the effort is better spent on selling more to current customers, or encouraging referrals from current customers so that you can find more good ones.

You can find your worst customers by sorting the information in your customer database on frequency and amount of purchases, as well as on frequency of on-time payment.

Collecting to Survive

It's great to talk about building wonderful customer relationships; the assumption is that everything will go along smoothly because you have taken great care to understand your customers' needs. Unfortunately, the marketplace isn't that predictable. Sometimes customers with the best of intentions don't pay you when they should. If you don't have a means of tracking their payment patterns, you could very quickly find yourself in a dangerous financial situation from which you won't be able to recover.

If you have created a customer database where you store all their information — what they buy, how much it cost, and so on — it's fairly easy to also include information about when and how much they pay. You can pull up that information to see if they're 30, 60, or 90 days behind in paying.

It wasn't that long ago that the only tools in your collection arsenal were the phone and the post office. Not any more. Today there is technology available even to small businesses that helps you do a better job of collecting payments from your customers. Three of these systems are online systems, calling systems, and scoring systems.

Using online systems

With online systems, you remove the hassle of paper files that could easily grow to several inches thick with particularly elusive customers. Today, using a basic database or contact management software, you can establish classifications based on criteria such as the following:

- Balance on account
- Age of delinquency
- Type of customer

An online system handles each classification differently. The most delinquent customers go directly to a collection agency. Customers who are merely a few days late receive a friendly letter encouraging them to pay. This can be a form letter that pops up, so the person handling collections can fill in the correct information. These types of systems usually display the oldest delinquent category with the highest unpaid balance first, so that you don't have to sort through all your customers to find those that need your attention.

Anyone can log in and see the history of the communication with a particular customer because the system records all communications as they occur. This process saves time and money.

When you purchase accounting software, make sure that it has the ability to generate collection letters and aging reports for you.

Using calling systems

You or your employees spend a lot of time in collection efforts to get ready to make the call to the customer. Typically, you pull the file, review background information, and the history of communications with the customer. After all this preparation, you dial the customer only to find no one on the other end of the line. The file goes back into the queue for the next attempt.

Calling systems help you save time by automating the dialing process so those doing the calling only receive live calls. This is how they work: Customer information feeds into the calling system and it starts dialing. The system skips busy signals, no-answers, and answering machines or voice mail, then signals the waiting employee when a customer answers the phone. Studies have found that you can increase productivity four times with this type of calling system.

Using scoring systems

In the best of scenarios, you don't want to call those customers who never pay or never intend to pay. You only want to talk to those customers who need a reminder or a bit of nudging to get them to pay their debt. Behavioral scoring systems are the most complex method of dealing with customers. They can tell you the odds that a customer will pay based on past history. When you're dealing with thousands of customers, this can be a real time-saver.

You can find these types of systems in very large organizations, but a small business may be able to lease this application from a hosting service for a much smaller fee. Your need for this type of system depends on the size of your business, the type of business you have, and the payment patterns of your customers.

Chapter 10

Using Technology to Create a Company Culture

In This Chapter

▶ How your company's culture impacts performance

▶ Ways that shared knowledge, facilitated by technology, impacts company culture

▶ How to your culture with the world

*A*fter looking at the title of this chapter, you're probably wondering if we're pushing this technology thing a bit too much. For that matter, what does the topic of culture have to do with technology in the first place? Remember that technology is a facilitator of business functions — marketing, finance, product development, and so forth. But it also facilitates the way people interact inside an organization with each other and outside with customers and business partners. In short, it helps make your company culture happen.

What is company culture anyway? In the simplest of terms, *culture* is the personality of your company. Walk into any business and you will sense its personality almost immediately. Is the environment formal, quiet, and highly organized or is it informal, noisy, and open? Is everyone working in private offices or are they all in an open, no-boundaries setup that forces them to work together?

Today, culture is not just about the environment that you work in; it's also about your competitive advantage. Today, workers leave better paying positions to move to companies that have cultures that more closely fit their personalities and work styles. That is certainly true in the Net culture where Silicon Valley companies even encourage corporate rituals and *technoshrines* to keep their employees.

For example, some companies like interactive tool developer Music Pen Inc. (www.musicpen.com) encourage their artists and programmers to make personal shrines of their computers to reflect their personalities and serve as a creative outlet. On any day, you may find an animator who has arrayed his monitor with traditional artist's tools like paintbrushes, paper, and chalk. Another will adorn his computer with paper-clip sculptures and fetish objects. Yet another designer creates a still life out of fruit and then eats it throughout the day. The purpose of technoshrines is to ground net gurus in real time and space. Because they deal so much with the virtual world, they need to remind themselves that there's a real world out there too.

Why a Company Culture Is So Important

There are two fundamental reasons that culture is an important attribute of your company. First, the culture that your company develops over time significantly impacts your company's performance. When everyone in your organization shares the same basic values, you find a sense of purpose and drive to achieve the company's goals that makes your business better.

Second, culture is the reflection of your company's commitment to its vision. (Refer to Chapter 2 for more information on vision.) The culture you sense when you walk into a business is essentially the implementation of the strategies that move that company toward its vision; therefore, culture is inextricably linked to the company's vision and goals.

Building a culture from core values

The culture of any company is also a reflection of the core values of its founders. *Core values* are simply those fundamental beliefs your company holds that do not change. For example, a core value may be that it conducts all its business dealings with integrity. This means that if the opportunity comes up to do something that violates your company's core values, you won't do it. Refer to Chapter 2 for more information on core values.

If you have an existing business and haven't thought about its culture, you may find that you have hired people with different values than the core values of your company. The advantage of understanding the importance of culture is that when you hire new people, you make sure that they share the values of your company. That is an important starting point for creating a shared culture. In the next section, we show you how trying to run a company with multiple cultures and goals that clash can keep your business from moving ahead and competing effectively.

Does your culture reflect your company vision?

If you haven't made a conscious effort to create a culture in your company, chances are one has developed on its own without your input. The challenge is that it may not be your company's ideal culture. You may even have multiple cultures in your company. For example, in some companies, people who work in technology have one culture, while people who work in, say, marketing or accounting display a quite different culture.

The contrasts in the two cultures stem from differences in their work environment, the way they interact with each other and the rest of the organization, and the general differences in the personalities of the individuals who chose a particular type of work. One group, for example, may spend a lot of time in front of a computer screen with little interaction with others in the organization, while the other group may be highly social, team oriented, and spend a lot of time out of the office interacting with people in the market.

When you force these two groups together, it's like trying to blend oil and water. The only common ground they share is the fact that they work for the same company. This type of multicultural situation occurs in environments where shared cultural norms deriving from the company's core values have not been encouraged. In this environment, it's difficult to channel all the energy of the employees in the same direction at the same time, because it's hard to get them to work together. Consequently, instead of the company driving forward in a unified fashion, it bounces along like an old Model T, sputtering, stopping, and starting on its way to its goals.

Realistically, you will always have some cultural differences among people in your organization (there's no way to make everyone exactly alike, and actually, you wouldn't want to), but the overall culture or personality of the company that is based on your core values should be shared by everyone so that your company has the strength it needs to achieve its goals.

Table 10-1	A Comparison of Two Cultures
Company A: *Informal Team-Based Culture*	*Company B:* *Formal Hierarchical Culture*
Teamwork	Individual
Celebrates change	Avoids change
Learns from failure	Avoids failure
Decisions made at all levels	Decisions come from top down

(continued)

Table 10-1 *(continued)*	
Company A: **Informal Team-Based Culture**	**Company B:** **Formal Hierarchical Culture**
Work priorities based on company goals	Work priorities based on external factors
Information shared freely	Limited access to information
Long-term focus on decision making	Short-term focus
Hires for organization fit and trains	Hires for skills
Freedom to disagree	Consensus management
Employees are most important asset	Employees are a necessity

Review Table 10-1 and ask yourself this very important question. *Which of these two cultures is most likely to succeed in a rapidly changing world?* It should be clear that the informal, team-based culture is more flexible and able to change on a moment's notice. Certainly, if you look at successful companies today, you will find that the best have company cultures similar to those in Company A. The Company A culture celebrates employees, celebrates change, and celebrates innovation. The Company B culture focuses on individual effort, control, and avoidance of change. Where does your company fit in the spectrum? One good way to find out is to not only take the quiz yourself, but also ask your employees to take it independently.

Culture is not something that you dictate. Culture is something that everyone agrees on and encourages. In the rest of the chapter, we look at ways to use technology to create and sustain an effective culture in your company. If you already have a company with multiple cultures, we show you how to begin to bring the two together.

Using Technology to Build a Community of Shared Knowledge

The infrastructure of any company culture is comprised of the communication channels that exist to bring information to everyone in the organization. It is through these communication channels that culture is reinforced. In a small company, about one to five people, these channels may consist of feet, mouths, and telephones — the proverbial "sneaker net." If you want to discuss an idea for a new project with your production expert, you jump up from your seat and walk the few steps to her office. The face-to-face discussion ensues and a decision is made. When you want to communicate the decision to the other three people in the office, you merely stand out in the hallway and call for everyone's attention. It works, and some companies have developed strong and successful cultures using the sneaker net to communicate.

However, times have changed. Chances are that some of your employees work some of the time away from the office, even from their homes or cars. Everyone may not be in the office when you have an impromptu meeting in the hall. Your company may have grown to such a size that it's difficult to get everyone together at the spur of the moment. That's where technology steps in to give your company an infrastructure that can keep everyone in touch all the time.

Creating a neural network

Think of your company as a giant brain or neural network with communication going in many directions simultaneously. Wouldn't it be nice to make your communication network work more quickly and effectively? You can do that by giving everyone access to all the information they need with a network (several computers connected together with cables to a common server; see Chapter 17 for more about Local Area Networks — LANs), which does for your company what your brain does for you — stores and processes information in a way that makes it useful. It also helps you create and maintain a company culture by doing several things.

> ✔ **You can share information in several ways.** Suppose you have some marketing statistics that you think everyone should know. With a network, you have several options for distributing these statistics:
>
> - You can send the file to everyone's computer individually.
> - You can send the information to a drop-off point (sort of a resting place) where each person can pick it up later.
> - You can store the information in a permanent place (a public folder called "Latest Marketing Statistics") on the central server where people can access it anytime they want.
>
> ✔ **You can share resources.** Suppose you don't have the budget to provide everyone with his or her own laser printer, modem, or CD-ROM drive. You can set up your network so that everyone has access to these resources.
>
> ✔ **You can share programs.** Some computer applications are very expensive and take up a lot of hard drive space. You can place these memory/storage hogs on the central server so that everyone can access them without having to put the complete program on each computer.

Notice that the common theme is *share*. Sharing information and resources compels everyone to work together.

Browse on your network just like you do on the Internet

After you have a LAN in place, it's easy to create an Intranet, which is just a smaller version of the Internet, but is private to your business. With an Intranet, you view everything through a browser like Microsoft Internet Explorer or Netscape Navigator. That means you can navigate through a document and create links to other documents in files or on Web pages on the Internet. It also means that you can create a common GUI (Graphical User Interface) that has a certain look and feel on the screen and reflects your company's culture just like a Web page reflects the company culture of an Internet business.

With an Intranet you can make your LAN as easy to use as surfing the Web. An Intranet takes you one step closer to keeping everything as consistent as possible. You can also designate sites where employees can post things of interest to everyone or to find such things as the Employee Manual or Company Policies. You can even have an online suggestion box and offer weekly prizes to the idea that saves the most money or does something great for your customers. Because pages such as these are already in a Web format called HTML (HyperText Markup Language) it's easy for you to transfer them to your Internet server and make them accessible to the public. No matter where an individual may be when she logs onto the network, she will see her company desktop and the company's logo and informational material. She will be able to reach anyone else in the company quickly and easily. For more about Intranets, see Chapters 11 and 17.

Digital dashboards can also be used in an Intranet to pull information from various places into small windows on a screen. It is essentially a more complex GUI that can get all the information you need to be displayed right in front of you all the time.

If a digital dashboard sounds like something you want, make sure you get someone who has some experience with them to build you one. They can be complex to set up, but once they are working, they are an extremely powerful tool to have. You can learn more about digital dashboards in Chapters 11 and 17.

Getting everyone together

One of the best things about a network is that it brings everyone together in the virtual environment. Whether you're working in the next office or miles away at another location, you can tap into the culture of the company every time you access the network.

If all employees see their company logo, notices of key events or information that's important to know — and maybe even a joke or two — when they log onto the network in the morning, it creates a mood that continues throughout the day. You can even set up your network to allow everyone to contribute to the calendar so all the activities of the company are known to and available to everyone. Similarly, using a centralized contact manager, which is very simply a database that contains all the information about the people you deal with — customers, suppliers, and so on — everyone can get to the people they need to contact quickly and easily.

Open book management: Who's making money?

Today many companies believe that in order to build a culture of openness and trust in an organization, you have to be willing to share the financial information as well. If people understand what they contribute to the profits enjoyed by the company, they are more likely to put out the effort to achieve them. By contrast, secrecy often results in employees feeling suspicious. It is difficult to build a successful company culture in an environment of secrecy and withholding information.

Technology can help provide the right financial information to the right people when they need it. Naturally, private companies don't want their financial information made public for their competitors to take advantage of, but through an effective password system you can better insure that only the people you want to see certain information have access to it.

Think how powerful your employees would feel if they had access to company budgets for the areas in which they work. In addition, they could modify those budgets as new information came in. Think how empowered they would feel if they could see instantly the effect that their decision may have on the company. With their department spreadsheets linked to overall company worksheets, they can play with options and alternatives to make better decisions.

Be sure to give modification access only to those people who need it. Others should have "read-only" access. And don't forget to keep backup copies of your original budgets in case someone makes a mistake.

Sharing Your Culture with the World

Once you achieve an effective culture in your company, it's natural that you might want to reach out and share it with people outside your organization. You can do this in two main ways: through a company Web site and an extranet, defined presently. The Web site lets you reach customers and others around the globe, while the extranet gives your company its own private Internet to communicate with all the various people and companies with which you do business. Let's look at both in more detail.

Give your company a home page

When you put up a company Web site, you're making a decision to communicate to the world something about your company. It's unfortunate that many business owners don't realize that the homepage of their Web site says a lot about the culture of their company. Moreover, what is particularly bad, is that it often does not communicate the real nature of the culture. Let's do a little experiment.

Look at the following home pages of some companies and see if you can identify a company culture. Here are their URLs:

Prairie Frontier: `http://www.Prairiefrontier.com`

New Pig Corporation: `http://www.newpig.com`

Cisco Systems: `http://www.cisco.com`

Would you agree that the Web sites express the following company cultures?

- ✔ Prairie Frontier definitely has a down home, simple feel — warm and friendly. The impression given is that these people don't believe in slick advertising, and their customers are down-to-earth people who love nature. There don't seem to be any pretentious people here.

- ✔ At New Pig Corporation, you see a company that sells products to other businesses, but doesn't take itself too seriously. It pokes fun at itself. After all, New Pig employees are in a pretty messy business, so why not find a way to enjoy it?

- ✔ Cisco Systems is in a completely different league from the previous two companies. This leader in network hardware devices presents a no-nonsense picture to its customers — other businesses. This site is the essence of the big company that's here to do a job and do it well. These people are very serious about what they do and it's apparent in the organization and presentation of their Home page.

Now, granted, the Web site doesn't tell you everything about the culture of the company, but it does create an image that sticks in the mind of its customers.

The Web site Home page is only one way you can communicate your culture to the outside world. Letting your customers tap into your Intranet is another.

Give your extranet access to your intranet

We have talked about the Internet, your Intranet, and now we're going to introduce yet another *net* term: *extranet*. No, it doesn't mean that you get more of the other two. An extranet is simply an online connection between your business and the other businesses you deal with in your distribution channel.

For example, take a look at Figure 10-1 to see what an extranet looks like visually.

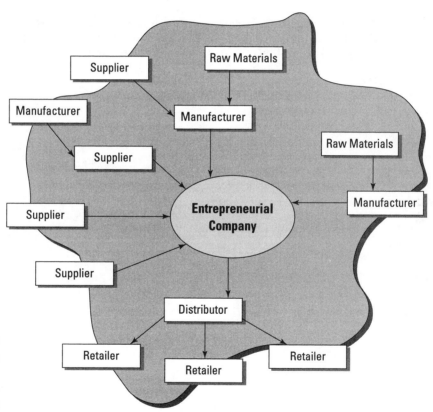

Figure 10-1:
Sample
Extranet.

This particular business outsources most of its activities to other businesses that include manufacturers, vendors, and distributors. Linking these businesses electronically with our sample company facilitates communication, making it quick and easy to keep everyone apprised of the latest information. For example, a supplier knows when the business needs additional raw materials because the computer program that links the businesses automatically triggers the request when the supply of raw materials reaches a critical point. The same is true for the distributors who trigger requests to the company for additional products when stock is low. All of the businesses have access to specific sites on each other's Intranets that pertain to the work they're doing. This process eliminates extraneous paper and makes it easy to organize, store, and find information when they need it.

As you can see, an extranet is really a group of strategic partners. And just like any partnership, you need to make sure that your partners have similar goals and are willing to work together for everyone's good.

Chapter 11

Using Technology to Form Strategic Alliances

In This Chapter

▶ Using technology to bring great minds together

▶ Fueling growth through technology alliances

▶ Managing successful partnerships

*H*aving strategic alliances is a great business strategy that has recently made its way to small businesses from large companies. No other strategy enables small businesses to grow as rapidly on limited resources. For many companies, forming strategic partnerships is the only way to acquire the talent, technical expertise, resources, and market access they need in order to grow.

A *strategic alliance* is a partnering of two or more companies with a vested interest in mutual success. Typically a company seeks a partner with a core competency that it is lacking. In return, the company provides the partner with one or more of the following:

  ✔ A skill set the partner is lacking.

  ✔ A new market that the partner would like to access.

  ✔ A way to increase the partner's revenues.

Strategic alliances work. How do we know? We know because entrepreneurs frequently use them. One study of over 400 of the fastest growing product and service type companies in the U.S. found the following:

  ✔ Growing companies that used strategic partners initiated 23 percent more new products over the previous two years than those that did not use partners.

  ✔ More than 51 percent of these high-growth companies used partnering to grow.

✔ Forty-one percent teamed with suppliers, while 24 percent teamed with marketing or sales partners, and 3 percent formed formal joint ventures.

✔ The rewards for partnering were that the average new product or service paid off its initial investment in 16 months.

The largest number of strategic alliances can be found in the software industry and in biotechnology, which is not surprising when you consider that technology, communications, and transportation have created an enormous number of opportunities in a fast-moving marketplace. The only way that smaller companies can take advantage of these opportunities is by working together.

Bringing Great Minds Together with Technology

Of all the new technologies from which small, growing businesses have to choose today, none has a greater impact than network computing. High speed communications and file sharing gives your business a power it never had before. Network technology lets businesses meet their customers' wishes even if they don't have the solution in-house. All that businesses have to do is seek out someone in the virtual world who can solve the problem, have that company send the solution to them and, bingo — they look like heroes.

Today, businesses aren't concerned with being large in terms of *scale*. They are more concerned with being large in terms of *scope* — being able to pull together a number of diverse resources that may come from a variety of locations outside their businesses, even from their competitors.

Described in Donna Fenn's 1997 article, "Sleeping with the Enemy," John Anson's business designs and builds equipment for large companies such as General Electric. In the past, when Anson secured a job that was too big for his small business to handle, he called on some of his competitors to help him. This precedent proved to be a stepping stone when GE and other big companies began to outsource more and more of their operations, and the size of the individual jobs more often than not were too large for Anson's company alone.

To solve the problem, Anson went to his competitors with a plan to do a $15 million project for GE that he would coordinate. They agreed and the group got the contract. Since then, Anson has created an agile web of strategic alliances with more than a dozen companies and they are now able to do projects with GE valued at more than $60 million. He has also kept those jobs from going to companies in other countries.

There are four primary reasons for making strategic alliances:

✔ You can provide better service to your customers and gain access to new markets.

✔ You can take on larger projects and share the risk rather than taking on the projects alone.

✔ Strategic alliances give your employees the opportunity to work on more interesting projects that challenge them beyond the things your company normally does, for example, to have access to new technology that the partner owns.

✔ You can grow your company.

If your business has any of these goals, read on because strategic alliances are just what the doctor ordered.

Creating the Digital Nervous System

Using technology to help you create and manage strategic alliances starts inside your own company. In Chapter 1, we introduced the concept of the "Digital Nervous System," which is the brainchild of Microsoft co-founder Bill Gates. We have repeated our graphical depiction of the system here for your convenience.

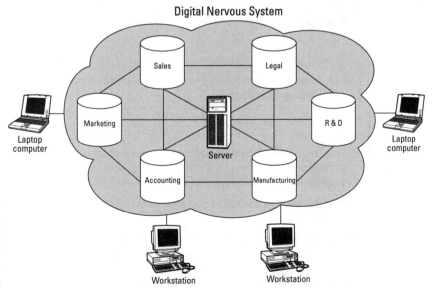

Figure 11-1:
The Digital Nervous System.

In short, the Digital Nervous System is a way to use technology to link all the information, processes, and people in your business together. It also helps you link with companies outside your organization — your strategic alliances. The goal is to create a system that resides in the background doing what it's supposed to do and supporting the activities your business undertakes. The basic technology components of the Digital Nervous System are the following:

- ✔ A server that is a central repository for company information.
- ✔ Workstations for everyone to connect them to the network.
- ✔ Modems or high speed connections such as DSL or T1 lines.
- ✔ Cables, hubs, and network cards to link all the workstations to each other and to the server.
- ✔ Network software.
- ✔ Office productivity software with basic spreadsheet, word processing, and database applications.

Making the Digital Nervous System work for you

The following list contains some ways to help information move throughout your business by using the Digital Nervous System:

- ✔ Have everyone use e-mail so that fast response to new information becomes a habit.
- ✔ Use PCs to do your business analyses and look for trends and patterns in your products, services, cash flow, and profitability.
- ✔ Use the network to create cross-functional teams that can share common information.
- ✔ Convert all of your paper processes to digital processes to speed them up, reduce errors, and free up your employees to do more important things.
- ✔ Use the network to provide constant feedback on products and processes with every employee having access to the metrics on which your company judges itself.
- ✔ Use the network to direct customer issues to the correct people to handle them.
- ✔ Use digital communications to define the scope of your business for any particular project or challenge. For instance, a customer complaint narrows the scope of the business to only the people involved in the situation, typically the customer, the customer service rep, and perhaps an appropriate manager. By contrast, a new product launch widens the scope to include customers, suppliers, and anyone who can give feedback to the company.

✔ Turn supplier transactions into digital transactions to allow for just-in-time delivery and to eliminate the intermediary between you and the customer.

✔ Use digital tools to let customers control their transactions with your business and solve some problems on their own.

✔ Use digital tools to connect with your strategic partners to facilitate communication and speed up operations.

Meeting virtually

Improved technology makes it possible for you to conduct meetings in virtual space with strategic partners that may be located anywhere around the world. This section discusses three ways that a small company with limited resources can conduct meetings online, from the most primitive method to the most advanced currently available:

✔ Hosted sites with private chat rooms

✔ Online meeting applications

✔ Hosted video conferencing

Hosted chat rooms

If your company has Internet access, then you already have the ability to have online chat meetings at no charge. Through sites like `www.e-groups.com` and AOL, you can set up a private chat room and hold a virtual business meeting. The advantages are that it's easy, fast, and doesn't cost you anything. On the other hand, it's rather cumbersome because it's like conducting a meeting using instant messaging. You post what you want to say and wait to see what everyone else posts.

Online meeting applications

There are several applications available that let you set up something similar to a phone bridge where everyone calls into a designated toll-free number and the company hosts a conference call. In this case, the "phone bridge" is a directory on your server and you call in from your computer. After everyone phones in, a window on your monitor acts much like a chat room.

The difference between using a chat room and an online meeting application is that the meeting applications have the ability to support digital video. If you and your team members have digital video cameras attached to your computers, you can actually see each other during one of these sessions. Two of the most popular and basic Internet communication tools are ICQ from ICQ.com and NetMeeting from Microsoft. Visit their respective sites at:

✔ `www.icq.com`

✔ `www.microsoft.com/netmeeting`

Keep in mind that the quality you achieve from this form of video conferencing leaves much to be desired. However, it's an inexpensive way to get up and running with local, regional, and worldwide communication over the Internet.

Hosted video conferencing

If you want real video conferencing, because the ability to see team members is critical, you may want to consider using a site like Kinko's. Many of their locations have video-conferencing facilities that you can rent. Everyone goes to the location nearest him or her at the same time, and voilà, you have a virtual meeting in real time.

Many small businesses that can't afford to invest in video-conferencing equipment (although the equipment is quickly becoming fairly affordable) or that don't use the technology very often use facilities like Kinko's on an as-needed basis.

Remember that the hardware is just one part of the cost of video conferences. The network connection also can be expensive.

Growing Rapidly with Technology Alliances

Network computing is the technology that has had the greatest impact on companies that are planning to grow. Networks have the ability to launch a company to the next level. For a relatively minor investment, small companies can gain access to state-of-the-art information management systems that rival those of much larger companies. Network computing is the first step in preparing your company to grow rapidly. But most smaller companies can't afford all the technology they may need nor can they handle growth all by themselves. To grow rapidly, whether you're a software manufacturer, an entertainment company, or a consumer products company, you must reduce cycle time.

Cycle time is the time it takes to design and produce your product or service and get it into the market. In today's fast-paced market — chaotic-paced in some industries — no company can take its sweet time about getting to market. To move fast enough, small companies need help.

Use a matchmaker

It's not always easy or possible to begin a strategic alliance on your own, particularly if that alliance requires that you gain access to the proprietary information of your much larger and very dominant partner. As described by Christopher Caggiano in a 1999 *Inc.* article, Richard Farrell's Boston-based company, Full Armor, produces a specialized software that enables the information technology departments of large firms to control and customize the applications their users can access via their desktop computers. Farrell was having difficulty, however, getting IT departments to purchase his product without assurances that the software was forward-compatible with future releases of the Windows operating system. To provide those assurances, Farrell needed proprietary technical information from Microsoft, not to mention the ability to share that information with his customers — a difficult quest at best.

It didn't take long for Farrell to realize that he needed help dealing with the impossibly complex maze that is Microsoft Corporation. Getting to the right people was critical to his potential success. That's when Farrell contacted Sarah Gerdes, CEO of Business Marketing Group Inc. (BMG), a specialist in matching small companies with large strategic partners.

The advantage of using a matchmaker was that Gerdes knew her way around the giant software company and also was an *insider* when it came to understanding Microsoft's strategic direction. She had their respect. Without the help of Gerdes, Full Armor may never have developed the strategic partnership that it needed with Microsoft.

We've worked closely with various groups at Microsoft and can vouch for the value of matchmakers like BMG. Here are some tips from our experience that may help you begin a strategic partnership with a much larger company:

- ✔ **Learn their language.** Every company has its own language — its own way of talking about things. You have to be able to read between the lines because often you won't receive direct answers to your questions. For example, when Microsoft says that it is casually investigating some new "buzz" they're hearing from the marketplace, chances are they have already designed a prototype product or purchased a small company that is doing what they're hearing about. Microsoft is often much farther along the learning curve than is apparent on the surface. Always assume the company knows more than you think they do.

- ✔ **Get to the right people.** While we have had the privilege of meeting and knowing the people at the top of many large companies, they are not always the right people to deal with if you want to get things done (in fact, quite the opposite is usually true). In companies the size of Microsoft, product managers and others may control huge budgets and make important product/market decisions — they are the ones you have to persuade to deal with your company.

- ✔ **Understand that your relationship will be measured based on return on investment (ROI).** You need to show your partnering company that they will make more money dealing with you than they would dealing with someone else or not dealing at all (opportunity cost). But, it's not just about money. ROI is measured in many other ways like joint marketing opportunities, access to a market the company hasn't tapped, or access to an expertise that they don't have.

✔ **Turn your company into Goliath.** Just because your company is a gnat relative to the size of your potential partner, doesn't mean you can't control what happens in the relationship. But to do that, you need to establish your company's value to your partner from the first day. Then continue to take control by setting goals and milestones that involve both companies. Get involved in activities that will bring added value to your partner beyond the scope of your current relationship.

✔ **Build your beachhead.** After you establish a relationship with one group of people at the company, extend your reach to others at every opportunity by suggesting ways that this relationship can benefit other groups in the organization. If you get on an e-mail distribution list for a group, you have instant credibility when that e-mail is forwarded to another area of the company.

Become an instant global company with partners

Although putting your company on the Internet can give you an instant global presence, success requires more than merely putting up a Web site and hoping someone in Italy will find you through a search engine. You need to develop strategic partners that will give you global credibility.

Unlike businesses in the United States, companies in most foreign countries will not do business transactions with your small company until they develop a relationship built on trust. You may fax information about your products and services to potential clients in Saudi Arabia and then not hear anything from them for months. They're not in a hurry. When you finally do hear something, it may just be the beginning of a long dialog leading, finally, to a sale.

To get around this problem and speed things up, you may want to consider partnering with a company that already does significant business in that country and has products or services that are compatible to yours. That strategic alliance may let you place their logo on your Web site and feature it in your promotional materials so that it's clear to your customers that you have a stamp of approval from a company they know and respect. If your partnering company happens to be located in the region of the world you're trying to reach, so much the better. It's all about who you know.

Partners and Knowledge: Managing the Three-Ring Circus

We are not going to tell you that if you set up your technology effectively, your strategic alliances will manage themselves — it's not quite that easy. Setting up a network of strategic alliances is analogous to watching a child play with Legos. While he may take great pains to patiently build a complex structure, there is never a sense that it will be permanent. More easily than it was built, it can be taken apart, leaving distinct pieces and no sense of loss.

Strategic alliances take a lot of effort on the front end because they're more about business than they are about technology. And when your partner is a much larger company, you have to protect your company against abuse and the belief by the larger company that it is in control of everything. When one company has more critical resources such as money, technology, or human capital than the other, then it has the most power in the relationship. However, if that company, because of the alliance, loses control over some of its resources, it loses its power. There are some things you can do to ensure that any strategic partnerships you have run as smoothly as possible.

- ✔ Always do your homework on the company you're planning to partner with. This will be an important relationship that will have a significant impact on your business. Investigate the company and its principals thoroughly by talking with customers, suppliers, competitors, and employees.

- ✔ Always create a written document that spells out the duties and responsibilities of the partners as well as how the financial part will work. It should also detail the ownership and rights to any intellectual property that either company owns or develops.

- ✔ Make sure that the other company has the equivalent (or better) technology to yours so that you can streamline as many of your communications and transactions as possible.

- ✔ Define a contact person in the other organization who manages the partnership from that end.

- ✔ If you have a good relationship with the customer, you have power even in a partnership where your partner is a much larger company.

- ✔ Make sure that the benefits of the partnership flow in both directions; in other words, make sure that it's a win/win situation. Define the strategic direction of the partnership.

Dealmaking in a virtual world

In some industries, technology has meant the difference between success and failure. It may surprise you to know that the cattle industry is one such case. A notion by Texas rancher Anne Anderson took cattle production into the virtual world. Anderson had tried for years to form an alliance among cattle producers so that they would be able to turn out steaks that were consistent in size, taste, and tenderness. But pulling together a bunch of independent cattle companies was like trying to herd cats.

Anderson looked for a company that could provide tracking technology, networks, and security to track beef from the range to the refrigerator so that she would have a better chance of influencing her colleagues in the industry. That value chain included ranchers, feedlot operators, packing plants, processors, distributors, supermarkets, and restaurants. Frustrated at her inability to find an adequate tracking company, Anderson decided to start her own. With three other people, she founded AgInfoLink. Operating as a virtual company was the only way to go because in the first year, AgInfoLink's clients came from Argentina, Australia, Canada, Mexico, and seven states domestically. Today AgInfoLink is one of several companies performing this type of service, which means that Anderson solved a real need in the beef industry.

Out of AgInfoLink's experience come several tips that you can apply to your business:

- ✔ Be sure that you have good reasons to have employees and partners in different geographic locations; make sure that those locations are near customers. AgInfoLink's programmers are typically located near ranchers in order to test new technology as the company develops it.

- ✔ It's not enough to rely solely on e-mail and the phone. Set up an intranet as quickly as possible. New employees, for example, should be able to get answers to their most frequently asked questions by logging onto the intranet instead of bothering their supervisor with messages by e-mail. You can even put your employee handbook online. Don't wait until you perfect your intranet to get it running. Put information, schedules, and anything else of interest to employees up as quickly as possible, so your employees can begin to enjoy the benefits of an intranet.

- ✔ Meet your new people in person first. It's worth the effort to have new hires and new partners meet key people in your organization before they begin working with you. This lends a personal touch and makes it easier to communicate with those same people in the virtual world.

- ✔ Wherever possible, try to place two people together in one location. As AgInfoLink found out early in its operations, it can get lonely at the "outposts" and having someone to bounce ideas off in a face-to-face mode can make all the difference.

- ✔ Control the potential for e-mail distraction. A good rule to follow is to encourage your partners and employees to check e-mail only twice a day. You should also ask them to configure their e-mail so that it doesn't automatically notify the user when new e-mail arrives. This notification tends to disrupt concentration and reduce productivity. Depending on the importance of e-mail to your daily business, checking two or three times a day at the most appropriate times for your business should be sufficient to keep everyone up to speed on what's happening.

- ✔ Create a daily "report card" on your business that gets sent to everyone. AgInfoLink's "Daily Flash" reports on the day's sales and cattle enrollments, and then compares them to the previous day's.

TIP

For a daily report like AgInfoLink's "Daily Flash," you can use a Digital Dashboard (described in the following section) to keep important information updated automatically on the user's desktop.

Knowledge management: Staying on top of everything

With information flowing freely and businesses partnering more, the sharing of proprietary information is crucial and knowledge management is a critical function of any business. Technology facilitates the sharing of information among partners, but technology alone doesn't give you the competitive advantage you seek. Knowledge management is the key.

Take a look at the desk in your office. It's probably loaded with information — everything from the morning newspaper to your schedule for the day to all those files you haven't gotten to yet. That's probably just a start! All that information with no organization or method to create knowledge from chaos means a lost opportunity. The following exercise can help you prioritize all that information piled on your desk. It's called the lifeboat exercise.

Suppose you're stranded on a lifeboat and you're only allowed to have four things with you. What would they be?

1. _____

2. _____

3. _____

4. _____

Modify the exercise to fit your office situation. If you could only have certain information visible to you at one time on your computer screen to make your most important business decisions, which four pieces of information would you absolutely have to have on that screen? Make a list.

1. _____

2. _____

3. _____

4. _____

This is a very real question because more and more business owners are finding value in something called a *dashboard*. All the things that are important to you (production stats, distribution status, e-mail, schedule, stock info, weather, news, and so on) can be presented to you in one screen on your monitor. Having all this valuable information at a glance increases the ability to make quick decisions which, in turn, increases your competitive advantage.

Dashboards

The dashboard, or *personal business portal,* can integrate all your typical business information and content from your local network, the Internet, and Extranet. Dashboards can work in real time giving you updates as they are available. They can also help you:

- ✔ Prioritize information that is important to you so it can be emphasized.

- ✔ Activate alarms that are triggered by information such as stock quotes, sales figures, and important reminders.

- ✔ Continue to collect less critical information in a designated area where it can be browsed on demand.

- ✔ Dispose of junk information before you even see it.

Figure 11-2 shows how you can choose which information to include in your digital dashboard.

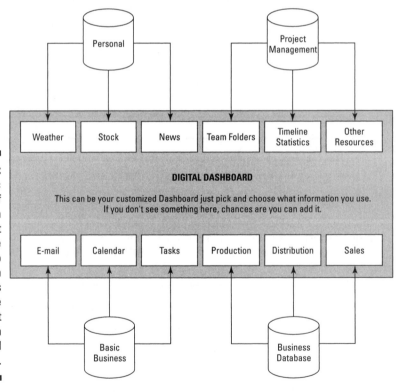

Figure 11-2: The basic types of information (boxes) that can be brought into one screen as well as the source of that information (round containers).

In order to view information from these sources, you traditionally had to look at separate programs and windows. Now, you can consolidate all of this information into one main screen. Placing a system in the middle that allows all this information to be shared enables your staff, customers, and partners to easily access the critical information they need to do their jobs — whether that information comes from the Internet or some other network.

Setting up this type of scenario takes some well thought-out planning and some serious tech skills. Chances are you will want to use the services of a solution provider for creating a dashboard that is right for you. Having a dashboard built from scratch can be very useful, but it can also be very expensive because of the time involved. Once you understand how much it might cost you, figure out how cost effective a dashboard will be. For most businesses, spending money on a customized dashboard is probably overkill. However, you now know another tool that may be able to help streamline your business awareness.

Chapter 12

Using Technology to Develop New Products and Services

• •

In This Chapter

▶ Developing new products in a digital world

▶ Creating virtual products and mass customizing by means of technology

▶ Outsourcing product development

• •

*B*ecause developing new products is a costly proposition and entrepreneurs are usually dealing with limited resources, they often have difficult times with product development. Small companies also don't have big teams of expensive engineers and in-house scientists who devote themselves exclusively to coming up with new products to expand the company's markets. Today's volatile environment has brought about an interesting change, however — now big companies are also having difficulty keeping up with the rate of change. They're having trouble keeping pace with their customers who are demanding the following:

✔ Superior levels of quality

✔ Extraordinary levels of variety

✔ Dramatic increases in reliability

✔ Significant decreases in cost

These demands are a challenge for any business to achieve, let alone a small business with limited resources. Not only do you have to design and develop a product that is viable in the market today, but you also have to create some basic technology that will live for several years so that you can get a superior return on your investment.

We don't disagree with that goal and it certainly still has its place; but today new variables have been added to the mix — the Internet and new information systems technology — and these variables affect product development in ways no one could have predicted. The Internet and new information systems technology have leveled the playing field, letting small companies enjoy the advantages of fast-cycle product development, early prototyping, and design-for-manufacture in ways they couldn't before.

In this chapter, you'll see how your company can become a product innovator or inventor using technology to speed up the product development process and make it more effective.

Doing Product Development in a Digital World

Let's start with a basic question. *Why should your company be doing product development in the first place?* Here are several reasons:

- ✔ New products enable your company to set standards and establish a brand that everyone recognizes and wants to buy. New products that enjoy patent protection also create barriers that prohibit competitors from legally copying your product for a certain period of time.

- ✔ An innovative company creates excitement within the organization, which makes it easier to attract good people, receive publicity, and draw more customers.

- ✔ If you integrate new products with new processes for producing those products, you make it much more difficult for competitors to copy what you're doing.

Whether you do your product development in-house or outsource it to someone else (we discuss this later), new product development should be an integral part of your growing business.

What's different in a digital world

Consider the following scenario:

Your company wants to produce a software product that searches the Internet to find small business owners who want to share resources. You don't know what the features of your product are beyond that basic idea. You're not sure exactly who the customer is outside the fact that it is a small business owner (SBO). You think you know how this software may benefit the SBO, but you don't know exactly what it will take or cost to build it.

You proceed to build a crude prototype of your new product and give it to a bunch of people whom you know like to try new software — beta testers. As you get feedback from your beta testers, you integrate their suggestions into the product and then send them another version to test.

This activity goes on for several more rounds and within six months, you have a product ready for market. You know exactly what the customers' expectations are, how they will use it, and what they like and don't like about it because you put it into the hands of your beta testers early in the game.

This scenario is an example of how product development takes place in a digital world that runs on Internet time. In fact, Netscape, the company that brought the power of the Internet to the mass market with its Netscape browser, used this very approach to develop its product. Had Netscape chosen the traditional route for product development, discussed later in this chapter, it would have taken much longer, and the company would have missed its window of opportunity to be the first mover in the market; someone else would have stepped into the gap to become the first branded interface to the Internet. When Netscape developed its product, it identified a market of potential customers who really didn't know much about the Internet. Netscape proceeded to give that market what it needed to become aware of the power of the Internet.

In summary, product development in the digital world means this:

✔ It's difficult to define markets clearly and precisely for new products.

✔ You should think of the market as a constantly moving target that you won't be able to hit for some time, if ever.

✔ You must quickly execute your product development.

✔ You need to get a product into the market in its primitive form as quickly as possible.

✔ You must continually improve the product. Change comes faster than you expect.

We contend that using technology can help you overcome obstacles and achieve desired outcomes. Technology also helps you develop your products much more quickly.

Why doing it faster matters

Today it seems that everything is happening faster — in Internet time, as it's called. The Internet and e-mail have changed people's perceptions about the speed of business transactions and business activities. Everyone expects mail and other documents to be delivered almost instantly. Everyone also expects to have information available at their fingertips. It's no wonder that the need for speed has filtered its way into product development tasks.

Two good reasons exist for why you may want to use technology to develop products quickly.

✔ First, if you develop products close to the time you introduce them into the market, those products are more likely to meet customers' current needs.

✔ Second, if you can gain a six-month product development jump on competitors in a market where the typical design-to-market time is 18 to 24 months, that head start can translate into as much as three times the profit over the market life of the product. Now, isn't that worth it?

We're operating on Internet time and customers' desires and preferences are shifting constantly, so your company must develop the ability to respond quickly to stay in the game.

The product development cycle: It's not linear

Product development may be the label under which we place all issues related to recognizing an opportunity — designing a product, creating a prototype, testing it, and developing a production-quality product — but it is not a function that takes place in a vacuum. Picture a team of engineers off in their own part of the building, working on something that no one else in the organization understands or may even realize is happening. That's the way product development took place in a traditional sense for years. The process was similar to the following:

✔ Opportunity recognition

✔ Concept investigation

✔ Initial design preparation

✔ Prototype building and field testing

✔ Initial test production run

✔ Market introduction and ramp up

Notice how the process depicts discrete tasks, one following the other. You don't build a prototype until you complete the initial design preparation. You certainly don't start your initial market test until you have a production-quality prototype.

In today's chaotic, digital environment, it doesn't work that way; in fact, it often can't work that way and succeed because that process is too slow. Today you need to involve representatives from marketing, finance, engineering, manufacturing, suppliers, distributors, and customers from the beginning so that you can move quickly with fewer design errors. Businesses in the digital age organize around a product rather than around departments. In this way, they can innovate rapidly.

Figure 12-1 depicts this dynamic process.

What the PD Cycle Really Looks Like

Figure 12-1:
What the PD
cycle really
looks like.

The product development process that Figure 12-1 depicts resembles a whirling dervish where inputs and outputs from many sources go into the design and development of the product. These sources may be located inside the organization or in geographically distant places, but you bring them together for the product development process by means of technology. We talk about the types of technology you can use to accomplish product development in the following section.

Using Technology to Create Virtual Products and Mass Customize

Technology is responsible for many changes in the way we conduct business. It also has been the precipitator of new types of products — *virtual products* — that businesses mass customize for individual customers. Virtual products are products that can be made anytime, in any place, and in any number of ways. In fact, the customer can actually take part in the creation of a virtual product. For example, digital cameras give customers instant pictures that they can manipulate on computer screens. Computers and software let users create all sorts of digitally based products. Some of the most sophisticated products that used to take months and cost hundreds of thousands of dollars to produce can now be produced on an engineer's desktop system and cost less than $10,000.

Virtual products are not just about putting control in the hands of customers. They're also about tailoring products to the needs of a specific customer in terms of features, design, delivery, and timing. The next section describes some of the technology tools businesses use to develop these new products and enhance the product development process.

The tools and rules of the game

Companies that understand and use information technology (IT) effectively tend to be better at developing competitive new products than companies that do not make use of IT's full potential. An investment in the specific types of technology that can speed up your product development process and get you into the market sooner is certainly worthwhile, and in some industries vital.

- ✔ **Rule 1: Get the customer involved in product development.** The potential customer for your product should be part of the development team from the conception of the product idea so that you don't waste time and money on features and benefits that the customer doesn't perceive as valuable.

- ✔ **Rule 2: Design right the first time.** The design of a new product is the biggest determinant of the product's final cost, so it's important to spend time on good design with a team that includes all the functional areas of your business, plus the customer.

- ✔ **Rule 3: Integrate product and process.** If you don't design a process to produce your product simultaneous to the development of the product, you risk designing a product that will cost too much to produce. Besides, integrating product and process makes it harder for others to copy what you're doing.

- ✔ **Rule 4: Get to a physical prototype fast.** The sooner you can get your product design into a physical form, the sooner you can put it into the customer's hands for testing, and that's when you really find out what works and what doesn't.

In the following sections, we briefly discuss a few information technologies, such as databases, simulation and calculation software, data integration by means of networking, and interfaces between design and production. Notice how companies use technology to follow the basic rules of product development.

Databases: Discovering the needs of the customer

One of the biggest boons to marketers has been database technology, which lets them look at and analyze customer information in a variety of ways. If you've been doing a good job of talking with your customers and recording the information you acquire, you have a tremendous source of knowledge about those customers. You can put that knowledge to work to develop new products and services that satisfy your customers' needs.

Even small businesses can mass customize

When David Meadows graduated from college, he never had a notion that he would someday own a successful software company that found its niche in developing corporate screensavers for promotional, incentive, and training purposes. He noticed that screensavers could really act like daily calendars, so he took the traditional screensaver concept and merged it with entertainment, information, and technology to produce a customized package that lets companies reach their target customers or employees. The screensavers incorporate text, photos, sounds, animation, and even time-released messages.

In 1997, he introduced his IncentiveScreen, based on the notion that goals enhance employee performance. His research found that screensavers are used 38 percent of the time that a computer is on, and those two pieces of information turned on a lightbulb in his head. Picture a company like Xerox with more than 6,000 employees competing for a trip to Hawaii.

Meadow's company will customize a screensaver with photos of Hawaii and motivational quotes, all designed to provide a daily visual reminder of the goal.

Oracle was the first to come to ScreenShop (www.screenshop.com) to produce a new technology for creating instant screensavers on the fly. With ScreenShop's proprietary technology, clients can have their own picture taken on location and within five seconds receive a 3½-inch floppy disk with their own photo inside a predesigned customized screensaver. Lycos, the online search engine, had ScreenShop create 10,000 screensavers, which they distributed at SuperBowl XXXIII in Miami, Florida.

Today, Meadow's clients include such major companies as Citibank, Sony, GlaxoWellcome, Lucent Technologies, and Hewlett-Packard. When you are the first in the market with a customized product, you establish the rules and you earn the brand recognition.

A relational database is an organizational tool that can match customer needs and preferences to product features. With the knowledge gained from the database, you and your team can make decisions about costs and benefits of including or not including certain features in your products. If you're not very familiar with databases, you may want to consider buying an off-the-shelf application that has easy templates to get you up and running quickly. One of the easiest database applications is Claris FileMaker Pro. You may want to contact a solution provider who can suggest an appropriate application that fits your environment and assist you in building a database that is tailored for you.

The database is only the beginning, though. You must get your customer physically involved in your product development process — Rule 1. Bring a focus group of customers into your design meetings, into your prototype building workshop, and onto your manufacturing floor. Let them test and use the product at every stage. Every piece of feedback they give you is worth its weight in gold because it will save you from having to go back and redesign your product after you think it's market-ready.

Simulation: Finding problems early

Product-development technology used to be solely focused on costly computer-aided design (CAD) software and engineering databases. Now the tide is turning to other kinds of applications that are equally important. Simulation and calculation software are being used in the earliest stages of product development to detect development and specification errors.

With this type of software, you can test the way your product functions in a variety of scenarios. You base the design of these scenarios on how the customer will use the product. For example, you may be designing a machine to be used at construction sites. You could set up the test defining weather conditions, level of stress to the machine based on continuous use, and even the way in which the customer handles the machine (some customers are very hard on machines). This is an example of Rule 2, "Design right the first time," in action.

Companies have found that using simulation software when designing product-assembly processes actually reduces the cost of manufacturing because they can incorporate the customer's ideas — no matter how wild — into the simulation and test them without incurring a big expense. It's a good way to narrow down the feature list for the product so that you can keep prototyping costs down. Sometimes a particular feature can cause the costs of assembly to increase enormously. Simulation software can help to discover those issues.

In general, the design of a new product represents about 8 percent of your product budget, but it accounts for 80 percent of the ultimate cost of your new product.

Integration: Bringing data and tasks together

Integrating data and tasks is another way to utilize technology in product development, and successful companies accomplish this integration. Because everyone is trying to reduce the time it takes to develop products in this fast-paced world, it's important to integrate the product development processes you perform in-house with those that your strategic partners conduct.

Integrating CAD and simulation databases and sharing that information over a computer network makes communication with partners easier and the entire development process go faster. There is an additional benefit to Rule 3's integration of product and process: It makes it more difficult for someone to copy your product without also understanding the process.

Many companies are resorting to Enterprise Resource Planning Systems, or ERPs, to manage their data and the systems in their businesses in the areas of scheduling, service, maintenance, manufacturing, and test protocols, to name just a few. ERPs are specially designed application packages that you can use to facilitate the communication of information between strategic partners and the business.

Essentially, ERP is a fancy term for business and data management software and systems. Until very recently, only very large companies could afford to use this customized software, but most of the major providers are now developing versions for smaller businesses as well. Two names you might recognize in this category are SAP and QAD.

Interfaces: Letting machines talk to each other

Another thing that the most successful companies do is develop interfaces between CAD programs used in design and direct numerical control (DNC) machinery used in production. These interfaces let you design a product, send that information to a DNC machine (very simply, an industrial machine that can be programmed to produce a specific part or a simple product), and — voilà — your design becomes a physical product right before your eyes! The machines typically use lasers to cut the raw material. Sometimes a part moves from one machine to another until it is completed.

We have an entrepreneur friend in the apparel industry who uses CAD programs to design fabric. The design is then transmitted over the network to advanced Stohl knitting machines that take raw yarn and transform it into a piece of fabric with the design in it.

Another technique being used is called *stereo-lithography,* where the device that produces the prototype from the CAD model consists of a vat of light-sensitive polymer in liquid form and a laser. The laser is used to solidify thin layers of the polymer, which build up to produce the part. This becomes a prototype that can be tested before it's produced in a more expensive form, such as metal.

The sooner you have a physical product, the sooner you can spot design flaws that you couldn't see on the computer screen.

For some types of products, nothing beats actually using the product for finding out what you need to change. This is particularly true when you're talking about the ergonomics of a product, that is, the ease and comfort of use. The only real way to insure that your product is comfortable and natural to use is by playing with a physical model of the product. The DNC makes the physical model available for testing much quicker than traditional methods can, thus facilitating Rule 4: Get to a physical prototype fast.

Some of the best companies in the CAD business today — like SolidWorks and 3D Systems — are producing mainstream versions of their very sophisticated 3D modeling applications. You can also outsource your 3D design needs if you don't want to invest in the application.

There are many technologies from which to choose. You need to decide which technologies are critical to your competitive advantage. Invest only in the technology that you need to gain superiority in your markets. Then look for ways to acquire other necessary technology through joint ventures and licensing.

Rightsizing is the way to go

One of this book's authors once dealt with an inventor who had designed and built an automatic tape dispenser that provided clean-cut strips of tape at the touch of a button. The prototype was beautiful to behold, and if you looked inside the machine, it was a wonder of engineering wizardry worthy of a place in the Smithsonian. The problem was that he engineered it to such a high degree that he had to price the product at $39.95 to make any money. To consumers, the product was merely a tape dispenser, and a price of $39.95 was way out of the ballpark. They didn't see the value and so weren't willing to pay for it.

This example brings to mind two questions you should ask yourself anytime you're developing a new product and considering adding a technological bell or whistle:

- ✔ Is the feature something that will excite customers so that they will pay more for it?

- ✔ Is the feature simply an add-on that entices customers to choose your product over another, but doesn't provide enough value for customers to pay more for the product? If this is the case, it is likely you won't get back the money you put into adding the feature.

Be cautious because sometimes simplicity does not equate with value in the customer's eyes. For example, purchasers of airplanes were shown a picture of a typical airplane cockpit with its hundreds of gauges, dials, and switches (the majority of which, by the way, serve no purpose). Then those same customers were shown a simplified version of the cockpit design — very much like that which you find in the typical automobile — that would result in ease of use, higher safety, and save money. Customers rejected it outright because it didn't look "serious" enough.

To counteract this problem, we suggest that you listen to the *signal-to-noise ratio* when it comes to product features. Your goal should be to provide just the features that customers perceive as valuable. You want to maximize customer satisfaction while minimizing cost. To accomplish that, consider the following four criteria for determining product features:

- ✔ **Attractive:** If you don't include these features, you won't lose customer satisfaction, but including them can greatly increase satisfaction. The classic example involves automobile cupholders. Automaker BMW put cup holders into its vehicles because customers complained about having nowhere to put their coffee. Customers would have still bought BMWs without cup holders, but they're much happier with them.

- ✔ **Apathetic:** These are features that customers may say they like, but the features don't really correlate to any degree of satisfaction. "Environmentally friendly" products are one example. It's politically correct to say that you like them, but most customers don't buy based on their inclusion in the feature set. Few customers will pay more for those features.

✔ **Necessary:** Absence of these features mean that you don't have a product and you have huge dissatisfaction among customers. For example, including a CD-ROM drive on a computer is quickly becoming a necessary feature.

✔ **Preferred:** These features actually increase customer satisfaction, so the more your product has, the better. The obvious example is Internet connections — you never have one that is fast enough.

How do you find out your customers' views regarding the features you're considering putting on your product? You ask them. That's why database marketing is popular with companies that produce consumer products. Creating a database of customer needs and preferences can provide a wealth of information to help you make decisions about product features.

Outsourcing Product Development: When You Can't Do It Yourself

It is very difficult for a small business to do all of its product development in-house because the development of a prototype product can cost as much as ten times the cost of the actual market-ready product. Why are prototypes so costly? The biggest reason is because you make prototypes in very small quantities, purchasing their components (parts, raw materials, and supplies) as individual units at full price without the discount you would normally get for a higher quantity. You also need to include the labor costs involved in getting the product to work the right way.

The other reason that doing everything in-house doesn't make sense when you're a very small company is that certain processes related to product development — like sheet metal forming, welding, powder coating, parts manufacture, and so forth — require expensive, specialized machines. Until you're producing in sufficient quantity to warrant the expense of purchasing these machines, you're better off outsourcing to a company whose core competency is the skill you require.

Tapping into consultants

Not all product-development activities that you outsource have to do with physical processes like welding and programming circuit boards. You can outsource many engineering design and design-related tasks if you don't have an engineer on staff. The following list contains some examples of consulting tasks that businesses often outsource to companies that specialize in specific tasks:

✔ Component design

✔ Parts integration

> ✔ Materials specifications
>
> ✔ Machinery to process
>
> ✔ Ergonomic design
>
> ✔ Packaging design
>
> ✔ Assembly drawings and specifications
>
> ✔ Parts and material sourcing

When you are outsourcing aspects of your product development, look for small engineering firms, solo engineers, and small job shops. They are usually quicker and less expensive than larger, name brand firms.

Thinking lean and mean

You have probably heard the phrase *lean and mean* in reference to the downsizing of large corporations. That was certainly true in the 1980s when corporations decided to trim down by firing many employees, thereby increasing profits. In today's Internet world, thinking lean and mean is something quite different. It is about ignoring traditional corporate structures completely.

A customer's main interest is value. Your company's size, the number of employees you have, whether you outsource many of your needs, and what your company looks like are not important to customers. All that matters to customers in terms of value is that you deliver what they want, when they want it, and in the way they want it. To deliver on that customer need, companies must be flexible in how they organize and use human capital.

Too often, companies create teams of employees or independent contractors to develop new products, and then never change the human composition of those teams. This is an internal focus rather than a customer focus and eventually it fails. Product development groups must be flexible and change to meet customers' demands not employees' demands. If the same people are always working together, they eventually develop "group think" and fail to innovate at a rapid pace. The only way to get people to upgrade their skills is to put them in new environments with new people. A company that is continually looking ahead to see what the next product will be will always have a place for its team members.

With today's network technology, bringing teams together, shifting them around, and providing them the information they need to do their jobs is easy and effective. Return to Chapters 10 and 11 to find out more about how to use technology to facilitate team building in your company.

Chapter 13

Making E-Commerce Work for You

● ●

In This Chapter

▶ Acquiring a dot-com site

▶ Helping customers find you on the Web

▶ Selling and buying through e-commerce

● ●

*T*oday it is no longer a question of *if* you should enter the e-commerce market, but of *when* you should enter. E-commerce is a phenomenon that perplexes many people and convinces others that they've found nirvana in a dot-com address in cyberspace. The reality is that the Internet is simply another distribution channel — albeit, a very effective one. It is faster, more efficient, and more global than any other channel you can utilize to buy and sell products and services.

In this chapter, we discuss the ins and outs of developing an e-commerce strategy. By the end of the chapter, you should have a good sense of whether or not your company should dip its toe into the pool or dive in headfirst and swim with the sharks. There is no mystery about what makes a successful e-commerce company. It's all in the details, and this chapter can help you understand some of those details.

Adding a Dot-Com to Your Name

For some companies, such as Pom Express (www.pomexpress.com), which supplies gear for cheerleaders, the decision to give up a traditional retail outlet and move lock-stock-and-barrel to the Web was the best decision they could have made. It means no overhead and the ability to sell globally. For Wine Country (www.winecountryonline.com), a company that didn't want to relinquish totally the traditional way of doing business, going online gave the company two profitable outlets and let it meet the needs of both types of customers: those that wanted the convenience of online ordering, and those that wanted to browse a real shop.

For most businesses today, adding a dot-com to their names is the logical next step in growing the business. For many start-up companies, it's the only way to go — low overhead, immediate global presence, and the thrill of making that first sale from the computer in your home office.

Before you get too excited about putting your business into cyberspace, though, consider the following:

- ✔ What you are trying to accomplish with your Web site.
- ✔ Whether your business is a good fit for e-commerce.
- ✔ What costs you will incur to set up the type of Web site you want.

Determining what you want to accomplish with your Web site

Knowing what you want to accomplish by going online is a critical first step in achieving an effective site. Yes, you want to make money, but the sites that are the most profitable are interesting to consumers and draw them in. Ask yourself three basic questions:

- ✔ **Whom do you want to attract?** Customers? Suppliers? Partners? Many different people and companies deal with your business. Which ones are potentially served by your having a Web site?

- ✔ **Do you want to offer information?** Many sites, such as www.prairiefrontier.com, www.women.com, and www.allbusiness.com, offer a wealth of information in particular areas of interest. PrairieFrontier seeks lovers of wildflowers and other natural environments, while Women.com provides a bounty of articles and resources of particular interest to women. AllBusiness, meanwhile, wants to be the best one-stop resource for small-business owners.

- ✔ **Do you want to create a sense of ownership in the business?** Sites like Raging Bull (www.ragingbull.com), which is dedicated to topics relating to investments, generate a sense of community by providing a place for like-minded people to gather, chat, and share information. Most of Raging Bull's content comes from the users of the site who post information, questions, resources, and so forth.

- ✔ **Do you want to educate people?** If you want to learn more about the fine art of tea drinking, Adagio Teas (www.discovertea.com) is on the Web to help you do just that. An online retailer of fine teas, Adagio Teas understands that you don't just sell products on the Internet; you have to provide added value to get people to return to your site over and over again.

Determining whether your business has e-commerce potential

Most businesses can justify an online component, if not a full e-commerce site. However, some businesses are easier to transfer to Internet mode than others. For example, businesses that require a high degree of personal service and depend on face-to-face interaction, or actually using a product before purchase, have a more difficult time adjusting to an online environment.

If you want a full e-commerce site where customers can purchase your products and services, here are a few criteria to consider when deciding if your business has e-commerce potential:

- ✔ Does your business have a product that you can easily deliver to customers?

- ✔ Do you have a product with broad market appeal?

- ✔ Do you want to reach a wide geographic area and have the ability to deliver product in those areas?

- ✔ Will you save money in terms of warehousing, retail outlets, and so forth by going online?

- ✔ Do you have the ability to get customers to your site?

Affirmative answers to these questions indicate that your company may be able to have a successful e-commerce site, but, again, your goals may be such that they don't require a full e-commerce site.

Determining the costs of starting up a Web site

You will find a lot of intimidating information about the costs of setting up an e-commerce site. Figures range from $5,000 to well over $1 million. One entrepreneur Kathleen works with set up a free site through his ISP, but he's just trying to provide a place where people can find out what he does (he's a consultant and writer) and how to contact him. Another entrepreneur Kathleen works with spent several hundred thousand dollars, but he needed a shopping cart and lots of graphics — essentially his catalog of products online.

It should come as no surprise to business owners that the biggest portion of the expense for an Internet site is labor, and that most companies use more than one professional service provider. So what's a small company to do to compete against these kinds of dollars? Costs of software and site design and construction are declining; however, the functionality needed to compete in this rapidly changing environment is increasing and becoming more complex. This means that your Web site must be able to do a lot more sophisticated things like provide a search engine, a shopping cart (if you're selling products or services), maintain a database of information and products, and so forth. All these functions add up to a lot of development time and money. Even on the low side, you're talking tens of thousands of dollars to get what you really want.

There are ways to bootstrap a good Web site, however. Here are a few tips.

Let a professional host your site

You can outsource the entire Web design and building effort to an application service provider (ASP). Companies like LoudCloud (www.loudcloud.com), the latest venture of Netscape founder Marc Andreesen, and Scient (www.scient.com) will gladly take the headaches of site design, development, and maintenance off your hands. Many of them will even host your site, which means that they will store and maintain all your Web pages on their servers.

When it comes to distribution, forget about doing your own; you have to hire too much expensive labor. Use the experts — FedEx and UPS — or find the best shipping rates and carriers through logistics experts like iShip (www.iship.com). Then track your shipments through companies like TanData (www.tandata.com). Spend a bit of time on the Internet exploring options. You will be amazed at how much information is out there waiting to be tapped and how many companies are ready to provide the products and services you need.

Managing e-mail from customers who visit your Web site can be a nightmare when your company starts growing and attracting more attention. Companies such as Critical Path (www.criticalpath.com) can make sure that you never have another sleepless night worrying about how to handle all the requests coming into your very successful e-business. They will manage your e-mail and respond according to your specifications.

Here are some of the advantages of using a hosting service:

✔ You normally get to market faster than you would doing it yourself. Remember, Internet time is the kind of speed that can kill if you don't know what you're doing. One of the most important things you can do is to get your site up quickly, but it also has to be well done — that's the catch. Most small companies can't achieve both on their limited resources. Furthermore, after you're up and operating, you can't slow down, and you have to learn how to move fast without spending a lot. So what's the solution? Get help; there's plenty of it out there.

✔ You have access to expensive services, such as multimedia, on an as-needed basis. Hosting services often provide the kinds of applications that a small business couldn't afford to purchase. You essentially rent them or pay a fraction of the cost for the development or use of a particular application. For example, accounting or human resource software can run into the tens of thousands of dollars to purchase. The software is designed for mid-sized and large business environments but retains every bit of value in smaller businesses. Small businesses can't afford to purchase software like this. However, that same small business is able to rent that software from the ASP for a price that it can afford and that is cost effective.

✔ You have access to higher bandwidths and more security than you could have afforded yourself. This means that your site will load faster, and the *applets* (little programs that load animated characters and other interesting things on your site) will pop up much faster. ASPs also maintain high levels of security on their servers so that your Web pages are protected from an unauthorized person going in and changing them.

✔ To provide the 24-hours-a-day, 7-days-a-week service that they need to provide, Internet hosts must have instantly available backups for disk storage, substitute Web servers, and alternative communications access routes. This means that your Web site is less likely to go down and be unavailable to your customers. It also means that if a disaster does occur, your Web site is backed up and can be recovered quickly.

How do you find the perfect host? Start with a free service called the Ultimate Web Host List, which catalogs and evaluates Web hosts and services. You can search hosts by category (Free, Budget, Personal, Small Business, Corporate, and so forth) or by a list of features in which the hosts specialize (such as RealAudio, which lets you listen to music).

To help you evaluate your potential Web host, we put together a list of questions that you may want to ask an ASP:

✔ **How big is the host's pipe?** The way your host connects to the Internet is important. For example, a T-3 line is faster than a T-1 line, which is faster than DSL. If your site has music, video, and/or animation, a server that is connected to a T-1 line is preferable. Web hosts perform a fine balancing act, among several servers running several sites, to maintain the highest performance levels for their clients. Make sure that you get your host to guarantee the bandwidth it claims to be providing to you. Sometimes other sites running on the same connection cause congestion, and your site may seem slow to the user at the other end.

✔ **What does the host do if its primary connection to the Internet goes down?** Does it have a backup connection that will kick in and keep everything online?

✔ **How much disk space does the host provide for you to store your HTML files?** Typically, a host provides between 5MB and 20MB of space in the basic fee. Beyond that, you pay a surcharge. Remember that up to about 800 normal HTML pages fit in about 5MB of space. Unless you're going overboard on graphics and animation or developing the latest graphical encyclopedia, 5MB should be a sufficient amount of space.

✔ **What kind of data and programs can you access?** If your company can't handle design and programming of the Web site and database management (where you store customer, product, and other information), you want a Web host that offers those services.

✔ **How secure is the site from hackers and viruses?** Look for at least these minimal layers of security on your site:

- Transaction security such as customer authentication, credit card checking, and electronic funds transfer. You want to be certain that the person using the credit card or electronic funds transfer on your site is the person who owns those rights, so you don't run the risk of losing money because of a fraudulent purchase.

- Online security such as Secure Socket Layers (SSL), Secure Electronic Transfer (SET), and data encryption (these software components help to protect information as it travels across wires).

Make sure to choose a Web host that can provide the services you need and that is easy to work with.

Helping Customers Find You

It's all well and good to establish a beachhead on the Internet, create an inviting site, and prepare those electronic cash registers to begin ringing; but, amid the crush of worldwide e-commerce businesses, how will customers find you? Remember the bricks-and-mortar adage: "Location is everything." The reality is that even your ability to be found on the Internet is a function of location.

Location on the Internet means that people surfing can find your URL or Web address (much like driving around a new city trying to find a street address). Several ways exist to increase your chances of customers finding you, and they vary in effectiveness. The following list gives you a few ideas:

✔ **Register with the major search engines.** Yahoo! (www.yahoo.com), Excite (www.excite.com), Lycos (www.lycos.com), MSN (www.msn.com), and HotBot (www.hotbot.com) are just a few of the search engines on the Web, some of which let you enter keywords that relate to your business. You can then retrieve a list of sites where those keywords typically show up.

✔ **Add keywords to your home page.** One of the best ways to ensure that your site comes up in the results of someone's search is to embed keywords, or tags, into the background of your home page. By doing so, virtually any query from any search engine will come up with a link to your site.

Sit down and brainstorm any and every keyword associated with what your business does. One strategy that many businesses employ is to add hundreds of other derivative keywords that may not be directly associated with their companies' products, goals, niches, or markets — but might be keywords that prospective customers search for.

For example, when you search on the Web and type the word *gym* to find a gym in your area, your results come up with links for workout clothes, vitamins, diets, and so on. Adding these keywords to the background of your Web page means that the words are hidden so the typical viewer can't see them; however, the words exist in the programming — which is what a search engine looks through.

✔ **Look for complementary Web sites and swap links.** If your target customer is on the Web, chances are she is going to all the sites that interest her. Go surfing on the Web and play the role of your customer. Try to figure out all the places a customer may go, and then contact those businesses for a mutually beneficial, barter-type deal. Offer them an opportunity to increase their traffic by placing a link to their Web site on your Web site.

Allowing another company to place a link on your site means that when customers go to your Web site, they see a banner advertisement for the other company's site. All the customer has to do is click on the banner, and the banner's link takes them directly to the other company's site. The other company — your potential partner — should reciprocate and place your banner on its site. By doing so, both companies increase Web traffic.

Cross-link on as many sites as you can — *it's free.* Cross-linking with complementary businesses provides long-term synergies and can do nothing but help your company and all the other companies involved.

✔ **Sign up to be in the Internet Yellow Pages.** Online directories like BigBook (www.bigbook.com) and BigYellow (www.bigyellow.com) function much like your telephone company's Yellow Pages. Customers can find your business by name, location, or product category.

✔ **Ask your customers where they go when they surf the Net.** Your customers may frequent online versions of their favorite offline magazines, newspapers, and retailers. If you're a customer trying to find a manufacturer of a particular item, for example, the logical place to go is the "bible" of manufacturers, The Thomas Register of American Manufacturers (www.thomasregister.com). The Thomas Register lists more than 155,000 vendors and 63,000 categories of products. It has users who perform well over 70,000 searches a day, which generate over 1,000 e-mail requests daily for information. Now that's a good way to get your customers to notice you.

✔ **Put a link on the sites that your customers visit frequently.** You may want to contact a site that your customers visit and investigate the possibility of putting a link to your site on its home page. Often, you can get a site to do so at no charge if there is a mutual benefit. In other cases, you have to pay for the link — how much is a matter of negotiation — usually on a monthly basis.

✔ **Don't forget offline publicity. It's free.** The best way to get your customers to notice you is through free publicity. Let the media, such as your local business journal, sell your business for you. If you have an interesting story to tell, the media will want to talk with you.

Also put your URL on anything from your business that goes out to customers, suppliers, and so forth: invoices, business cards, brochures, and catalogs, as well as in the signature section of your e-mail.

Avoiding Mistakes

In terms of Internet time (which is measured much like dog years), e-commerce has been around for a lifetime, so there are ample examples of what *not* to do. Here are some of those examples:

✔ **Don't price your products and services too low.** Doing so — a common dot-com pitfall — creates erroneous expectations on the part of your customers. You probably won't be able to cover your costs, which means that you won't be profitable. Some companies, such as Buy.com (`www.buy.com`), have used this strategy to attract people to their sites but now are having to find a way to increase prices so that they can make money. (What a concept!)

✔ **Don't think that merely spreading your dot-com domain name everywhere ensures the survival of your brand.** Music Boulevard and Cdnow were recognizable names, but no one knew which one was better or why. In other words, customers didn't know where the value was. The two companies merged because they seemed so homogenous to customers, but even that didn't work, and Columbia House, the well-known mail-order house, finally purchased them.

✔ **Don't forget that satisfying the customer is the most important thing.** The Christmas season of 1999 was famous for two reasons in the Internet world: First, online retailers racked up more sales than ever in the history of e-commerce; and second, online retailers failed to satisfy more customers than ever before. Many e-tailers didn't understand that the biggest and most important component of their businesses was fulfillment — warehousing, distribution, and delivery. E-tailers weren't prepared for the huge demands Christmas placed on that component of their business.

In the online business, supply-chain management is at least as important, if not more important, than the Web site itself. Be sure your warehousing, distribution, and delivery can keep pace with increased sales.

Winning on the Web

Here are some things you can do to increase your chances of success in the world of e-commerce:

✔ **Keep graphics to a minimum, but use them effectively.** Graphics should be kept under 12K so that they load quickly, keeping impatient visitors happy. Most monitors display graphics at 72 dpi, so you're wasting your time posting graphics at much higher resolutions. Also, remember that animations (those cute little moving icons, dancing babies, and other attention getters) really don't have a purpose that warrants their loading time. Unless you have a graphic arts site, choose graphics that are critical to your business's message, and keep them to a minimum.

✔ **Make your site easy to navigate.** Make sure that you have an easy-to-understand navigation bar on your site, one that appears on every page. You want to ensure that no matter which page customers land on, they will know where they are and where they can go from there.

✔ **Optimize your site.** How many times have you gone to a site and clicked on a link, only to find yourself in the twilight zone — the page no longer exists? Be sure to clean your site regularly of dead links so that pages load faster. If you developed your site yourself with WYSIWYG (what you see is what you get) applications like Macromedia's Dreamweaver or Microsoft FrontPage, you need to use a good code editor tool or hire someone to do it for you. If you absolutely must do it yourself, try using some great tools like WebsiteGarage (www.websitegarage.netscape.com) or Doctor HTML (www2.imagiware.com/RxHTML).

✔ **Watch your color selection.** Some colors do not translate well as they move over the Internet. Browsers can read 216 colors, so stick with those. You'll probably find what you want. To get color help, try Lynda Weinman's site at www.lynda.com/hex.html.

✔ **Make it easy for customers to contact you.** Be sure to put a contact page on your Web site that lists your company's e-mail address, phone number, fax number, snail mail address, and any people customers can contact for specific issues. Also, let users e-mail from your site directly to the company through a pop-up form.

✔ **Update, update, update your site!** We can't be more emphatic about this point. Customers will not keep coming back if they don't find anything new on your site on a regular basis. Keep it fresh, and your customers will visit often.

Part IV

Dealing with Tech Consultants and Other Wild Things

"TECHNICALLY HE'S A WIZARD, BUT AS A MANAGER HE LACKS PEOPLE SKILLS."

In this part . . .

One of the critical elements of a great technology strategy is the input of a tech consultant. You definitely don't want to create this strategy alone. But finding a great tech consultant is not an easy task. In this part, you get some help in choosing a tech consultant and knowing what to expect from the relationship. You also discover ways to avoid the problems that many business owners face when dealing with technology people and technology itself.

Chapter 14

Understanding Your Tech Consultant Choices

In This Chapter

▶ Knowing when to call in the professionals

▶ Deciding on the type of tech consultant you need

▶ Searching for the right tech consultant

Keeping up with technology is one of the greatest challenges that small-business owners face as they look to the future. How do you stay on top of what's new, and how do you know which technology may be beneficial to your business? Enter the technology consultant, the guru who can solve all your problems and get you on the road to technology nirvana, right?

If it were only that easy. The real problem is that consultants live in a world of DLL conflicts, revisions, patches, hot fixes, and crashes, but business owners typically don't. Skip the discussion and the techno-jargon — you just want the problem fixed. Right?

Dottie Hall, who sells marketing advice to software companies and buys equipment for her business, doesn't study computer magazines — she doesn't have time. What she does is call Tony Wainwright of ExecuTek, Inc in Phoenix and she takes his advice almost without question. Hall is not alone. In fact, the majority of small business owners (93 percent in one survey) rely on consultants and computer resellers to help them make their purchasing decisions, design and maintain their systems, and perform miracles in emergencies.

In this chapter, you can discover the many solutions available to help fill the gap in your need for technology expertise. You also gain an understanding of the world of the tech consultant so that you can find the best one for the money and deal with him or her in an effective way: a win/win situation for both of you.

Beam Me Up: Calling in the Professionals

You know it's time to call in the professionals when everyone else in your industry is racing by you because they've improved their business operations with technology. You know it's time to call in the professionals when you're spending too much time away from the business trying to solve tech problems. You know it's time to call in the professionals when you haven't had time to keep up on the latest technology and you're about to make a major purchase. You know it's absolutely time when the problem you're facing makes no sense whatsoever and nothing good can come from your sitting in front of the keyboard trying to wade through a mass of confusion.

You also need a tech consultant if you don't have anyone with technical knowledge in-house and you're thinking you can provide for your own technological needs (and do it cheaper) yourself. Trust us, you can't. Even if you have some experience with computers and networking issues, you probably can only see the smallest part of the whole picture. Unless you derive masochistic satisfaction out of staying after hours, late into the night, trying to configure the new network you just cobbled together in a piecemeal fashion, forget about doing it yourself. Getting things running the way you want will take you ten times longer; you will spend countless hours figuring out how to do it; and through it all, who will be running your business? At some point, you just have to accept that you're too valuable to spend time doing the tech tasks.

To save money, you may be tempted to use someone like your administrative assistant's son as your informal tech consultant. He's been playing around with computers since he was in diapers, and the cyberdude even has his own Web page, and maybe he actually can do what you want him to do. However — face it — this is your business you're talking about. This is serious stuff. Call in a professional; in the end, it will end up costing you much less in money, time, and frustration.

Determining your reasons for needing professional help

For every business, the reason to use professionals may be different. For example, you may have no one in your organization who really knows anything about technology, or your company is about to grow very quickly and you need to have the right systems in place to make that happen. Here are a couple of real life examples of why professional help is a worthwhile investment.

One financial services company in San Francisco decided it was time to call in the professionals after its own makeshift efforts at setting up a network failed and it needed to set up an officewide e-mail system and company Web site. The company decided to end its frustration by working with a Santa Clara–based company, CenterBeam, Inc. CenterBeam provided all the hardware, software, security, backup, and 24-hour tech support for about $165 a month per user on a subscription basis. What was attractive to the financial services company was the predictability and reliability of CenterBeam's service. When one of the PCs in its accounting department died unexpectedly, the company was able to pull a spare out of a closet, call CenterBeam, and ask them to transfer the backed-up data to the network. They were back in business in a very short time.

A company that provides automated systems management software didn't want its expensive software engineers troubleshooting its PCs or helping the rest of the employees. The company wanted them spending their time creating products, so its CEO signed up with Everdream Corp. of Mountain View, California. Now when he gets hung up in a program he's using, he contacts Everdream and lets a tech consultant access his computer remotely so that they can both see the screen and the tech can guide the CEO through the fix.

Like many other functions of your business that you outsource, the tech consultant's business is probably your information technology department — your chief technology officer (CTO) of sorts. He or she helps you devise your technology strategy and make decisions about hardware and software purchases. Your tech consultant also handles the installation of your technology and maintains the system. In fact, he or she does as much or as little as you want. Some tech consultants also do database development and other types of programming specific to your needs. Do you have time to do all that and your job too?

The complexity of today's technology and the speed at which business is conducted combine to produce a situation that screams for professional help. Where technology is concerned, bad things can definitely happen to good people. We want to encourage you to either hire that help in-house or outsource to a company that is used to working with small businesses.

Deciding on in-house or out-of-house help

Hiring your very own CTO (chief technology officer) probably ranks right up there with buying your very own corporate jet in terms of being within the realm of possibility. You can barely afford to pay yourself and your employees the salaries you would like to pay, so spending big bucks to get your very own tech consultant is just a pipe dream. Or is it?

That's what one entrepreneur thought. After all, his company was just a nine-person company dealing in a lot of paper in the form of industry profiles, news stories, and résumés in 1996 when he made the decision to take the leap and recruit a CTO for his company. His philosophy? He needed someone to drive the company's use of technology strategically. His advice? If your knowledge assets (customer lists, intellectual property, employee skills, and culture) are greater than your capital assets (equipment and facilities), then you need your very own CTO.

Getting champagne tech help on a beer budget

As more and more small businesses are seeing technology as a strategic asset rather than as an equipment expense, many of these businesses are considering the value of having a tech consultant on call 24/7. They realize that this person must not only have technology skills, but understand business as well. That's not always easy to find. Here are some resources for those who want an in-house tech but have a limited budget:

- **Students:** Business and engineering schools are full of eager students wanting to ply their trade — namely doing your tech work to help build their résumés or maybe start their own consulting companies. Students may work for as little as $15 an hour and you can hire them on an as-needed basis for projects or full-time for a one-time fee, if that's what you need.

- **Professors:** Many professors, as well as high school teachers, take on technology jobs over the summer months, and some continue those positions part-time throughout the year.

- **Your employees:** Within your own business, you may have a tech wannabe, someone who has a smattering of technology knowledge, but clearly has the potential to learn more. Get that employee some training and you may be able to develop a homegrown CTO for less money and fewer headaches.

- **Interns:** Many people who are choosing to work in new industries because they've left or been laid off from a job in another industry often need to start towards the bottom again. They need to be in the environment to learn the ins and outs. You may consider bartering with those who possess hardware or software technical skills. They provide you with their computing skills (these are usually common across all industries) and you can teach them about the industry.

Even on a limited budget, you can find creative ways to get the technology expertise you need.

One entrepreneur we know was faced with a dilemma. His customers were asking him to join the Information Age and get e-mail and an Internet site. The problem was that his Minnesota-based company, an engineering firm, was not wired. He knew he had to look for different options to satisfy his customers, because he couldn't afford to have his expensive engineers spending their time surfing the Web for solutions.

The way he solved the problem was to hire a $10-an-hour intern from a local college. He explained his goals to the intern, who then did all the research and came up with a recommendation. It cost $1,280 for the intern (that's 128 hours of work) and $25 a month for unlimited full Internet service, which included a connection, an e-mail account for the company, and some Web hosting space. All in all, this entrepreneur figures that he saved about $2,500 dollars by using an intern.

Determining the Type of Tech Consultant You Need

Tech consultants are as varied a species as you ever want to find. They come in all shapes and sizes, with the whole spectrum of personality traits and skills.

Unfortunately, finding a really good tech consultant is not easy. The demand for skilled programmers, resellers, and consultants has far outstripped supply, so everyone with even the slightest bit of technology knowledge is hanging up a shingle and going into business. Furthermore, the industry has no formal accreditation procedures — there are no licenses, and no one monitors performance and ethics. It's hard to know who is incompetent because tracing the trail littered with botched jobs, unhappy business owners, and inflated budgets is difficult.

To be fair to consultants and programmers, it's not that they're intentionally spiteful and incompetent. It's more likely that they aren't good at estimating what they can actually deliver. Often consultants face business owners who aren't realistic about budgets and fail to plan for technology. It is estimated that for every hour you spend planning for technology, you save about five hours in implementation — so in this section, we're going to help you raise your chances of finding that one tech consultant in a hundred that is a keeper and will help you implement your technology plan successfully.

Identifying the many species of tech consultant

Consultant is a broad term, so you need a field guide to the various types that populate the consultant domain. In general, think about consultants in terms of four species: independent consultants, very big consulting firms, value-added resellers or solution providers, and tech temps.

Species #1: Independent consultants

Independent consultants are either lone wolves or run in packs, sometimes of 100 or more who band together under one name to create strength — but who still operate basically as independents. These types of consultants tend to specialize in a particular industry or segment and classify themselves based on whether they are hardware experts, application experts, networking experts, or programmers. Some brave souls still call themselves generalists and try to cover all the specialties within technology. Being a generalist is difficult because technology is moving so fast that keeping up with it is hard.

The important thing to know about independent consultants is that they do not represent any particular vendor, which means that they have to stay up-to-date on all the new technology from all vendors. Most of the time, they charge on a flat-fee basis that can range from $80 per hour to $250 per hour depending on their expertise and the region of the country in which they are located. But you can also hire a consultant on a *retainer* (paying the consultant a monthly fee for a specified number of hours of service) or on a project basis.

Species #2: Very big consulting firms

You can always call in the big boys if you're looking for a prestigious consultant. Andersen Consulting, Boeing Information Services, and IBM — to name just a few — are good to use if you must have the signature of a name firm. Generally, if you're planning for a fast start-up of an Internet company that is going for a public offering (IPO) in the near future, your investors may require that you associate with a name-brand company. You can find these top-tier firms through the Information Technology Association of America, where they all hang out.

You may or may not get the more personalized service that you can get from a smaller firm, but you need to weigh the advantages and disadvantages of both. How important is the name versus personal service? Also, recognize that these large firms will not take on just anyone. You will probably need to have an exciting business with huge potential for growth before they will consider working with you.

If you hire one of the big firms that sport thousands of consultants, as a small business you probably won't be getting their most seasoned employees. What you'll likely get are the new hires right out of college who are working their way up to the top by starting in the trenches. And you won't necessarily pay less for them, so do your homework and be sure that if you are getting the firm's less-seasoned employees, you are being charged less for the service.

Species #3: Value-added resellers or solution providers

The difference between VARs (value-added resellers) or SPs (solution providers) — the most common terms for sellers of computer hardware and services — and independent consultants is that VARs and SPs get a percentage of everything they sell from the vendors they represent, so the technology solutions they recommend usually involve their respective vendor's products. Good (and ethical) VARs disclose vendor relationships, but don't expect them to recommend products other than the ones they carry, even if other products would be better for your business.

VARs make money through consulting fees, commissions on sales, and discounts. For example, a VAR may purchase a particular application at a discount from a vendor and resell it to you at full price, but then add value by customizing the package for you.

A VAR has a stake in selling particular hardware and software to you, so their opinion will generally be biased. But if they are selling the brands you prefer, this relationship might be good. Because VARs generally have a close relationship with their vendors, they're often first in line for tech support.

Species #4: Tech temps

Like other forms of temporary help that your company may utilize, you can hire temporary technical help from agencies that specialize in providing consultants for projects that generally last six months to a year in any area of technology. The National Association of Computer Consultant Businesses (NACCB) estimates that 3,000 companies are in business in this area. Try the following sites to find temporary help:

- ✔ I-Tech Futures, Inc. (www.jobs-ct.com/itech/)
- ✔ C-Net (jobs.cnet.com/Main/PostJobs_m.jsp), where you can post the position that you're looking for
- ✔ Courtney Services (www.courtneyusa.com/recr_techsupport.htm)
- ✔ ASD Inc. Technical Services (www.asdinc.com/htmdocs/flyers/techs/)

The good thing about temps is that they enable you to be flexible — you can hire the specific skills you require on an as-needed basis. The kinds of people you find working for temp agencies in technical areas are a different breed from their brothers and sisters holding down full-time jobs: They are every bit as qualified but prefer to lead a more freelance life and like moving from job to job.

Understanding the different types of certification

You find many certifications in technology consulting — everything from software development to database administration, computer repair to advanced networking, support to training. Some of these certifications take a good chunk of time and a lot of money to achieve. Many tech consultants find themselves buried in thick books or in classrooms learning this material before taking exams. These certifications are designed to build the skills of solution providers and generate a level of confidence and comfort in the business owner knowing that they have a skilled professional.

Understanding vendor-specific and general certification programs

Many vendors offer certification programs to insure that the VARs and SPs who sell their products know what they're talking about. The certification considered universal for small and medium-sized businesses is the Microsoft Certified Professional (MCP) and Microsoft Certified System Engineer (MCSE) programs.

For example, MCPs have been certified because they have had hands-on courses in successfully implementing different Microsoft products into a business. By contrast, the MCSE certification is the higher end of the Microsoft program and means that the certificate holder is skilled in considering business needs and then implementing the appropriate technologies for them.

Consultants can build their skills by taking other courses on different topics. For instance, MCSE + Internet adds on to the role and responsibility to include creating, implementing, and managing an Intranet or Internet site. Take a look at www.microsoft.com/trainingandservices to see the breadth of education solution providers must go through to call themselves certified.

This is just a taste of what certifications are out there. Other programs are designed for skills in other operating systems for medium to large companies such as Novell, Oracle, and Sun. Here's a brief list of some of the other certification programs you might run across:

- ✔ **The Learning Tree** (www.learningtree.com) provides certification in such things as Windows, Intranet/Internet, PC support, Networking, and Oracle.

- ✔ **Certified Computing Professional (CCP) from the Institute for Certification in Computing** (www.iccp.org), a prestigious organization, provides certification on a common body of knowledge in computing.

- ✔ **Disaster Recovery Institute International** (www.dr.org/certification.html) provides a Business Continuity Planner certification in helping businesses to recover from disasters.

Finding out about certified companies

Although the company you hire may be labeled an MCSP or a CCP, the reality is that it can send any of its employees to provide services to you. More often than not, the company will send employees who are not certified at all, because these employees are cheaper. These technicians usually end up being the culprits when problems occur. You know the scenario — you think you hired the best of the best, but now everything is going wrong. If a consulting company charges a premium for its services, you are entitled to get the most qualified people it has.

Ask that at least one of the people working on your project be an MCSE (Microsoft Certified Software Engineer). We're not claiming that because someone has an MCSE title, your installation will be foolproof, but chances are you will at least be working with one of the company's experts. Sometimes an MCSE is the leader of a group of technical people who come out to your site to do an installation. The MCSE can do all the hard work in configuration and allow the others to do the more straightforward tasks.

Just because a company has been certified doesn't mean that a certified technician will walk through your door. In some cases, a company needs only two certified engineers to call the entire company certified; in other words, the rest of the employees are not certified. We're not saying that a consultant has to possess a certificate in order to be skilled and talented in what he or she does. However, if a company claims that it's certified, it makes sense to make sure that at least one certified engineer is working directly on your project.

Certified tech consultants are high on the list for recruiters because they have specialized skills on specific equipment or applications, so don't be surprised if your certified tech consultant changes companies just when you become comfortable with him or her. Of course, you can always rehire your tech consultant from the company that he or she joins.

Locating a Tech Consultant

Consider these things before beginning your search for a competent and reliable tech consultant:

- ✔ Don't limit yourself to your immediate geographic area. The best consultants often travel, and they can do a lot by accessing your system remotely. However, a consultant who is not in your area may not be the best choice if you think that you may need 24/7 support.

- ✔ If you're used to working with certain brand-name hardware or software from companies such as Microsoft or IBM, you probably want a consultant who's certified for those vendor-specific products.

✔ Get a reference from someone who has had a positive experience with the consultant you're considering. Referrals are the best source for tech consultants.

✔ If you can't get a referral, try professional organizations, the Better Business Bureau, or your local chamber of commerce. In addition, don't forget your accountant, banker, and attorney; they hear a lot from their clients.

Two sites may be worth your time if you're looking for technical help. They help you find a tech consultant for the particular type of technology solution you're looking for, and they cover all types of consultants, from temporary to permanent.

✔ **Independent Computer Consultants Association (ICCA)**
(www.icca.org): This national not-for-profit organization is based in St. Louis. It provides professional development opportunities and business support programs for independent computer consultants. You can review more than 1,500 consulting firms.

✔ **Information Technology Association of America (ITAA)**
(www.itaa.org): The ITAA, with more than 11,000 members, is the only trade association representing the information technology industry. This site provides information about the industry and its members.

Chapter 15

Hiring and Working with a Tech Consultant

. . . .

In This Chapter

▶ Understanding your contractual agreement

▶ Hiring an in-house technical consultant

▶ Maintaining a good relationship with your technical consultant

. . . .

Solution providers constitute one of the biggest determinants of how successful a small business is in adopting technology. They bring wisdom and knowledge on how to apply specific technologies to individual business processes that help increase productivity and efficiency. Just as your interest and core competency probably are in business, these providers are interested in technology and all the products and services that fall within it. They are skilled professionals when it comes to understanding the best products and services that are available and are also aware of those products and services that aren't worth the money. So it's important to understand the perspective of the solution provider who can potentially make your world a lot more manageable.

In this chapter, we discuss what solution providers expect from their small business clients, the contracts that bond the two, and how to nurture a win/win relationship.

Contracting with a Technology Consulting Service

Anything you do with a consultant will probably require a service contract. The purpose of that contract is to spell out in detail the terms of engagement — that is, who is responsible for what and how much it's going to cost. This document is important because it tells you what to expect out of your relationship with your tech consultant. It also tells you what is expected of you in that relationship. Here's a list of some of the typical things included in a service contract with a technology consultant.

Consultant availability

Part of your contract will deal with when the consultant (the firm) is available to come to your site or respond by phone. This is important, because not all firms operate on a 24/7 basis. If you need that kind of availability, you should make sure that it's in the contract. Other issues that the contract should address relative to when you can contact your consultant include the following:

- ✔ A definition of service hours — normal, after-hours, and emergency.
- ✔ How to request service for nonemergency issues.
- ✔ How to request service when you have an emergency (these are issues related to the down time of your server and what to expect).
- ✔ Who backs up your tech consultant when he or she is not available.

Because you never know when you're going to need your consultant, it's important to find someone in your local area so that 24/7 emergency service is available if you need it.

Scope of work

The contract will probably outline the boundaries into which the work provided falls. That way the consultant is protected from being asked to do things for which he or she is not paid, and you can better understand what is an appropriate request. Here are some of the things that are dealt with in the scope of work:

- ✔ Which of your operating systems, applications, and hardware are within the tech consultant's scope of service and which are specifically out of scope.
- ✔ If you hire a consultant as an on-site administrator for your company, where his or her job ends and your company's job begins.
- ✔ Whether or not training is included within the scope of the service.

Execute a contract that sets the work out in stages, so you have points at which you can stop if things aren't going the way the consultant projects. That way you won't get so deep into problems that it will take a lot of time and money to get out.

Levels of support

Your tech consultant can respond to your need for service at three levels, depending on the nature of the problem and whether or not it's an emergency — defined as a situation in which your business has shut down as a result of the problem. Talk to your consultant about which level of support is appropriate in any given situation. Every consultant has his or her own preferences and will recommend the most appropriate response.

- ✔ **Phone response:** It's rare to find a tech company that will respond immediately to a phone call, but if you're facing an emergency situation — you have a server down and a major project with an imminent deadline — you should be able to get a call back within 15 minutes to a half hour. That's standard in the industry. For example, the tech consultant calls back and walks the most tech-savvy person on your staff through the process of logging all the employees off the network and rebooting the server, if that's necessary. If that doesn't solve the problem, the consultant will tell you what he or she is going to do next.

- ✔ **Remote response:** If you have given your tech consultant the ability to access your system from a remote location, he or she can dial into your system and do some remote diagnostics to detect any problems. It can take up to 90 minutes or more to get this type of response from your tech consultant after you've made the call requesting help.

- ✔ **On-site response:** This means that you want the tech consultant to come to your place of business and solve the problem. The trouble with this is that it costs significantly more for a house call, especially if you can handle the problem by phone or remote response methods. Tech consultants typically price their on-site visits significantly higher than the other two solutions to force small business owners to use the other two first.

Understanding how tech consultants price their services

As you research the best tech consultant for your business, you should be aware that there are basically four different types of pricing arrangements. They include fixed price, time and materials, per incident, and hybrid arrangements. For example, drawing up your technology plan might entail a fixed price, while implementing the plan through the installation of technology might involve time and materials and an ongoing retainer.

Most consultants like to define a set amount for a certain number of hours per month. If you use more than the specified number of hours, you are charged an hourly rate above that. Here are some of the issues that affect pricing:

- ✔ Whether the service is provided at the your site, by phone, or though remote support (the tech controls your computer from his or her own and walks you through the problem).

- ✔ Whether the service provided is routine or out of the scope of work (we cover this distinction later in the chapter).

✔ Whether the service provided is an emergency requiring an after-hours visit to your site.

✔ Whether the consultant is working on a special project outside the scope of the original contract, for example, designing and building a customized database for your company.

Fixed-price services

This approach has been called the all-you-can-eat pricing arrangement because you have access to all the resources of the tech consultant within limits that are spelled out in fine print — be sure to read the fine print! The kinds of things typically included in fixed-price service are the following:

✔ Hardware repairs

✔ Software upgrades

✔ Troubleshooting sessions

✔ Informal training questions

✔ Help desk calls

Because client businesses on fixed-price deals have the freedom to call for tech support a lot, fixed-price services work well only when offered by a large, well-staffed, consulting firm. If your consulting firm doesn't have a big enough staff to handle the help desk, you may find yourself waiting in a cyberline while your consultant takes care of other customers — which can be frustrating and a waste of time.

Because of the need for more staff, these types of contracts are usually priced to include a buffer for the risk the consulting firm takes in giving clients unlimited access. Some tech firms let you have a fixed-price contract only if you have someone inside your company who has technical knowledge and can fix minor problems.

Time and materials services

Most VARs (value-added resellers) and VAPs (value-added providers) prefer time and materials contracts because you — the customer — pay for all the service hours you use in addition to any parts you require. Billing is by the hour plus materials. You should know that this pricing option can get quite expensive if you run into a complex problem that takes a lot of time to solve.

Per-incident services

This arrangement is pay-per-use of the tech consultant. Expect one fee for phone support, another for remote support, and another for on-site support. VARs don't usually like this arrangement because it forces them to clearly define what's included in an incident, which isn't always clear-cut.

Hybrid services

This arrangement may be the best all around for both the technical support and the customer. Here you may have certain services under a fixed-price contract and others on a per incident basis; still others are handled by hourly fees. This arrangement is probably the most common in a small business situation because it provides the most flexibility in pricing.

Handling disputes

Be sure to include a method for dispute resolution. This usually involves bringing in a third party to arbitrate — someone you both agree will give an unbiased view of the situation.

By having some form of arbitration, you may avoid having the tech consultant get the last laugh by popping a time bomb or time lock in your software that prevents you from using it. This is usually done when the business owner hasn't paid off the contract. The bomb "explodes" and erases all the programming. Depending on what the software was designed to do, that explosion could literally shut down the company. We're not saying that tech consultants routinely do this; just be aware that revenge is a remote possibility, and always seek ways to resolve a conflict amicably.

Hiring a Technology Consultant

Hiring technical help is a tough task at best. More than skills, it's about the person you hire, whether that person is an independent or part of a large firm. Will that person work well with your organization? What's your gut feeling when you talk to this person? Always trust your intuition; if the person doesn't seem like he or she fits with your value system and the culture of your company, don't hire him or her — it won't work.

In this section, we deal with the things you need to do that will lead to hiring the best tech consultant for your business. Some of those tasks include reviewing a résumé, checking references, preparing for the interview, conducting the interview, and making a decision to hire.

Knowing what a résumé tells you

The first thing you should know about résumés is that most of them are puffed up; that is, people make themselves look much more grand and accomplished than they really are. So if you think that you've found a gem, temper your enthusiasm until you check the candidate out.

Always verify a candidate's résumé by calling references and checking with customers.

Here are some of the things you want to look for in a résumé:

- **Look for a summary of the consultant's specific skills and expertise.** You want to know if the candidate has the basic tools to do what you want him or her to do. A cautionary note here: Consultants will routinely list every technology, program, or system with which they have experience, but you have no way of knowing the depth of that experience. A general guideline is that the farther the item is down the list on the résumé, the weaker the skill is.

- **When reviewing the candidate's experience, look for specific projects and specific outcomes.** Anyone can say that he or she was a particular company's tech consultant; the question is, what did he or she do for the company, and what was the outcome? If it's not stated in the résumé, you may want to bring it up during the interview.

- **Check to see if the consultant has done a lot of job hopping in permanent positions or has big gaps in his or her résumé.** That could signal someone who is either unreliable or incompetent. Recognize, however, that it is common today for technology people to move from job to job, but if it's happening every few months, you may not want to deal with that level of instability.

- **Note the level of his or her education.** Evidence of some business coursework is definitely a plus, because at least the candidate will have some understanding of how businesses work. Some of the best tech consultants don't necessarily have college degrees but do have lots of experience building and maintaining technology. If the type of work you need is fairly routine from a tech's perspective, then a degree in computer science is not really a requirement, and may cost you more. Do look for certifications in the specific technology that you need because that usually means that the person has focused in that area and will be better at it than someone who is a generalist across many types of technology.

Getting ready for the interview

If you strategize a bit before the interview, you'll get a lot more out of it than you would have otherwise. Part of that strategy should be to prepare a game plan that the consultant can't prepare for that reveals his or her strengths and weaknesses. That way, you can better judge how he or she would perform inside your company.

One strategy is to give your potential tech consultant a small task to do before the interview takes place. For example, ask him to review your Web page so that you have a basis for beginning a conversation during the interview. If he comes back with glowing reports of how great it is, be wary. By contrast, if he comes back with some suggestions for how to make it better, you may have a winner on your hands.

American Golf Corp., which operates over 250 golf courses in North America and Europe uses this tactic. They require that a candidate visit one of their golf sites before the interview so they can ask for their comments at the interview. One savvy 27-year-old tech candidate wrote a four-page report evaluating everything from the concessions to the management team to the course itself. He then gave practical suggestions. Ultimately, he was hired. (We're not surprised.) Granted, as a small business owner, you will probably not get a candidate to do what the one in the above example did, but on a much smaller scale, you can, and it's worth the effort to do so.

If you use the "test the candidate" strategy we just described, be sure not to ask more of the candidate than is reasonable. You haven't yet hired him or her, so you're asking the candidate to do this for free. Keep the task small, something the candidate can do quickly — such as looking over your Web site.

In the interview, you can ask the consultant to rank his or her skills from strongest to weakest. That way, you and the candidate together can identify his or her strengths and weaknesses.

It's important to decide what you want to achieve from the interview. What are the most important things you want to learn about the candidate during the interview? An interview tells you how well and in what manner a person answers a series of questions. A great interview starts with great questions.

Questioning a potential tech consultant is an art. You want to gain a lot of information, which the consultant may or may not want to reveal. The kinds of questions you ask in one situation may not be appropriate for another — and may actually give you bad information. The following list presents common questioning techniques that you should employ in your interview:

- ✔ **Open-ended questions:** This type of question forces the interviewee to respond with more than yes or no. *What do you do to handle pressure on the job?* is a question that requires an explanation, thereby giving you information about the applicant.

- ✔ **Questions about past performance:** These questions solicit information about the candidate's past performance so that you can make inferences about future performance. They are worded in such a way that the candidate has to talk in detail about his achievements. *What was your greatest achievement on a previous job and why?*

- ✔ **Negative-balance questions:** Don't assume that a candidate who is strong in one thing is strong in everything else. If you find yourself becoming overly-impressed with your potential tech consultant, stop and ask the following: *What do you consider your biggest weakness?* or *What is the biggest mistake you ever made and how did you handle it?*

✔ **Negative confirmation:** If the answer to your negative-balance questions raises flags for you, you may want to follow up with a negative confirmation question. For example, if the tech consultant claims to have ignored the wishes of a business owner for which he was working, you may want to pose the following question, *That's interesting. Were there any other times that you felt it was necessary to ignore the business owner's wishes?* What you want to find out is if ignoring the client's wishes is a habit.

✔ **Hypothetical questions:** Hypothetical situations gauge the consultant's decision style — *What would you do if . . . ?, How would you react if . . . ?*

✔ **Leading questions:** It's wise to avoid leading the consultant to a specific response because then you never know if that's what the consultant actually believes. *We are a company that puts the customer at the center of everything we do. How do you feel about customer service?* Don't be surprised if the candidate answers that he believes it's central to everything he does. Now, what have you learned? You can use leading questions to confirm what you've heard, but only later on in the interview.

These are just a few of the types of questions you may use to structure your interview. If you use the right questions at the right time, you can stay in control of the interview and learn enough about the candidate to make a decision.

Many people think logically, so if you ask them a specific question, they'll give you a precise and truthful answer, but they'll only answer the question that you ask. Therefore, if you don't ask the right question, they may seem evasive. This doesn't mean they're lying — they're just being very precise about the question you asked.

Finding out the right information in the interview

The following is a list of the important things you want to do at the interview:

✔ **Pick out your six best questions and ask them all at once.** Then sit back and listen to the responses. You can always follow-up later in the interview. Using this technique keeps you from being too impressed by the candidate too early in the game, and it forces you to listen — something that many business owners have a hard time doing.

✔ **Ask questions about things you're familiar with and avoid areas where the tech consultant could snow you.** Any good attorney would tell you to ask questions to which you already know the answers, and this is particularly true in tech situations where it would be easy for the techie to take the conversation into an area about which you know nothing. That will serve no purpose because you won't be able to make an informed decision about the tech's competency.

✔ **Ask the tech consultant for examples of projects he or she has worked on.** The tech should be able to describe some problems businesses like yours were facing and how he solved them with technology. If he can't, he may not have the experience will small businesses that you need.

✔ **Find out if the tech consultant is used to working under tight budgets.** Don't be shy about telling your tech that you have a limited budget — believe us, he's used to hearing it. But the question is, is he willing to work with you under those circumstances.

✔ **Ask how the tech consultant handles stress and pressure.** While you may not plan to have your consultant work under pressure, it does happen, even with the best planning efforts. You want to know that the tech can remain calm and get the job done.

✔ **Notice how the tech consultant communicates.** Is he understandable? Is he trying to impress you with his technical jargon? Is he uncomfortable dealing with some of your questions? Communication is one of the most important skills your consultant can have. Make sure that the one you hire has good communication skills.

✔ **Does the consultant have knowledge of how businesses like yours work?** Asking about previous jobs the consultant has handled should give you a good idea if he or she has knowledge of your type of business.

✔ **Has the consultant ever solved problems like yours?** Specifically, you want to know if the types of problems you need solved are similar to the types of jobs the consultant has dealt with previously with other companies. You want someone who is familiar with these issues.

✔ **Ask the tech consultant about his or her documentation skills.** With technology consultants moving around these days, it's critical that you be left with documentation on what was done and where things are.

When you give your five-minute warning that the interview is about to end, don't be surprised if your tech consultant candidate suddenly says, "I almost forgot the most important thing." It happens all the time and usually reveals vital information about the consultant. So pay attention.

Making the selection

After you've done all the work, it's time to make a selection. This is the tough part, because whether you are hiring this person as an independent contractor or an employee, you are still bringing him or her into your company and putting him or her in charge of important processes in your business. To choose, you may want to use a simple rating system based on the criteria that are important to you. For example, set up a table with the criteria listed. Then list the candidates across the top. Rate each on a 1–5 scale (5 being highest) on each of the criteria.

Table 15-1 gives you a sample of what that might look like.

Table 15-1	Criteria for Technical Consultant Candidates	
Criteria	*Candidate 1*	*Candidate 2*
Required skills (you might list them)	5	4
Level of experience	5	3
Business knowledge	1	3
Communication skills	2	5

Then you can add up the scores and see how they rank. In this case, the first candidate earned 13 points and the second earned 15 points. The second candidate, although she doesn't have the experience of the first, has more business knowledge and is a far better communicator, which could definitely tip the scales. If you have a mathematical bent, you could even weight the criteria according to their level of importance to you. That would further refine the analysis.

If you can find a consultant who has years of successful experience, and reams of positive client referrals, that alone probably says more about the consultant's abilities than any certification can. When it comes down to it, nothing beats hands-on experience. But don't forget those communication skills. When times get tough, you have to be able to talk with your tech consultant.

Building a Long-Term Relationship with Your Tech Consultant

Building a long-term relationship with your tech consultant — whether he's an independent consultant or someone you hired in-house — requires communication and mutual respect.

Discuss with your tech consultant what you're both trying to accomplish. After you agree on that, give the tech consultant the freedom to do his job in his own way. In other words, you can tell your tech consultant what to do, but don't tell him how to do it. When you do that, you're treading on his territory and you'll offend him. Just give him a problem, agree on objectives, and then leave him alone to find the solution. You might want to look at Chapter 20 to find more ways to effectively work with your tech consultant.

Although you may leave your tech consultant alone to solve the problem, don't forget that it's your job to keep your project on target and within the agreed-upon budget, and it's your right to ask for regular reports (they should definitely be written) and documentation. This way you have a paper trail should anything go wrong.

If you're lucky enough to have technical people in your organization — engineers or programmers — you can ask your consultant to present his update reports to them. Tech consultants care a great deal about how they're perceived among their peers because it's a close community, so they'll definitely do their best if they know their peers are watching or could trace the mistake back to them.

If you want to keep your tech consultant happy, be sure to show your appreciation, give credit where credit is due, and pay on time.

Knowing what to expect of your tech consultant

We know what you really want from your tech consultant. You want him or her to read your mind, anticipate your needs, do what you want, when you want, and where you want — and do it all with a smile and a sense of humor. Right? Good luck. No one could meet all those demands and still maintain a sense of humor, so be realistic. Here's a list of what you should expect from your tech consultant:

- ✔ Do expect your tech consultant to be a lifesaver when things go wrong.
- ✔ Do expect your tech consultant to define milestones for your technology project from his or her perspective with consideration to your perspective.
- ✔ Do expect your tech consultant to outline all of the tasks he or she will have to perform to make good on a proposal.
- ✔ Do expect your tech consultant to look at your business differently than you do and give you suggestions to improve your processes.
- ✔ Do expect your tech consultant to be your teacher or to help you find trainers who can teach you what you need to learn.
- ✔ Do expect your tech consultant to enhance the quality of life around your office, as he or she gives employees the ability to be more effective on their jobs.
- ✔ Do expect your tech consultant to help you maintain your competitive advantage and even gain advantage.

Conversely, here's a list of what *not* to expect from your tech consultant:

- Don't automatically expect your tech consultant to come running instantly every time you call. You aren't his or her only client. If you need this kind of service; find a tech consultant that specifically offers it.

- Don't expect your tech consultant to go above and beyond the call of duty until you have established a good relationship over time.

- Don't expect your tech consultant to read your mind. You should clearly ask for what you want.

- Don't expect your tech consultant to ask about how your business operates. It would be nice if he or she did, but often that's not the case. You must take the initiative to make sure that the tech consultant understands your business's operations so that he or she can provide the technology and services that best fit your business.

- Don't expect your tech consultant to perform miracles. Know when you or your employees have done something wrong and admit it. Covering up what you did can lead to several hours of your tech consultant searching fruitlessly for solutions in all the wrong places. He'll get frustrated, and you'll end up paying.

- Don't expect your tech consultant to knock on your door every time there is a new technology that may be good for your environment. Your tech consultant probably has several businesses she is dealing with and although yours should always be a priority (at least in your mind), the reality is that you're just one of many businesses wanting her attention. Do your own research and when you find something that looks interesting, give her a call and get some feedback.

CASE STUDY

Hearing from a real tech consultant

Mark Mosch is the founder and president of Aims2000, LLC (www.aims2000.com), a full-service solution provider. We met Mark through some research we were doing on small business technology strategies. Because his company sets the benchmark for the ideal solution provider, let's hear what he has to say about the ideal customer and more.

EBusiness Technology Kit: *Mark, Describe for us your ideal small business customer.*

Mark Mosch: I think that the ideal small business customer is someone who takes a little

time to plan for more than just the immediate moment. The biggest issue is someone who evaluates the total cost — what his best cost of solution is over a year's timeframe — rather than just looks at the purchase price and sees it as a loss. We like a customer who is communicative. We feel that a client that can communicate can help us get to what their expectations are. We can give them a happy installation process. That would be our perfect client.

ETK: *What's the first thing you want to know when you visit the customer's site?*

Mosch: When we visit the site, we want to assess the state of the current system. Until we know that, we don't have a way to figure out where they [the owners] want to go. Everything flows from where they are and where they're moving to. The design is based on the gap between those two areas. You need to know the state of knowledge of the clients because if they don't know anything, there are sophisticated solutions that we won't offer because the clients will be unhappy because of their inability to use it — it's a waste of money.

ETK: *What are some of the biggest problems small business customers face, in your view?*

Mosch: Small businesses have small to mid-sized staffs, and they don't have people assigned to take care of this [technology]. They are running around doing so many things themselves; it's difficult to get their undivided attention for an hour or two.

Budget is a real hindrance. For example, we used clones [off-brand machines] to support . . . a lot of clients with small budgets, but we started running into a lot of problems. When we replaced clone machines with brand-name machines, we no longer had machine problems. The reasons we had problems is that the small business owners had such small budgets; they passed on doing the solution [we recommended] to save a couple thousand dollars, but [they got] less quality and more problems.

ETK: *What are your top ten pet peeves about small business customers?*

Mosch: (At this point, Mark brought in his production manager, Lynn Rosario, who "holds the hands of customers" during the installation process. This list represents their joint contribution.)

1. Clients who don't understand that there will be problems — that technology is not perfect.

2. Business owners who are cheapskates and think they can get everything from Circuit City for 10 cents less.

3. Clients who need to know everything about the software just because the software is marketed as a do-it-yourself product — they can't do it themselves.

4. Clients who want to become a network administrator in one hour — without any classes.

5. Clients who take all the work you've done before a sale to analyze their business, and then give the order to the lowest bidder.

6. Business owners who think all of their people are stupid, so they refuse to put the time and energy into training employees.

7. Customers who don't understand the need for downtime. Whenever there's a problem, they expect the system to remain up.

8. Clients who expect tech consultants to work after hours (after midnight) for regular rates.

9. Small businesses that have only one person who knows the system, and that person is not the owner. Then when that employee leaves, the owner expects the consultant to step in and manage the system.

10. Clients who don't understand the need to pay for a pre-installation review after the sale has been made. (In other words, who refuse to pay for consulting time.)

We asked for the top ten pet peeves, but Mark and Lynn had one more that they thought was very important:

Customers who lie — play with the system and mess something up, then call to say they didn't do it. What they don't understand is that there are logs in the operating system that tell a consultant who did what.

(continued)

ETK: *You have a potential new client. How can that client prepare for your visit? What should he or she do?*

Mosch: Take an inventory of what [he or she has]. A lot of people don't know what types of systems they have. Also, they should look at the state of licensing and the legality of their software. We've had clients that have taken one copy of MS Word and copied it to ten computers. We tell the clients that we will legally reinstall software with original disks only, so they're stuck.

ETK: *From a business operations perspective, what can business owners explain to you?*

Mosch: The more they have their systems on paper, the better. As long as they know how things are supposed to happen, we can address how they should happen with the support of technology. One of the big challenges is that most of the time, it's [the business operations] not in writing.

ETK: *Do you find that most business owners understand their operations?*

Mosch: The owner has an overall perspective of the business's operations and viability, but, in general, the people who work in the business don't have an overall perspective.

ETK: *Have you ever had a business that had graphical depictions of their company information flow, and would that help you?*

Mosch: We have never found a business that had a graphical depiction of their company's operations. If they did, we could pinpoint bottlenecks and make them more efficient.

ETK: *Can you suggest other types of documents that could help improve communication between you and your customers and allow both parties to understand what is expected?*

Mosch: We have certain policy statements that we give to clients from the minute they call for information. They are generally in the form of disclaimers and disclosures. It's better to be up front. Networking is a complex process involving hundreds of hardware, software, and configuration choices, and we can't foresee everything that might go wrong. It might be that the things that come up will require additional fees.

ETK: *Is there anything that small business owners can do to help keep a good tech consultant?*

Mosch: One thing is for them to be a bit more educated about computers in general. A lot of the older generation business owners are reluctant to learn [about computers]. They become antagonistic when forced to learn. The best clients understand that over the life of the relationship, there will be legitimate problems that occur. If someone is reasonable and understanding, you will go out of your way to help them, even give them free time and products. On the other side, there are clients who need everything in writing to maintain the relationship.

Handling conflict

If you need to criticize what your tech consultant is doing because he made assumptions and is heading down the wrong road, get another tech consultant — someone who understands the mindset — to do the critique for you. This technique will get a much better reception from the tech consultant under attack because the two tech consultants can talk through the issues from the same perspective.

If you need to make a business decision that conflicts with what your technology consultant wants to do, couch it simply as a business decision and she'll understand. However, if you tread into the technology arena and make a technology decision, you may run into resistance because you won't have your tech consultant's respect — you're a business person, not a technical expert.

Saying goodbye: Terminating the relationship

There may come a day when your relationship with your tech consultant must end. It could be for a variety of reasons, from a change in the direction of your company or the consultant's company, to a falling out with the tech consultant, to a budgetary crisis. The reason really doesn't matter; whatever the cause, saying goodbye is never easy.

If you have a written contract in place (and you should), you may have already prepared for this by stating the conditions under which you can terminate the contract. If you don't have a written contract, then you certainly want to give your tech consultant some notice (2 weeks to 30 days) to be fair. (Unless, of course, there is fraud or some criminal action involved — then you must terminate his contract immediately.) Likewise, you should have language in the contract that specifies that your tech must give you reasonable notice before ending the agreement.

If you choose to terminate the relationship, be sure to sit down with your tech consultant and state clearly, confidently, and precisely why you are ending the relationship. Don't make excuses and don't tell him that he did a wonderful job and you would recommend him to others. If that were true, why would you end the relationship? On the other hand, if you no longer need his services because you can now afford to hire an in-house technical person, for example, you should definitely write a letter of recommendation for your consultant (assuming that you were happy with the services) and tell him that you will be happy to refer other business owners to him.

Never end the relationship on an angry note. It may come back to bite you. Recall that your tech consultant may leave a gift for you when he leaves in the form of a time bomb in your software, or you may find that all of a sudden glitches surface in your hardware that were not there before. Tech consultants always get the last laugh, so end the relationship in a way that doesn't put all the blame on the tech consultant. Depress your own ego for the time and take some of the blame yourself. *I know I haven't been easy to work with . . . my company is going through a tough time and we need to tighten our belts . . .* whatever you can say to take the blame off the tech consultant and put it onto you will soften the blow and end the relationship in a civil manner. Besides, something small may come up that a two-minute phone call can resolve, and your departing tech consultant just may be willing to oblige if you handle the termination well.

Getting a technical consultant online

Picture this scenario (which, by the way, is all too common — it has happened to us, and we've seen it happen to the big guys at Microsoft): You're just about to make the most important sales presentation of your business's life. You even came in early to load your carefully constructed PowerPoint slides into the presentation computer. It's show time. You smile at the audience and confidently click the mouse to display your opening slide, designed to wow even the most skeptical of customers. What's this? An error message? A fatal error message? Who are you going to call? Where is tech support when you need them most? If you can find one, hold onto your wallet because it's going to cost you big bucks.

There is another solution (assuming you've decided not to check your tech manuals while the audience is getting restless) — online tech support, and it's the biggest cyber-shopping mall around. Here's how it works.

When this problem occurred you were using PowerPoint, which is a Microsoft product, so it makes sense to start your support search at www.microsoft.com. When you get there, do the following:

1. **Rest your mouse over the Support tab at the top of the page.**

   A drop-down menu appears.

2. **Choose Knowledge Base.**

   You are taken to the Knowledge Base Search page.

3. **Click the arrow to the right of the My Search Is About box.**

   A drop-down menu gives you choices of Microsoft products.

4. **Choose PowerPoint.**

5. **Type your question in the My Question Is text box and click Go.**

   Within seconds, you find yourself facing more responses than you thought possible, among which may just be the answer you are looking for.

Of course, there is always the chance that your answer won't be there. In that case, there are other options. Some very philanthropic technology consultants have banded together to give frustrated business owners a chance at solving their own problems quickly and easily. Here are a couple of sites to try:

- ✔ **PC-Help Online** (www.pchelponline.com): This site is a clearinghouse of support and forums to connect you with your fellow frustrated business owners. If nothing else, you have virtual friends who will commiserate with you.

- ✔ **No Wonder! Inc.** (www.nowonder.com): This site offers free tech support, with an answer within 24 hours.

Visiting do-it-yourself hot spots

You may want to put your most technically savvy employee in charge of figuring out how to solve the little problems that could save an expensive call to the tech consultant. The Internet is friendly to do-it-yourselfers. There are places you can go to solve those annoying problems that keep cropping up. The reason we say that you should put someone in charge of this task is that we know that you're probably no different than we are. You're so busy trying to keep up that you just put up with the annoyances rather than take the time to solve them.

So get a newbie in your office to go on a scavenger hunt and solve everyone's little glitches. He or she will become a hero, and so will you for coming up with the idea in the first place. One great place to look is Windows 95 Annoyances at www.annoyances.org/win95/index.html. You can find a list of the most annoying features of Windows 95 and ways to work around or fix them.

If you like getting e-mail and want computer tips to come to you, try ElementK at www.elementkjournals.com/zdtips/. This great site promises to send you tech tips daily. An e-tip a day keeps the techie away!

Many of the problems you have with software are not your fault; they're caused by *bugs* (defects) in the software. In other industries, we would attribute this to poor quality control, but for some reason, we all expect and accept bugs in software. To get the bugs out, try BugNet (www.bugnet.com) the leading resource for computer bugs. Here you will be able to download *patches* — files that fix problems — for free so you can get your software in good working order.

Using a tech consultant to help you plan and implement your tech strategy is always a better choice than trying to do it yourself. But there are times when you face tech problems and a tech consultant is not close at hand. For those times, the support available online may help you, but only in the short term.

Chapter 16

Crashes, Bugs, Viruses, and Other Nasty Problems

In This Chapter

▶ Keeping viruses away from your system

▶ Defending against hackers

▶ Using backups as protection

*Y*ou thought that all you had to do was get a professional to set up your computer network and you would be home free — nothing more to worry about. Well, nothing could be further from the truth. Getting your network, desktops, and Web site in good working order is only the beginning. Keeping them that way is a daily struggle. That's because computers and networks are complex animals with lots of potential for glitches, problems, and all-out disasters. You can't fully prevent bad things from happening, but you can take preventative measures that lessen the chance of them happening, and help you recover quickly should they occur.

In this chapter, you find out how to prevent a catastrophe from wiping out your business's vital information, whether it be through natural disaster, computer malfunction, or malicious intent.

Vaccinating Against Viruses

In business today, pretty much everyone uses e-mail and downloads files from the Internet, even if it's just the latest patch for your new software. Most people don't realize that if you do these things, you're actually at risk for letting a virus enter your computer and destroy your data. What exactly is a computer virus? A *virus* is simply a program that may or may not attach itself to a file and replicate itself inside your computer. After a virus invades a file, it may or may not corrupt the data in the file. In other words, the virus could be harmless, or it could do a lot of damage. There's just no way of knowing.

Understanding the many types of viruses

Because viruses do not come in only one flavor you should be aware of several major categories of viruses:

- **Boot-sector viruses:** These nasty predators infect files that let the computer load the operating system. They are transmitted through human contact (it's not the computer's fault) in the form of floppy disks or zip disks. If you get one of these viruses, you may not be able to boot up your computer.

- **Macro viruses:** This virus buries itself deep into the codes of applications such as word processors, and it's unique in that it can cross platforms. What is frightening about macro viruses is that they can actually lie dormant in your computer for years and then suddenly appear and bring down an entire network. The first known and most prolific macro virus was the concept virus. It prints a secret message in the computer's code. The message? "And that is enough to prove my point." Beyond that, it's harmless.

- **Worm viruses:** Worms spread through e-mail at a breathtaking pace. They typically arrive in the form of an e-mail attachment, which, when opened, causes the script in the file to insert other files into Windows system directories and automatically sends copies of itself to all the addresses in a Microsoft Outlook directory. This is the fastest spreading type of virus anywhere because — like the ILOVEYOU virus (alias The Love Bug), which cost companies in the billions when it raced through computers in May, 2000 — it arrives in the form of an innocent message from someone you know. That particular virus didn't just jam up e-mail systems; it also sought out .jpg graphics and .mp3 music files and overwrote them with .vbs files.

Your network administrator needs to set the filters on your e-mail servers to filter out known viruses.

Combating viruses

So what can you do to keep your computer or your network virus-free? First, you need to know that you can't keep your computer totally virus-free. We found that out when The Love Bug hit everyone from the Pentagon on down. Because viruses often come disguised as harmless or even important mail from people you know, it's easy for someone in your company (and it only takes one person to infect a network) to innocently open a file that then replicates itself instantaneously to do its damage.

The virus-busters do it again

When you need to solve a crime, sometimes those who have been perpetrators of similar crimes become your best source of information. Certainly, that is true when it comes to crimes involving breaking into computer systems and setting off viruses. In the best tradition of Dick Tracy and Sherlock Holmes, three unlikely characters joined together to find the author of the Melissa e-mail worm. Richard Smith, the eldest member of the group is a retired programmer who also started Phar Lap software. His success is legendary. In 1999, he discovered RealNetworks' unethical data gathering practices, revealed Microsoft's suspicious registration procedures, and was also the first person to publish the identifying numbers in digital documents.

Smith met his two virus-buster partners, former hackers Fredrik Bjorck and Jonathan James, through a Usenet group during the time that Smith was trying to track the author of the Melissa virus. They shared information and began working as a team to track down the virus.

As described in two *Wired* online articles (Leander Kahney's May 12, 2000, "Who Do Cops Call? Virus-Busters" and Lynne Burke's May 10, 2000, "The Multi-National Love Bug Team"), when the next virus, the Love Bug, hit on May 4,

2000, these three ex-hackers set to work immediately to locate its author. Bjorck was the first to pinpoint an apartment in Manila, the Philippines. The trio then zeroed in on the perpetrators, identifying them. It seems that one of the virus authors had left his resume embedded in the source code, which indicated that he probably hadn't intended for the virus to be released on the Internet. The trio worked with FBI investigators to identify all of the suspects.

But doing the sleuthing to find the perpetrators of an international virus is a global process. While the virus-busters were doing their research, a Frenchman, Jean Francois Gagné, was tracking logs of ICQ, an instant messaging service. He believed that the virus was launched from multiple locations including Australia, the Philippines and Tanzania. His ability to come at the situation from a different point of view helped the FBI to ultimately track down the perpetrator, who was charged on June 29, 2000. But the story is not yet over, because the Philippines has no laws that directly address this crime (the government signed a new law on this issue just before charging the suspect); thus, he was charged with related crimes.

Although hackers are generally thought of as people who skirt the law, many of them use their talents to stop crime.

Installing antivirus software is the best way to ward off known viruses and even some unknown viruses that work in the same way as the known ones. Antivirus software works this way: After you install it on your computer, it runs constantly in the background — checking files, Web pages, CD-ROMs, diskettes, and e-mails against the virus definitions written into the software — in an attempt to detect matches.

After you have your antivirus software running, you breathe a sign of relief — you're protected, right? Wrong! That's what a lot of people think, but the fact is that unless you continuously update the software by going to the vendor's

Web site and downloading the new virus definitions, you leave yourself open to attack. An average of six new viruses are created every day, so you really ought to update your program at least once a week. It's only going to get worse as more unscrupulous people use their programming skills to do harm.

How would you like to return from lunch to an e-mail that said "I love you" and came from someone you know and trust? You open it and unknowingly have unleashed a virus in your computer that buries itself in your system files and destroys all your graphic and MP3 music files. That happened to one of your authors who is usually very careful about opening attachments.

If you use a cable modem or DSL connection to the Internet, you inadvertently leave yourself open to hackers. One of our author colleagues had his American Express card hijacked by a hacker and only noticed it when he started to spy unusual charges on his card. The solution? Put up a firewall (sort of a moat around the castle). Companies like Norton Utilities produce Internet security software that is affordable for small business owners. Once you have it installed, it will notify you if someone tries to get into your computer (that in itself is scary). Our author friend was the victim of 25 hacker attempts in the first week he had the firewall, but he is now protected.

The following are crucial components to fighting viruses:

- ✔ Back up religiously.
- ✔ Scan for viruses at least once a week.
- ✔ Use Internet security software.
- ✔ Update your virus and security software once a week.

Choosing your antivirus software

You can find antivirus software nearly anywhere you look, including online retailers, computer stores, and discount stores. The leading brands are probably Norton and McAfee, but there are some criteria you should consider when choosing among them.

- ✔ Find a package that lets you update easily — the top-of-the-line packages offer automatic updating. Essentially the software downloads the latest definitions from its Web site and incorporates them into the software on your hard drive.
- ✔ You may want software that removes zipped viruses from e-mail messages without destroying the entire message.
- ✔ Your software should issue a warning about an infected file before you download it.
- ✔ Check to see by how much the software degrades your computer's performance (remember, it's running continuously in the background). You may need to add more RAM to your computer to make up for the loss of performance.

Some final warnings

Okay, you've done everything we suggest. That's a great start. Now here are some final warnings:

- ✔ No foolproof antivirus programs exist; you must back up regularly — daily is a good idea.

- ✔ Don't use pirated software. It may be cheaper (or free), but it will cost you in the end because it's more likely to contain viruses.

- ✔ Make sure that your network administrator grants to employees write privileges only for the areas they need to do their work. Doing so prevents unlimited access to all your documents and accidental or malicious changes.

Protecting Your Computer from Hackers

In February 2000, several major Web sites were attacked by hackers — sites like Yahoo!, Cnet, and e*Trade. Hackers are computer nerds that find it challenging and amusing to see if they can penetrate the security of major companies and institutions like the federal government. The unprovoked and sudden assault on major Web sites in the spring of 2000 proved that no matter how much money you spend on your Web site, you're still vulnerable to clever hackers.

The good news is that a small business's chances of having its computers hacked into are miniscule. They just aren't worth the hacker's time. Professional hackers typically go after much bigger game. Nevertheless, no one is immune, so it's a good idea to protect your business.

If you're operating your business from home (as more and more people are doing), you probably haven't considered security very carefully. Computers in home offices generally don't have the firewalls and other Web security devices that businesses do. If you have an always-on connection like cable modem or DSL, your computer is vulnerable even from the kid hacker on the same local cable loop. Software like Norton Internet Security 2000 exists to provide protection to home computer users. It creates a private firewall to ward off hackers and monitor what comes in and goes out over the Internet. You can customize the settings for different types of users.

The various species of hackers

Although hackers come in several varieties, this section covers the three major categories, which include network hackers, software hackers, and virus-building hackers.

✔ **Network hackers:** These hackers are probably the elite members of the group. Movies usually depict hackers as either introverted, unattractive, and socially inept, or — conversely — as hip and sexy. The truth is that network hackers are average people with an above-average understanding of computers and an intense desire to test their abilities in ways that often step over legal boundaries.

Their activities include two types of attacks. The first type is the denial-of-service attack, where they tie up a Web site with fake requests for pages. The server spends so much time processing these fake requests that it's impossible for the network to respond to legitimate requests, ultimately bringing it down. This is what happened to several major sites like e-Bay in February, 2000. The other type of attack is a mail bomb, which targets mail servers and unleashes a virus when the mail is opened.

Network hackers also attempt to penetrate secure networks, usually by setting up a program that tries millions of passwords until they get one that's accepted. Often they do so just to test their skills, but some hackers actually get into files, change data, and then erase the evidence that they have been there.

✔ **Software hackers:** These people break software security. When you installed your word processing software, for example, you probably had a serial number that you had to enter to be able to install the program. A hacker will set up a serial number generator to find a serial number that will open the program.

✔ **Virus-building hackers:** These hackers build viruses — worms, Trojan horses, and logic bombs — that invade your computer system or network. Some viruses do damage. Others are harmless. See the section about viruses earlier in this chapter.

How to avoid being hacked

You can do a lot to prevent hackers from getting into your system. Here are just a few suggestions you should consider:

✔ **Stay up with the news in the world of computers.** You should be reading at least one technology-related magazine on a regular basis. In addition, you may want to check out these two Web sites that give up-to-the-minute updates on what's going on in the world of hackers, www.hackernews.com and www.securityfocus.com.

✔ **Disconnect anything you're not using.** If you don't use it, get rid of it. If you have a modem, go offline when you're not using the connection. If you have an always-on connection like a T-1 line or DSL, you should have some kind of firewall and/or proxy server that helps prevent people from getting in.

> ✔ **Never open e-mail attachments from people you don't know.**
>
> ✔ **Get to know your ISP.** They aren't equal when it comes to protecting you from hackers and viruses.

Be careful about whom you hire. Most hackers have been disgruntled employees somewhere. Before they leave the company, they put a back door into the company's system so that they can enter later from a remote location. That's why it's important to get to know the person you're about to hire to set up and manage your information systems. Also, check the upcoming section called "Practicing Safe Computing."

Backing Up So That You Can Go Forward

No matter how careful you are to protect yourself from hackers, viruses, power surges, crashes, and all the other nasty things that can go wrong with your system, something bad can still happen. For that reason, you need to back up your data regularly and systematically. If you ever have to reconfigure your complete hard drive set-up from scratch, you'll learn quickly that having a full copy of the hard drive on tape, removable cartridge, rewriteable CD (CD-RW), or second hard drive is essential. A four-step process ensures that you're better protected:

1. **Copy everything from your hard drive onto the backup medium and store it in a safe place.**

   Do a complete backup of your hard drive at least once every six months.

2. **Back up new and updated documents with an incremental backup on a weekly or daily basis, depending on how often you use your computer.**

3. **Use your software to set up an automated schedule for doing incremental backups.**

   You can run these backups at night. Be sure to restore your backups periodically to make sure that they're working properly.

4. **Archive data that you don't need to use but don't want to lose.**

   Archiving is long-term or permanent storage of things like invoices, old contracts, and so forth. You can write these to permanent media like CDs and take them off your system.

Practicing Safe Computing

Computers are machines that need to be taken care of. A little time and effort spent now in cleaning up and protecting your computer from malevolent forces, be they human, computer, or natural, can prevent problems down the road. This section covers such topics as housekeeping — both inside and outside the computer — protective measures against hackers, protective measures against being your own worst enemy (where the computer is concerned), and buying insurance.

Essential environmental computer care needs

You can start by looking at the environment in which your computer resides. In general, you want it to be located in a room that has a constant temperature, where it is not in direct sunlight and is not affected by airborne contaminants. Don't jam the computer up against a wall or below a low-hanging shelf, because the fan needs plenty of air.

Finally, be sure to plug your equipment into a UPS (uninterruptible power supply) with a built-in surge suppressor. Doing so not only protects your computer from electrical spikes, but also gives you a constant source of power should your power go out.

Make your computer secure

As you can see, it's easy to get into someone else's computer and play havoc with his or her data. Computers don't come with deadbolt locks, unfortunately. To protect particularly sensitive data, you may want to consider parking it in a secure folder on your hard drive using an encryption program. These programs scramble data in folders that you specify and make it extremely difficult for someone to access without a password.

Network Associates produces two programs designed to deal with security issues:

> ✔ **CyberMedia Guard Dog** is a personal security system for the Internet. It prevents others from monitoring your Web-browsing habits and cleans up after you. It can also cause an alarm to go off if someone accesses sensitive files.

✔ **McAfee PGP Personal Privacy** is designed to stop the rise in mobile computer theft. Its encryption program stops hackers and computer thieves from gaining access to sensitive data on your laptop or corporate network. It uses 128-bit encryption to create a vault on your hard drive where it stores your sensitive data. It also has an e-mail encryption utility that works with popular e-mail programs and lets you encrypt a message (scramble it so that no one can read it without a key) with a simple click on the toolbar button. So go ahead and sign your message with a digital signature and lock it with an electronic key (a key being a complex code of numbers and letters). After you've done this, only those who know what that key is are able to open the messages.

Clean up your desktop

One thing you can do to protect your computer and your network from itself is to get rid of unnecessary files and empty the Recycle Bin. This is not an easy task if you use the Windows operating system, because it spreads files across many directories on your hard drive. This makes it nearly impossible to do the job manually. Fortunately, there is software that can do it for you by searching through your system to find fragments of files, corrupted files, and other files that don't do your system any good. It then displays these files and recommends whether or not you should delete them. Some good products are

✔ Norton's CleanSweep Deluxe

✔ Symantec's Uninstall Deluxe

✔ CyberMedia's Uninstaller

Don't mess with registry files unless you know what you're doing. If you do even one thing wrong, you may not be able to use your system. Talk with your tech consultant about these files.

Another thing you can do to help yourself out is create an emergency disk that will let you boot your system, even if a disaster occurs. You also want to make sure that your hard drives are working correctly, so if you're using Windows, you can run ScanDisk. If you want to do an even better job, try a maintenance utility such as Symantec's Norton Utilities, CyberMedia's First Aid, or Helix Software's Nuts & Bolts. If you're a Mac user, you already have a bootable CD-ROM or floppy disk to use in the case of emergency, but you can also use Norton Utilities for the Mac.

After checking your hard drives, you need to defrag them. *Defragmentation* helps you arrange your files and allows them to open more quickly, and increases the performance of your hard drive. The more that you use your system to install, delete, move, and change files, the more likely it is that you have a fragmented hard drive. This fragmentation slows your computer's performance and makes it possible to lose files.

If you notice that your computer seems to be a bit sluggish, it's probably because you haven't defragmented the hard drive in a while.

Like everyone else, you have probably experienced your computer crashing and losing the document you were working on. The experience is frustrating, but certain utilities can recognize when a Windows application is about to freeze — Symantec's Crash Guard Deluxe, Quarterdeck's RealHelp, and Artisoft's ConfigSafe, to name a few. The software will make repairs and save your document.

If you forget to save your documents and then lose them when your computer freezes or a program locks up, there is a software utility for you. It's called Wild File's GoBack (`www.goback.com`), and it's an invaluable recovery tool that resurrects your system by sending it back in time, even if Windows won't start. It keeps track of changes you make to your computer and lets you instantly restore your hard drive to the way it was minutes or days ago. It also lets you look back in recent time and see your hard drive as it was at that time — sort of like a picture from the past.

Avoid the bad things that computer users do

We all do things to our computers that we shouldn't do, including spilling coffee and Twinkie crumbs on the keyboard and not regularly cleaning the equipment and removing harmful dust. These things are minor in the grand scheme of things (although we have it on good authority that keyboards are not coffee drinkers). Most of us are not aware of the really harmful things we do, or at least we're not aware that we're doing damage. If you choose to do some of the things mentioned in the following sections, you must weigh the risk and decide whether you're willing to take it.

Bootlegging software

Have you ever borrowed software from someone? On the other hand, have you ever gone to a Web site like Hotline Communications (`www.hotlinesw.com`) to download software from some stranger's server? That's like eating food off a stranger's plate. What you've just done is something that is patently illegal. Besides that (and that's really enough in itself), you may contract a virus and you'll get no tech support. We recommend that you "just say no" and practice safe computing instead.

Companies like Microsoft are coming down hard on businesses that pirate software. Just visit their antipiracy page at www.microsoft.com/piracy and you'll be amazed when you read the statistics on how much money software companies lose each year to pirates. If you decide to pirate software, be aware that the fines for piracy can range up to $250,000 and you could end up in jail for up to five years.

To make sure that you're doing everything according to the law, you might want to visit the site of The Software and Information Industry Association (www.siia.net).

Unplugging your peripherals while the computer is running

Another thing we all do from time to time, especially when you're trying to run two different printers off the same port, is unplugging peripherals while the computer is still running. You take a big chance, doing this. If you unplug or plug in your monitor while there's power to the plug, you could ruin the video card or the monitor itself, especially if you simultaneously generate static. When you disconnect a peripheral that the operating system recognized when you booted up your computer, the OS goes crazy trying to figure out where it went. Chances are your computer will freeze up and you'll have to reboot anyway.

Some laptops have what are called hot-swappable drives that enable you to switch peripherals mid-stream, but check your manual to make sure that your manufacturer explicitly says it's okay to do this. A good rule is to shut everything down, if you can, to make your changes.

Automate your utilities

Not too many computer users remember to use the various utilities that we talk about in this chapter. With everything else you have to remember, it's no wonder defragging your hard drive is not high on your list of things to do. Fortunately, the software companies that provide the utilities designed them with you in mind. They can be set to prompt you to perform certain tasks or do them automatically without prompting. Some of the tasks that can be set for automatic reminders and automatic operation are backups, updating virus files, and defragmenting the hard drive.

Insuring against cyber-liabilities

Did you know that when you get into e-commerce, you open yourself up to all sorts of liabilities — everything from stolen credit cards to computer crashes to lawsuits? Internet insurance is becoming big business. With more businesses relying heavily on computer systems and other expensive technology for their daily operations, business insurance needs are no longer standard.

Suppose your e-commerce site crashes because of an error, a virus, or a hacker. If you had standard business insurance, you would not be covered. Insurance geared toward technology and e-commerce, however, can compensate you for lost revenues, and pay for the costs of disinfecting your system, repairing your computer, or other related tasks. If you have a pure Internet site with no brick-and-mortar backup, you're in big trouble when things go wrong — you're immediately out of business. On the other hand, if you have a brick-and-mortar site that is lost to a disaster, the Internet may save you.

In addition to the standard property insurance on your equipment, there are two types of coverage businesses should consider and you need to talk to your insurance carrier about them.

✔ **Professional Errors & Omissions (E&O):** This policy protects you against a negligent act, error, or an omission you make while delivering your professional services particularly over the Internet. Some E&O products also cover trademarks and copyrights.

✔ **Directors and Officers Liability Insurance:** This type of insurance is important for both public and private companies. Shareholders and employees tend to be litigious these days — not to mention competitors, customers, and the government.

Insurance can cover almost any kind of exposure you may incur — for a price. Like any other insurance, you have to get a physical — in other words, a technology checkup. The insurance carrier inspects your site and its security — which, by the way, provides you with a lot of information on which you may want to act.

Part V
The Part of Tens

The 5th Wave — By Rich Tennant

"NO, SIR, THIS ISN'T A DATING SERVICE. THEY INTRODUCE PEOPLE THROUGH A COMPUTER SO THEY CAN TALK TO EACH OTHER IN PERSON. WE INTRODUCE PEOPLE IN PERSON SO THEY CAN TALK TO EACH OTHER THROUGH A COMPUTER."

In this part . . .

In this part, we tell you about such things as buzzwords that you can use to test someone's tech IQ, technology mistakes that small-business owners make, ways to make your tech consult love you, and reasons to get a Web address. We finish this part with the best technology resources on the Web.

Chapter 17

Ten Buzzwords You Can Use to Test Someone's Tech IQ

In This Chapter

▶ Familiarizing yourself with the jargon

▶ Defining types of networks and types of nets

*Y*ou have no doubt found yourself in conversation with people who have an interest in technology or work in the field. As if the whole world understood and was immersed in technology, they gleefully throw out terms you're supposed to know: ASP, domain name, DSL, intranet — you get the picture. We want to save you some embarrassment by giving you a list of ten buzzwords that you may hear at your next event or around the water cooler. Add them to your vocabulary and see how fast you gain of bit of respect (but just a bit) from your techie friends.

ASP: This Is Not Cleopatra's Snake

Any business owner who maintains a network knows how much work it can be to keep the network running optimally. What if you could get all the applications and benefits of a network without having to worry about hardware maintenance and software upgrades? Well, such a solution is available. An *application service provider* (ASP) can offer you the use of software applications and the necessary network hardware/software that your business needs to run its operations effectively.

The nice part about outsourcing the service to ASPs is that all the applications run from a server that is set up, administered, and maintained by information technology professionals outside your office. This means that, as a business owner, you don't have to go out and buy a server and then spend the time and money to get it up and running. You still need to do basic network wiring in your office to connect all your computers and, more important, focus on connecting to your potential ASP. However, a business that normally wouldn't be able to afford a heavy-duty server and really expensive software has the chance to have valuable services at a fraction of the cost of installing, maintaining, and upgrading a large system when it uses an ASP. Lastly — and perhaps best of all — a professional technology group takes care of almost everything.

Look at the possibility of an ASP providing services for your business. ASPs take on a lot of the burden that most small businesses struggle with when it comes to technology.

Database

Believe us, if you're not using a database right now, you're making business much harder on yourself. A database is a great place in which to assemble, manage, and organize similar pieces of information. The two most popular database programs are Filemaker Pro from Claris Corp. and Access from Microsoft Corp.

Most databases use something called *fields* to store this data. An example of a field is "name." "First name" would be one field and "last name" would be another field. "Phone number" would be one field, and "fax number" would be another.

Following are two examples of typical databases:

- A telephone directory stores fields of information such as name, address, telephone, and fax. Every person you add to your directory creates a new record.

- Your check register is another database. The fields here are check number, date, payee, amount, and balance. For every check you write, you enter the information into your database as a new record.

If your business uses order forms, a database is a wonderful way to store all that information. An order form may contain fields such as company name, purchase order number, shipping address, and item descriptions.

Once the information is in the database, you can do a search according to any field. For example, a repeat customer calls and wants to know if her current order has shipped. You can do a search, or a *find,* in your database by entering your customer's name. The database then pulls up all past records associated with that customer, including the current order. The more specific your request, the more accurate the results will be.

Databases are essential tools for managing information. Many database samples are included with the programs you buy, and you can start using them right away. On the other hand, the value of most databases is realized when they're customized and created just for you. They come in two basic types: relational and flat. The difference lies in how you build them.

- ✔ Flat databases are not very difficult to build. *Flat* means that you can add several fields without having complex relationships between them.

- ✔ On the other hand, a *relational* database is more sophisticated and complex to put together, but it gives you added benefits because each record in the database can relate to every other record with common fields. These relationships make the database run more efficiently and facilitate searching for the information you need.

Domain Name

A *domain name* is your identity on the Internet. This name is usually what comes between the www and the .com in a Web address. For example, www.domainname.com is the traditional format of a Web site address. You also see other domain name extensions, such as .org, .gov, .edu, and .net. Associations and nonprofit organizations usually have .org extensions. The .gov extension belongs to governmental agencies, .edu is used for educational institutions, and .net belongs to a telecommunications company or networking company. The domain name itself is just an easy way for people to find a Web site, just like your home address or telephone number is the way that people find you.

Before domains caught on, the way to get to a Web site was to type the address of the computer. The real address of a computer on the Internet has many numbers in a row, like a telephone number. Remembering the words and phrases that have become common parts of domain names on the Internet is much easier.

If you have a great idea for a name for your business, you may want to register it right away. Unscrupulous "cybersquatters" are out there grabbing up domain names and then trying to sell them for thousands or even millions of dollars. You should know, however, that if you have trademarked a business name, you will have first rights to the domain name for that trademarked name, even if someone else is using it. The laws are changing rapidly, so it's important to keep up with them if you want to have an Internet business.

Domains are not free, unfortunately, but they aren't expensive, either. The official price is $75 a year, but some services provide registration at a cheaper rate. If you want to get a domain name, look up www.networksolutions.com on the Web. Once you're there, you can find out whether someone else already has taken the name you want. If not, and you want to register your domain name, Network Solutions will be happy to take your money and lock in the name so that nobody else can take it.

Keep in mind, though, that this isn't all you have to do to get onto the Web. You need to sign up with an Internet service provider (defined later in this chapter) who will host your Web site on its server and give you access to it so that you can make changes and update it whenever you want. (You can hire the ISP to do this for you if you don't want to be your own Webmaster.) Then you need to design your site and test it (you can hire a consultant to do this, too). The whole process can take from a day to several months depending on how complex your site is. If you're new at the Web site business, get some help from your tech consultant.

DSL

Digital subscriber lines (DSLs) give businesses and homes an "always on" connection to their ISP (Internet service provider, described later in this chapter), who in turn gives them access to the Internet. A DSL is a high-speed replacement for dialing up over a regular modem, and it uses the same wiring on which your telephones run. For businesses that can't afford the traditional $2,000 per month charge for other "always on" types of connections, DSLs empower them with the technological ability to get their offices up and running with larger competitors.

Ask yourself these questions when considering a DSL connection:

- **Is DSL available in my area?** Check with your local telephone carrier to see if this service is available in your area. The telephone company office must be within a certain required distance from your office or home in order to provide you with this service. The telephone company must also test the wires that already exist in your home or office to make sure that they meet the requirements of this service and that they're not so old or rusted that they will give you problems.

- **Do I need special equipment?** You need to get a DSL modem and a network interface card (also known as a NIC) for your computer. You have the option of either purchasing or renting them from your provider.

- **What type of DSL should I order?** Several different flavors of DSL are available. The most typical is called ADSL (asymmetric digital subscriber line) that gives you higher speeds when downloading files and graphics and a slower (but not as slow as a modem) speed when uploading items like e-mails or files.

GUI

A GUI is a *graphical user interface*. A simple analogy is to think of a GUI as a pair of glasses that lets you to see things a certain way. If you wear glasses (and if you don't wear glasses, just go along with us for a second), imagine looking at something with your glasses off. Chances are everything looks really fuzzy. But when you put your glasses on, everything becomes clear.

Information in a database is just words and numbers; looking at it can make your brain a little fuzzy. A GUI can help take those words and numbers and put them into a user-friendly screen called an *interface*. An interface is simply the screen that sits between the incomprehensible and confusing computer language and the person using the information. Most people find it easier to click on a picture of a folder to see its contents than to type a line of code. That picture of the folder is a piece of a graphical user interface.

A small business can really leverage the strength of GUIs by using one on the home page of its Intranet (discussed in the following section) or Internet Web site. Businesses can also use GUIs to ease the use of databases, along with many other applications. You can design the GUI to have whatever look and feel you want. Maybe you can find a way to convey your company culture through the design of such an interface.

Intranet

Yes, there is a difference between Intranet and Internet. The Internet is an enormous network of networks (and all the computers connected to those networks) that circles the globe. An Intranet is simply a private Internet inside the walls of a company. You can use an Intranet to take data sharing a step further by displaying information in one place that everybody can access. This streamlined source makes it easier to provide better and faster customer service, for example. You can even get fancy by incorporating databases, group scheduling, and shared contact managers into your site, just to mention a few options.

Keep in mind that an Intranet is not different from a client/server network. An intranet is a *service* that is added to your client/server network. Users make their way through the Intranet by using the same Web browser that they use to surf the Internet. As a result, you can navigate all your business documents the same way you navigate Web pages on the Internet.

Even though it may start out simple, an Intranet has the potential to become a beast because of how useful it becomes. You can start off with something small to see how it might work, but in order to do it right you may want to bring in some help. One suggestion is to outsource the development, management, and maintenance of the Intranet to skilled professionals. If you choose the right group, you'll probably have something up and running faster, and you'll be able to shift the burden of responsibility off your shoulders and onto theirs.

A new trend in Intranets is the use of a *digital dashboard*. A digital dashboard is an interface, or screen, designed specifically for you and your company. It displays all the different pieces of information you need and puts them right in front of you on one screen. The dashboard can incorporate personal information such as your calendar events, e-mail, and daily tasks. It also can provide a great way for project team members to have a common place to go to for project resource data, timelines, and milestones. For more information on digital dashboards, see Chapter 11 or visit the Digital Nervous System section of Microsoft at www.microsoft.com\dns.

ISP

An *Internet service provider* (ISP) is your ticket to surf the Internet. ISPs pay a lot of money to have very fast connections to the Internet that can accommodate many people. Why can't end users like you connect to the Internet directly without having ISPs in the middle? Spending thousands of dollars per month for connections like this doesn't make sense when ISPs can buy these big connections in bulk and then charge you a small, monthly access fee.

The most common way that customers connect to ISPs is by standard modems over normal telephone lines or advanced modems over DSL connections. (See the section titled "DSL" in this chapter for more details.) Most ISPs also offer email accounts and space on their servers to put up your own personal or business Web pages. Many packages are available, and the one you choose depends on how many e-mail accounts and Web pages you want.

LAN, WAN, Have a Plan

A LAN is a *local area network,* or, more simply, it's the formal name for the networks we talk about in this book. What's it good for? Well, a LAN lets you connect all the computers in your office so everyone can access and share information locally. By contrast, a WAN is a *wide area network* that allows you to connect multiple networks or computers in different locations within a city or around the world. For instance, a company could have multiple regional offices they want to connect so they can share information. Once those offices are connected, regardless of how they are connected, you can say you now have a WAN.

LANs can be set up in two ways:

✔ A *peer-to-peer network* connects two or more desktop/laptop computers so they can share information and resources with each other.

> ✔ A *client/server network* includes the same types of computers you would use in the peer-to-peer, but one or more servers (the queen bee computer that runs all the programs that give you the services you need — like sharing files, sharing databases, e-mail, and so on) become the center of the network. Several computers, all connected to a common place called a network hub, can then use the services the server provides. All the company data gets stored in the server so it can be easily accessed and managed.

The client/server model is usually the better way to go, because you store all your information on the server and use your desktop simply to access the information. In the peer-to-peer network, information has a tendency to be stored on whatever machine is being used, which means everyone has to remember where it is.

Centralizing your information on a server makes it easier to find and to back up (make copies of) your files so that you always have a safety net (see Chapter 16 for more information on backing up files). Regardless of how your LAN is set up, the sharable information can be files such as company letterhead, forms, and contact or calendar information. Depending on what you want and need to do, the LAN is the physical foundation for how you share information. You can continue to add servers and other machines (printers, modems, and scanners) that can add value to your network.

A LAN gives you the ability to share and not have to spend more of your precious dollars buying more equipment. Of course, as we say throughout this book, you need a plan so that your LAN will accomplish your business goals. Look at Chapter 3 to find out more about how to create that plan.

Portal Mania

The World Wide Web has so many Web sites that you probably can't even count them all, but you have to start somewhere. That's why so many companies are creating *portals*. Portals started out as search engines that let the user find what they were looking for on the Internet. Yahoo! and AOL are examples of these types of portals. Today, however, portals have become much more than mere search engines. Portals are now about branding, content, and distribution — in other words, new ways to create value.

Companies such as Excite, Yahoo!, and AOL want you to consider their portals as your main start screen. This screen, or page, offers links to all sorts of other sites, allows you to search by keywords or phrases for sites that interest you, and also gives you the feeling that you have a home (or base) to go to while surfing the Web.

In any Web browser (your glasses to see the information on the World Wide Web) that you use, you can set a certain page to be your home page. Companies that create portal sites know that the best way to grab a Web audience is to control where that audience goes from the second they log on. They want you to set your home page to their site so every time you log on, their logo is the first one you see. You may find that a substantial player in your industry has created a portal with links to sites that are helpful and are of interest to businesses such as your own.

You may want to visit some portal sites to get firsthand experience as to how they work. While you're there, ask yourself if you can picture using something similar to a portal for your company intranet. Better yet, think about becoming the number-one resource of needed information that other businesses in your industry can go to. Having *your* Web site as *their* home page enables you to gain an audience that needs useful information and will see your branding of products and services.

VPN

A *virtual private network* (VPN) enables people or offices that are located around the corner, in another state, or in another country to connect over the Internet in a somewhat secure "private network." VPNs provide a great option to businesses that need a WAN (wide area network) but can't afford all the equipment and people needed to custom build one.

Remote offices, traveling employees, and employees working at home can get a regular Internet connection with their local ISP and then establish a connection to the local network at the company's main office. A VPN connection uses various forms of encryption to keep information passed through the Internet secure and to keep others from peering into your business, so to speak. Because you can get a connection to the Internet from virtually anywhere now, a VPN allows your local network to be accessible to anybody you want, anywhere around the world, almost instantly.

Chapter 18

Ten Technology Mistakes Small-Business Owners Make

In This Chapter

▶ Acquiring the right technology

▶ Using your technology efficiently

▶ Staying informed

*W*e've spent a lot of time working with small-business owners on their business and technology needs, so we've gotten pretty good at predicting the mistakes we'll find when we first visit a business. Running through a short list of questions tells us quickly whether this business needs help — and what kind of help it needs:

✔ Do you have a business plan?

✔ Do you have a technology plan?

✔ How do you buy technology?

✔ Have you had any training on your technology?

✔ How are you allocating your resources?

✔ Are you backing up your information?

✔ How are you securing your information?

✔ Do you have a disaster recovery plan?

✔ Do you have a maintenance plan?

✔ Do you document your network?

✔ Do you stay abreast of new technology?

In general, most small-business owners do none or very few of these things. What they don't realize is that they're putting their companies in jeopardy. Think about how you would answer these questions — and keep reading. In this chapter, we look at the most common mistakes small-business owners make.

Failing to Plan

You're not going to get away from technology, no matter how hard you might try. It's going to be part of your business life from now on. Nevertheless, you don't have to let every tech advertisement or salesperson that crosses your doorstep seduce you. You don't have to buy every new application or new device just because it promises more speed or efficiency.

You can make wise decisions about technology if you take the time to plan. The old saying that "people don't plan to fail; they fail to plan" couldn't be more true. In fact, that's what this book is about — planning. Take us seriously. You need to create a plan that matches technology to your business goals. Then choose those pieces that can help you achieve those goals.

Buying Technology for the Wrong Reasons

Rule #1: Don't buy even one piece of technology — a cell phone, a laptop, or a network — unless it solves a problem or fills a need in your business. Technology is a facilitator, a means to an end, not the end itself.

In addition, when you purchase technology, never buy more than what is necessary to help your business. For example, if you have a three-person office, setting up a network to share files and hardware may be overkill. Doing so won't make sense financially, and it won't make sense if you consider the time it takes to overhaul all your manual processes. When you get to five or six people and some of them work from remote locations, investing in a network may make sense.

Rule #2: Never buy technology just because it's on sale. You always get what you pay for, and the technology you find on sale through that enticing Web site you encounter while surfing one day may not meet your business's needs.

Rule #3: When you purchase technology, be sure to plan for growth. Some people also refer to this as being able to *scale* later. In other words, buy technology today that won't constrain you down the road, when you need to add even more technology. Most people find themselves wondering if spending money on something they may not need right now is worth the investment. More often than not, the answer is yes, if you think you can justify the need for the technology over the long-term. And you *will* need it — count on it!

Not Getting Enough Training

We can't emphasize training enough. You must get training to use your new technology to its fullest advantage. But who has time to spend hours trying to figure out how a piece of equipment or a new software program works? While you're figuring things out, you're losing sales because you can't keep up. Bite the bullet and spend the money to hire a trainer or attend a class that will help you learn how to use the technology that you have in your business.

Most people don't use all the capability available in their business technology because, frankly, they don't know that it's there until someone points it out. All it takes is a couple of days of training to make you feel in control of the situation and let you see the potential of your new technology.

It's important that the training you purchase not only trains you on standard applications but also teaches you how to use the components of standard applications that will help your business most. For example, if you need to create a database of customer information that everyone can access, be sure that you purchase technology that allows you to do so. Make sure that your trainer shows you the most effective ways to access and use that technology.

Not Leveraging Available Resources

Make sure that your computing resources are being used by those who need them the most. Say your engineer, who's juggling several projects, has the same type of computer as the receptionist, who uses her computer primarily for word processing. The receptionist's computer breaks down, so you decide to purchase a new one for her. But because new computers are faster and can handle more processing, you should give the engineer the new machine and give the receptionist the computer that the engineer had been using.

Resource allocation is important if you want optimum efficiency with limited resources. Take inventory of what you currently have and make sure that there is no misallocation of resources. It's amazing what you can do after you rearrange some of your equipment to suit your employees' needs and responsibilities.

After your employees start working on machines, they tend to feel as though they own them. Handle the reallocation of this equipment with respect for your employee's feelings, at the same time that you meet their functional needs.

Failing to Back Up and Restore Business Information

Back up, back up, back up! We can't say enough about the importance of backing up your files. One big problem with having a paperless office is that you don't have all your information available to you if your systems go down. You can avoid this horror by backing up your system regularly.

You can back up information several ways:

- **Full backups:** The term *full backup* refers to backing up all files, including system files (the ones that make your computer run), application files (the ones that make your programs run), and other files (such as documents, databases, and so on).

- **Incremental backups:** An *incremental* backup is a backup of only the files that you created or changed since the last backup. This quicker form of backing up lets you back up the information that you use and change the most. System and application files don't really change that much, so it's okay to do them once a week.

Keeping your backup media in several different places is good practice. If the current backup is at the office, bring last week's backup home with you and try to find a media-safe place to store it. By placing the media in several places, you reduce the risk that a disaster in one place will destroy all your data. For example, some kind of natural catastophe could occur in your office that would destroy your server and all the backup media that was sitting on top of it. If some of those backups were offsite, you would be able to replace the server and restore all your data quickly.

Restoring your data is more important than backing it up. Doing a restore proves that your backup is good. The best-case scenario lets your information reappear like magic. Most businesses, however, don't make restores a part of their regular routine. That's why some business owners have been shocked to find that their backups were no good.

Bad backups happen for several reasons, one of which is a bad tape or disk. Using the same tape or disk over and over may corrupt it. Use fresh tapes or disks as often as you can. Isn't your business information worth at least that?

Failing to Pay Attention to Security

"The revenge of the nerds" is upon us. Every week you hear about hackers who prey on unsuspecting businesses just for the thrill of it. Moreover, some of these hackers are experts at making their way into your computer system, your files, and your databases. They don't get in by magic, however. The only way they can get in is through your modem or other connection you have to the Internet. A DSL or any other connection that's always on is the most prone to attacks. Just like expert car thiefs, these hackers make it their life's work to break into the most secure systems.

While a professional hacker is unlikely to attack your small business, plenty of teenagers and others out there may try to do it just to see if they *can* do it. The way to keep unwanted people out of your company's private network is to set up security walls known as *firewalls*. To do so, you need professional help from your technology consultant. In addition, you want user accounts, passwords, user rights, and file rights. Several layers of different security devices make it more difficult for unwanted visitors to access your system.

Hackers are not the only challenge you face. Some people enjoy setting loose a host of alien creatures known as *viruses* that attack your files and systems by way of the files you download via e-mail. These viruses come in many colorful forms: Michelangelo, BubbleBoy, and ILOVEYOU are examples. Don't let a charming name fool you. Malicious programmers create these viruses, and they replicate quickly and travel through network cables to destroy your data. The key to stopping them is to control outside access to your network, which happens through the Internet. Viruses spread when you either download a file containing the virus to a network drive or open an e-mail attachment containing the virus.

You must install antivirus programs and update them regularly. Norton AntiVirus and McAfee are two well-known brands. To date, more than 48,000 known viruses exist, from the relatively benign "gotcha" kind to the kind that deal an instant deathblow to your operating system or hard drive. Scan everything that comes into your system from the outside, whether it's through the Internet or from a floppy disk. You can set your virus scanning software to do so automatically on a regular basis (at start-up or shut-down, or at specific times if your connection is always on). Also, be sure to update your virus software at least once a week. You can set these programs to remind you to update, or to do it automatically. The effort is definitely worth it.

Never open an e-mail attachment from someone you don't know, or even from someone you do know if you weren't expecting it. The Love Bug caught a lot of people unaware because it came from people they knew.

No site is totally secure. The best you can do is to provide as many layers of security as possible. Security devices and software cost money. You must identify a level of security that is sufficient for you and your information. You must be secure, but you probably don't need to be as secure as the Pentagon.

Not Having a Disaster Recovery Plan

If you've ever spent hours agonizing over a business report only to have the computer freeze up and crash, causing you to lose all your work (and your sanity), you know the importance of preparing for technology failure. Fortunately, some major components of your computer system have potential for *redundancy*. Redundancy in this case simply means that if one device fails, a duplicate is there to pick up where it left off and keep going. It is a backup if the worst happens. For example, if you have an e-commerce business whose life depends on an Internet connection, you should definitely make sure that your host has a redundant (alternate) connection so your Web site can stay alive if the first connection goes down. Or if your office has a DSL connection, identify a regular telephone line and modem as a dial-up alternative to resort to until you're back up on your faster connection.

Hard drives are another point of failure. That's why you should consider investing in a mirrored hard drive for your network server that creates a backup for everything you do on the server. Yet another source of failure is power. Keep backup batteries on hand. Some business owners have gone so far as to have backup power supplies such as a generator on hand in parts of the country where power goes out frequently — places that often incur the wrath of Mother Nature or have overloaded power stations and grids. Think of redundant systems as insurance you can't afford to be without.

Having backed up data is an important part of your recovery. At the *minimum,* back up your data files to disks, back up to CDs, or use a tape backup system. Then store your backups in a fireproof safe, which you can buy at most office supply stores.

If you use tapes or disks to back up your information, you must put them in a safe that is media proof. Tapes and disks are made out of materials that melt much more quickly than paper, so the safe you put them in needs to be better insulated than a normal safe that protects paper. When you purchase a safe for media, buy one that specifies that it is intended to be used for that purpose.

To make sure that you can respond quickly in a disaster, create a procedure manual that describes everything you should do (or not do) to get your system back to normal. Keep the following in it:

- ✔ All your network documents
- ✔ All your operating system disks
- ✔ The phone number of your tech consultant(s)

Having this information on hand will lower your level of stress during a disaster.

Not Having a Plan for Maintenance

Not planning for the maintenance of your technology will catch up with you at some point. Maintenance can be as easy as having scheduled times to restart your server to clear out any issues that may have built up during use over a month. For example, as you use programs and files in a computer, they get stored in the machine's temporary memory. With so many files going in and out of that memory, things can get a little confusing — even for computers. Little bits of information may get stuck in that memory and not free up the space for other data to be stored. Over time, there is less and less space in which information can get processed. The computer eventually starts complaining by doing abnormal things and sometimes just ends up saying, "That's enough."

Planned restarts help prevent a machine from crashing, freezing, or just running too slowly. Some administrators also run what's called a *disk defragmentor.* This program looks through the files on your hard drives and rearranges them so that your computer runs as fast as possible.

From time to time, software companies release a *patch,* or upgrade. Patches contain resolutions to problems the software has manifested in its previous versions. Install these patches. If you want to understand more about maintenance, check your hardware and software manuals, or ask a technology consultant for advice.

Not Tracking How Your Network Works

If the in-house tech-consultant-wannabe in charge of your network suddenly left the business, would you know enough about your network to be able to talk to a tech consultant? It's crucial to document all the relevant information about your network configuration, including such things as network addresses and schematics. Doing so saves you time, money, and frustration. Keep this network diary with your other important documents in that fireproof safe we recommend earlier in this chapter.

Not Looking at New Innovations

Even if you own a piece of software that you think does the job, don't stop researching new products or services. Many small businesses get stuck at certain levels of productivity and efficiency because they don't take the time to explore what's new. Don't be afraid to change with the times. As technology tools become more sophisticated, the potential for supporting some of your business processes increases. Keep an eye out for new and innovative methods and learn how you can integrate them into your business.

Chapter 19

Ten Ways to Grow Your Business with Technology

In This Chapter

▶ Getting your customers' attention

▶ Making your company more efficient

*B*eing flexible and quick to respond to change is important in today's business world. You may be wondering how your company can achieve the high level of flexibility that is necessary to be competitive. We believe that technology is an essential component in the growth strategy of any business; therefore, we've compiled a list of ten things you can do from a technological standpoint to help your business grow.

Install a Local Area Network

Using technology to grow your business starts with building a local area network (LAN) in your business environment. A LAN links all your computers with cables so that they can share information and hardware from a central source. If planned, installed, and set up right, networking technologies can increase productivity and efficiency almost immediately, especially if you incorporate training into the installation mix.

Network environments allow you to share hardware and software, but — more importantly — they enable you to collaborate with others in your organization by sending e-mail, sharing files, and remotely accessing company information. Once you have the basic pieces of a network (desktop computers, a server, and the hubs and cables that connect everything together), you have the option to add on other technologies mentioned in this chapter, such as shared databases, Internet applications, and digital dashboards.

When determining what you need, don't decide on something that only meets your needs right now. What you invest in should provide room for growth — or, as technical consultants say, it should be able to "scale out."

Build an E-Commerce Site to Increase Market Reach

A Web presence for your business is not a difficult, expensive, or problematic project anymore. Today, with lots of support from the Internet itself — places like bCentral (www.bcentral.com) and Yahoo!Store (www.store.yahoo.com) — you can build a Web site and accomplish business transactions online in a matter of minutes.

If you don't have an e-commerce site, you need to get one up and running, because e-commerce can expand your market reach to include customers who are looking for your product or service on the Internet or who can't get to your bricks-and-mortar site.

Think about all the time, energy, and effort it takes to get a customer to the cash register in your store. E-commerce enables you to extend that cash register to people's desktops at home or at work, 24 hours a day. The number of potential customers you can reach worldwide is in the millions, and they're available as soon as you post your site on the Web. Now that's a growth strategy!

Remember, building a Web presence is similar to opening another store to service customers in a new area. The major difference is that these customers reside all over the world. Many services can help you every step of the way; you'll be opening up new marketing, sales, and distribution channels in no time.

Spread the Word about Your Company by E-Mail

In the past, large companies used mailing lists and postal services to send flyers and brochures to people's mailboxes. These mailers cost $2 to $3 apiece to print and ship. Today, e-mail is a great way to get word out about your company and its products and services — and you don't have to pay for shipping.

You can access a number of services that will send daily, weekly, or monthly e-mails to your customers informing them of new products, services, or promotions. Telemarketing firms have evolved into e-marketing firms that assemble lists of e-mail addresses in addition to street addresses and phone numbers. You can increase your return on investment because e-marketing lets you target your mailings and virtually eliminates the cost of shipping.

For a fee, e-marketing firm Postmaster.com (`www.postmaster.com`) lets you access a list of names and addresses of people in your target market who have consented to receive materials. For an additional fee, Postmaster.com also can distribute your materials via e-mail to the people on the list. This e-mailing service costs a fraction of what the traditional U.S. Postal Service and other carriers charge.

Visit these sites to learn more about direct e-mail marketing:

✔ The Direct Marketing Association, Inc. (`www.the-dma-org`)

✔ Listbot Email Marketing (`www.listbot.com`)

✔ Exactis.com (`http://find-on.exactis.com`)

Increase Customer Awareness with Internet Branding

Just as the need to brand a business's products or services in the real world is important, the need to brand products or services offered over the Internet also is important, even crucial. You can increase your presence and boost sales in many ways, including by posting billboards — known as *banners* on the Internet. After you design your banner, you have two choices for getting it out into the e-world:

✔ **Swap.** One way is to contact other businesses that have Web sites that market to any part of your customer base and make an agreement with them to swap banners. What you're saying is, "If you place my banner on your site so that customers can see that I exist and click on the banner to access my site, I will place your banner on my site to give your site the same benefit." Because both sides provide additional revenue streams for each other, the agreement is a win/win situation.

Don't stop at one agreement, though. Surf the Web and look at all the sites on which you can envision your banner placed. Before you know it, you may find yourself building an online community of vendors who complement each other with products or services that can increase sales.

✔ **Enlist the services of a professional placement company.** You pay a fee to a placement company, such as Advanced Marketing Corp. (`www.ultimate-promotion.com`), and it places your banner on sites that participate in the same program. Placement companies also place links to your site with search engines (described later in this chapter) and other sites that enable you to really leverage the reach of the Internet.

Use an ASP to Expand Your Services

Until now, if you wanted to provide certain services for your in-house employees or your out-of-house customers, you needed to purchase hardware, software, and the skills of professionals to make it happen. As much as you may have wanted to provide the services, the bottom-line dollar amount may not have made the purchase affordable.

Application service providers (ASPs) provide a new model that enables small businesses to expand their breadth of services by using solutions that they traditionally could not afford. Think of an ASP as a large information technology group that you would find in a large corporation. In other words, ASPs take the burden of technology off the shoulders of the business owner.

ASPs are successful because they

- ✔ Enable you to rent software on a per-use basis, as opposed to buying a more expensive full license.
- ✔ Can handle all the installation, setup, scheduled maintenance, and hardware upgrades for your environment.
- ✔ Can provide all the system administration, software upgrades, and customized databases that you require.
- ✔ Can provide access to application-specific software (human resources, accounting, quality assurance, and so on) that has traditionally been too expensive for small businesses to purchase.
- ✔ Can provide consultants, designers, and other skilled professionals who can make the technology portions of your ideas reality.

Use Internet Search Engines to Help Customers Find You

Most people, including your customers, use search engines to find what they're looking for on the Web. These wonderful inventions send their software robots out over the Web to search for the keywords (see the next section) you've entered in your search request and return a list of links ranked according to how close the search came to what you wanted. Register your Web site with the major search engines so that the people looking for the products or services that you offer can find you. Here's a brief list of some of the major search engines on the Web:

- ✔ www.about.com
- ✔ www.altavista.com
- ✔ www.askjeeves.com
- ✔ www.excite.com
- ✔ www.goto.com
- ✔ www.hotbot.com
- ✔ www.infoseek.com
- ✔ www.lycos.com
- ✔ www.northernlight.com
- ✔ www.webcrawler.com
- ✔ www.yahoo.com

Internet marketing groups make registering easy. These groups either charge a service fee to do a single placement of an ad on a Web site, or charge an annual fee to promote your site for the year. Here are a couple places to start:

- ✔ MoreVisibility.com (www.morevisibility.com)
- ✔ 1st Place Search Engine Positioning (www.1stplacepositioning.com)

If you register with the major search engines, a link to your Web site will appear and let your customers go right to your site.

When you search for a topic by means of a search engine, you enter keywords in the box that the search engine provides, and the search engine uses the keywords to compile a list of sites containing that topic. Although every search engine has its own personality, many actually look through *every* word of *every* page of content available on the Internet and let you know if they have found any content that contains the keyword or phrase that you're looking for.

You likely have experienced what it's like to enter a search for a subject and get a list of Web sites that don't seem to have anything to do with that topic. This is because keywords are hidden behind pictures and backgrounds of many Web sites. These keywords reside in the programming, placed there by the people who built the Web pages. The programmers put them there so that they can get the site in front of as many people using search engines as possible.

You, too, need to put keywords in the background of your home page. Brainstorm and come up with a list of every single keyword anyone could associate with your business. Think broadly rather than narrowly. When somebody enters a search for these keywords in a search engine, a link to your site will come up.

Build a Database to Manage Growth

The word *database* alone often scares people off, but it shouldn't. A database is essentially just a file cabinet with a lot of information in it that can be organized and viewed many different ways, depending on your needs. Databases are often used when you have forms into which you must place information. For example, a doctor's office uses patient information forms, which become the structure of the database. In this case, each patient is a record in the database (form) providing specific information to the questions on the form.

The most common uses for databases are the following:

- Contact information for customers and vendors
- Tracking
- Billing
- Scheduling

All the information in your business that can be written down can be entered into a database and managed from it. As you expand your customer base, increase your inventory, and/or increase the number of locations you're operating from, a database becomes an increasingly critical tool that saves you time and helps you better manage that information.

Two of the most popular brands of databases are the following:

- Microsoft Access (www.microsoft.com/office/access)
- Claris FileMaker Pro (www.filemakerpro.com)

Track Inventory with Bar Codes to Achieve a Perfect Balance

Many small-business owners believe that using a system with bar codes is only for large organizations. That may have been true once, but it's true no longer. Implementing a consistent way to keep track of your inventory ensures that you have the right amount of inventory when you need it.

You don't need fancy machines to run the software that generates bar codes. All information associated with tracking can be held in a database, and most low- to medium-range desktop computers and printers sold today can handle the job. You also need some kind of database software, such as Microsoft Access or Claris FileMaker Pro (discussed earlier in the preceding section).

You also need a bar code scanner to scan the barcodes that you print out. Here are a few sites to check out to see what sorts of bar code scanners and services are available. These sites provide bar code devices, software, accessories, and services related to your tracking needs.

- ✔ BarCode.com (www.barcode.com)
- ✔ BarcodeDiscounters (www.barcodeddicounters.com)
- ✔ Label Solutions (www.barcodekit.com)

If you want to get sophisticated, call in a consultant and have him or her build a bar code tracking system that is customized to your business but utilizes off-the-shelf hardware and software.

Use Digital Dashboards to Manage Growth in Real Time

Digital dashboards enable you to keep an eye on your business's operations from your desktop by incorporating several pieces of information into one portal or screen. Close-to-real-time information about manufacturing, delivery, sales, and other important business data helps you make better decisions more quickly. You get to choose the specific pieces of information that your digital dashboard provides so that it can help you to make your decisions on a daily basis.

This screen brings together a stock ticker, e-mail, sales warnings, a company calendar, and a real-time view of the traffic you may get stuck in on your way home from the office. If you were in manufacturing, you would probably want to look at the output of production lines, finances, and client information instead.

Another growth strategy is to use a dashboard to bring your independent contractors together to work on your projects. You can create team folders that let each business involved in the project look at the same screen with the same information. As information is updated, so is everyone's screen.

Develop Your Own Electronic Mailroom

How many times have you found yourself standing in line at the post office, watching the clock tick away and the dollars you lose by standing there add up at a rapid rate? Mailing and shipping are big parts of most businesses, and accomplishing these functions effectively can help your business grow. Unless you've gone the virtual route and provide only digital products and services, you're probably going to have to rely on the Postal Service or a private mailing service at some point.

When savvy entrepreneurs recognized this problem, they began to provide business owners with the equivalent of full-service mailrooms online. For example, E-Stamp (www.estamp.com) enables you to buy stamps online, download them, and print them on your company envelopes — all from your desktop.

You can now print and ship documents online as well. NowDocs.com (www.nowdocs.com) offers services ranging from two-hour delivery to overnight or two-day shipment of your documents anywhere in the world. You upload your documents to a filing cabinet on the NowDocs site, attach your requirements for printing, binding, and duplication, give NowDocs your delivery instructions, and it's done.

If you want to compare shipping rates for packages you're going to send, try SmartShip.com (www.smartship.com). You can compare the services and prices of major shipping companies online (including the U.S. Postal Service), pay for packages online, print your shipping and priority mail labels, and track your packages.

Chapter 20

Ten Ways to Make Your Technology Consultant Love You

*I*n the current market, technical consultants are in demand. There are more of *you* than there are of *them,* so the consultant doesn't seem to have any incentive to try to build a long-term relationship with your business. There are always more businesses out there, eager to hire the consultant.

But times are changing. Business owners expect more from their tech consultants, and they deserve to get it. Companies that work closely with tech consultants are attempting to improve the situation through training and workshops, and over time, the good consultants will survive and the bad ones will be forced out of business.

But, for the time being at least, market pressures dictate that you should do your best to keep a good consultant happy. The good news is, you don't have to do much to help your consultant appreciate you and want to continue to work with you. In this chapter, we give you our ten best ways to create a great relationship with your tech consultant.

Make Yourself Available

Granted, you pay technology consultants, and they work for you — but keep in mind that the happier they are, the better your chances that they will do a good job. For example, consultants typically ask questions of you while they work, such as, "Do you have a methodology or any system for storing your files?" or, "What information would you like to have in front of you all the time?" Time is money, and consultants certainly don't mind charging you their hourly rate while they wait for you to answer their questions so that they can continue their work. Nevertheless, they would rather get a quick response and continue their work than to cool their heels while you ponder your answer or make time to deal with the question.

Be available to answer questions. The less time a consultant waits for you to make decisions, the less frustrated he or she will be, and the fewer hours he or she will charge you for.

Be Consistent

Consultants, for the most part, base their work on a plan. Therefore, it is important to agree on a master plan and stick with it. Sometimes a consultant gets halfway through the work at hand only to find that the client has changed his or her mind about the task and wants to add new features to the system. That's okay the first couple of times it happens — it just results in additional hours on the bill. However, when the client's mind changes repeatedly, the issue is no longer just money. It develops a case of *consultant frustration,* a psychological state likely to cause poor relations between consultant and client.

The consultant may grin and bear your indecisiveness to a point because you are the customer. But put yourself in the consultant's shoes and imagine how frustrating it would be if you had to redo a project you were working on over and over again because someone couldn't make up his or her mind.

Try to ask as many questions as you can up front so that you know what you want and can stick with the plan.

Think Long-Term Relationship

When you work with the same consultant over a long period, he or she really understands your business. The consultant will be able to give you better suggestions and use up less of your precious time as a result. In general, the relationship that you develop with your chosen tech consultant is about three things:

- ✔ Designing and implementing the technology strategy for your business
- ✔ Maintaining the technology you have in the business
- ✔ Making new suggestions based on changes in your business strategy

If you develop a good working relationship with your consultant, try to keep that consultant over the long-term because doing so will save you time, money, and, most important, your sanity. Consultants look for business clients whose businesses are growing and have the potential to add new technologies in the future. Letting your consultant know that he or she is your guide to using technology to maintain your competitive advantage and treating your consultant like a business partner will pay off for both of you.

Be Patient: Know When to Call

Consultants should take care of you no matter how demanding you are. Unfortunately, many business owners misuse and abuse consultants in various ways. The most common form of abuse is calling the consultant to complain about something before you understand the nature of the problem: "I'm not getting any e-mail off my Web site." "My computer froze for no reason at all."

Too often, problems like these stem from not understanding how things work or how to use certain pieces of technology. Maybe your entire network seems to be down simply because you didn't type your password correctly when you started your machine. Perhaps the reason you aren't getting e-mail off your Web site has nothing to do with technology; it may be that you never let customers know that your company is out there on the Web, so they're not finding your site when they search for businesses like yours.

Talking with your employees may uncover the source of these problems without your having to make an expensive call to your tech consultant. You could troubleshoot the network problem by asking anyone else if the network seems to be running okay. Knowing that all other machines are working normally tells you to focus on your own machine. Try restarting your computer and going through the normal steps. You may find that in most cases, you can solve your own problems.

Sometimes, however, you definitely want to call the consultant. If a server is down and everyone in your business suddenly does not have the tools that they need to do their work, you need to call the consultant. Your consultant would expect you to call.

Let the Professionals Work

Have you ever seen that big sign on the wall of your auto mechanic's repair shop? NO CUSTOMERS BEYOND THIS POINT! It's there for a reason. A mechanic hates working with a busybody customer looking over his shoulder and providing color commentary and armchair quarterback advice at every turn. The situation is no different with technology consultants. Your consultant is a skilled professional. Do not second-guess. Let the consultant do what you pay him or her to do.

At first, consultants may find it amusing when their clients, who don't know a lot about technology, tell them how to do their job. After a while, however, they get annoyed because the client is trying to control their environment. That makes it difficult for the consultant to do his or her best. Trust that you have chosen a professional, back off, and, if you have to say something, tell the consultant that you appreciate the good job he or she is doing.

Provide Incentives

Although you may be paying a premium for your consulting company to do the work promised, think about providing a bonus. In the same way that you provide incentives to your employees to encourage them to do more than the minimum — to strive for excellence — you can motivate your technology consultant by means of incentives, particularly when you want to develop a long-term relationship with him or her. Your technology consultant is another member of your team, and you should treat him or her accordingly.

One very important point: You should provide incentives for the person who is actually on site doing the work for you, not the company itself. Providing incentives for the company is as misguided as tipping the owner of the restaurant as thanks for the service your waitperson gave you. Good management requires that you reward the person who performed the service.

What kinds of incentives are appropriate? They don't have to be big, because it's the little things that count. For example, if your consultant is going to be spending a lot of time in your office, find out what he or she likes to snack on and make that snack available. If your company deals in products or services that the consultant could use, give that as a gift or provide a special discount. The gesture will pleasantly surprise the consultant (companies don't often think to do these things) and make him or her feel important and appreciated.

Another incentive that companies often provide their consultants is a bonus for completing a project quicker than planned and under budget. If you need something completed fast and it requires that the consultant work odd hours and use a lot of resources, consider providing a bonus on top of the original amount stipulated in the contract. How much depends on the size of the job. The bottom line is to treat your consultant as you would like to be treated.

Give Business Referrals

The argument that marketing and promotion are essential to growing a business is certainly as true for your tech consultant's business as it is for yours. Word of mouth is the strongest way for consultants to expand their clientele because the customers they gain from referrals are generally the best kind. Assuming that your consultant has done good work for you, give his or her business card to other businesses you deal with.

This is a win/win situation for both of you because providing referrals doesn't cost you anything, and your consultant will give you the best service possible because he or she knows you are a fountain of future business. And when the day comes that you're in a tight situation and have to ask your consultant to go above and beyond the call of duty, chances are you will get what you need because you were thoughtful enough to refer other business to him or her.

Give Your Consultant a Road Map

When consultants first arrive, they know little about your business, yet it's their job to associate the right hardware, software, and services to meet your needs. One thing you may do to help your consultant get off the starting block quickly is to draw a flowchart illustrating what your business does — what the various processes are that people in your business undertake on a daily basis. This chart helps your consultant understand your office environment, which is critical to making decisions about technology.

Talk about a day in the life of your business (refer to Chapter 4 for a complete discussion of this topic). Explain the types of information you use, how that information flows through your organization, and the roles and responsibilities of your employees. The more a consultant understands about your business, the more knowledgeable he or she becomes in providing you not just any solution, but the *right* solution. A good consultant can figure out how your business operates on his or her own, but you can speed up this process. More importantly, you can emphasize particular areas that you think need the most support. This orientation will save the consultant time and frustration — and save you money.

Keep an Emergency Repair Kit on Hand

Consultants don't always come in to install a new system from scratch. Sometimes they're called to alter or care for an existing system that someone else originally set up. (Lucky them — this is the maintenance side of tech consulting.) Consultants don't enjoy having to fix somebody else's mess, especially when they need to spend several hours trying to understand what the previous person did.

The frustration of trying to resolve problems in an existing system may prompt your consultant to recommend scrapping the whole thing and starting fresh with a system that he or she builds and installs. That solution is certainly easier for the consultant, but your budget may not be ready to handle such a large, unplanned expense. To avoid this dilemma, be sure to make all the resources describing your current system available to the consultant. Examples of such resources are manuals, software license information, and emergency repair disks. Keep these items together in a safe place so your technology consultant can get your system back in great running shape, and so you can protect your budget.

Follow Directions

Consultants provide services based on their experience and knowledge. You essentially pay them to tell you everything they know, so you may as well listen to what they have to say and follow directions. For example, your consultant may instruct you in certain things you can do periodically to assure that your network remains up and running. Please do these things. They will save you time and money in the end.

More important, you also should adhere to the suggestions your consultant makes about staying away from certain equipment. One cable can mess up an entire network and disrupt everyone's work. If the consultant says to stay away from the server, for example, stay away from the server. Believe us when we say that you probably don't have anyone in your office who's skilled enough to do anything positive with it, and you could actually harm it.

We have seen too many instances in which a tech consultant has received a phone call from a business client saying that his or her network has just gone down and someone needs to come out right away. Through a few well-chosen questions, the consultant often finds out that people at the business didn't heed the warnings and did something they weren't supposed to do. Consequently, the consultant has to come out to the business, fix the problem, and charge the business. Following directions can save you a lot of time and trouble, not to mention money.

Chapter 21

Ten Reasons to Get a Web Address

In This Chapter
▶ Enhancing your business's image by having a Web presence
▶ Increasing your sales and/or visibility via the Net

*W*e firmly believe that not every company needs a Web site. It doesn't hurt to have one if you don't need it, but it doesn't necessarily help. Having said that, we could probably look at any entrepreneurial business with growth opportunities and discover a way to make the Web work for that business.

Some people are nervous about getting their site up and then being deluged with requests that they can't handle. First, let us assure you that it doesn't happen that way. Just because you put up a site doesn't mean that people will come to it, if they can find you at all among the millions of Web sites around the globe. Search engines won't pick you up on their radar if you haven't done the right things to let them find you. (Check out Chapter 13 for more about setting up a Web site.) So relax; you can do this slowly. In this chapter, we give you our best reasons for getting a Web address for your business. See if they entice you to do it.

You Get to Put Dot-Com After Your Name

Admit it. Aren't you just a little jealous of all those people sporting dot-com (.com) after their companies' names? Have you ever wondered if dot-com is the secret to your business success? Well, we can't guarantee that, but dot-com will definitely give your business a new identity. So why not just do it? Besides, for most businesses, it is the next logical distribution channel for their products or services.

If you haven't already registered for a *domain name* (the most common way that people refer to and remember Web sites), you may find that getting a Web address that is *yourbusiness.com* is more challenging than you thought.

If you're in the process of building your Web presence and you still haven't registered for a domain name, go to www.networksolutions.com, a representative of Internic, the organization that supervises domain name registrations. First, you have to do a lookup to see if anyone else has already registered the name you want. If someone has already taken that business name, there isn't much that you can do about it. If the name means that much to you, however, call the person under whom the name is registered to see if you can buy it from him or her.

Buying a domain name is often a costly proposition, so think long and hard about how valuable that specific name is to you. There is relief on the horizon though. Now there are several other extensions (.net and .org are two of them) that allow you to get the name you want. The downside is the initial risk you take that people won't remember the new extension because they're accustomed to everything being dot-com. Over time, however, they'll get used to other extensions because the dot-com realm is getting too filled. No matter what, claim your real estate and start operating on the Web.

Everyone Else Has One

The 1990s put more computers on home and small business desktops than ever before. The digital divide started to shrink as the power that was once only in the hands of large companies worked its way into the offices of small businesses. If you owned a small business in the 1990s, you definitely felt the pinch to get involved with computers to stay current and offer the same efficiency and quality that everyone else had.

Now it's all about the Web site. Regardless of size, most businesses need to have a Web site just to keep up with the evolving state of business. Look at what your competitors are doing with their Web sites on a regular basis. At a minimum, you should consider doing something equivalent but uniquely yours.

It Gets You Worldwide Attention

After your Web site is up and running, it is available to everyone all over the world. We're not saying that this automatically makes everybody part of your market or that people will find you easily on the Web, but it certainly has the ability to get your business in front of a huge audience. The ability to stir business up in various regions worldwide is something that only large corporations have been able to do until now.

Today, the world is at everyone's fingertips — literally. Expand your market research from local, to nationwide, to worldwide, and identify new revenue potential. You've have heard us talk about how much time, money, and effort it takes to start a business. Needless to say, it takes a lot of everything, so you may as well do it big. On the Internet, your business can be as big as you want it to be.

You Can Provide Great Customer Service

A Web site builds a better bridge between your business and your customers. It lets your customers interact with your business 24 hours a day, 7 days a week. For example, customers probably call your business for answers to similar questions or solutions to the same problem. You can post frequently asked questions (FAQs) on your Web site, thus giving customers the answers they need when they need them. You also can integrate e-mail into the site so clients can send unique questions or problems directly to you.

Your site can give your customers the ability to track their orders, look at their account status, and post comments that can help you improve your operations. But perhaps most importantly, your Web site can be used to collect information on your customers that can be put into a database, sorted and analyzed, and used to provide better products and services to them.

It's a Cool Way to Market and Promote Your Business

Imagine that you're out to dinner. You start talking about business, and someone asks for more information on what you do. Instead of getting an address from them to send out a brochure or package of materials you say, "Go to my Web site at www.yourbusiness.com and you can find everything you need; if not, let me know." This is the way most businesses are doing their marketing and promotion now.

There is no reason to send an expensive fold-out brochure anymore. Besides being expensive, people who receive them tend to throw them away, and if you need to change any information in the brochure, you're stuck. The static information that you find in a brochure belongs on a Web site, where it can become dynamic, along with all your other marketing materials including press releases, information about the company (which may be just you), and a look back at the products and services you offer.

Promote Internet-only discounts on products and services. Make agreements with other Web sites to place links on their pages that people can use to get to your site. Needless to say, the dot-com phenomenon won't be over for a while. A large percentage of commercials and advertisements have the dot-com brand name on them. It speaks to people when they see it, and customers' perceptions are that this company is up with the times and going places.

It Lets You Turn Your Business into a Resource Site

There is a lot of value in information. There is even more value in having several different pieces of information in one easy-to-find place. Businesses realize that information attracts their customers and other business associates. As a result, many Web sites are becoming industry-specific portals that offer a one-stop shop for information on a particular subject or a particular industry.

For example, a contracting company responsible for building schools deals with a number of different subcontractors, equipment vendors, and state agencies. This particular company has built so many new schools that other contractors, vendors, and government officials from around the world constantly call to ask questions and find solutions. A contractor may want to use a particular vendor he worked with on another project, or a state agency may need the resources of a smaller vendor for another job. To take advantage of its unique position, the contracting company built a Web site to serve as a information resource for projects pending and in progress.

In addition, the company formed a knowledge center where they store public information that they have gathered over the years. The site is now a place for current news in the industry, a place to do research on new products or services available, and a place to honor those in the industry. These types of facilities and activities will attract people to your site. They may come for information initially, but it is your company they are coming to and learn to trust.

It Makes It Easier to Make Friends

In today's rapidly changing business world, strategic alliances are the name of the game. With transactions occurring at Internet speed, and companies constantly changing, it's no wonder that most businesses are seeking partnerships with other companies that can provide some of the products and services they need. In fact, some enterprising individuals have even created Internet companies that make it easier for you to find partners.

For example, Guru.com (www.guru.com) is a place where consultants and businesses seeking a particular expertise can find a match. The venerable Thomas Register of American Manufacturers (www.thomasregister.com) is a great place to find companies that can make anything you may need. Everywhere you go, people are writing about the value of strategic alliances. In fact, you may want to check Chapter 11 where we tell you how to use technology to make it easier to create a strategic alliance.

It Helps Boost Your Sales

Many small businesses have found that adding a Web site to their distribution and promotional mix is just what they need to boost sales and help them get into new markets. For most businesses, marketing in new geographic areas is a costly undertaking because you have to learn all the marketing nuances of that region. What do customers like to buy? When do they like to buy? How do they like to buy? It can be a very complex task, and it takes a expert to sort through all the differences in customer tastes and preferences region by region.

On the Internet, however, regional differences seem to fall away. That's because business Web sites must be user-friendly on a global level — in other words — universal in appeal. The Internet is also a great place to test market products, services, and ideas because you can get a sense of who is interested in your products and services and which region of the world holds the most promise for potential customers.

It Can Make an Old Business New Again

Do you have a business that needs a makeover? Many businesses have been reinventing themselves as e-commerce businesses. The Internet is the new frontier, and it welcomes all sorts of innovative business models. You may want to take your traditional brick-and-mortar business and give it a new twist on the Internet. For example, catalog companies were very popular in the 1980s, when they delivered their colorful catalogs to a majority of doorsteps all over the world. Customers ordered by mail or phone and within weeks their order was on their doorstep. The business model worked, but it was inefficient, and the customer had to do too many things to complete a transaction. Moreover, the old method wasn't too conducive to impulse buying.

The Internet delivers a shot of new life to catalog companies, which are now publishing directly to the Web. Customers can browse through all the products or search for specific things they want. All it takes is just a click on the product and the system instantly adds your item to your virtual shopping cart. Punch in your credit card number and your order can be at your doorstep the next morning. Catalog companies can update stock information frequently and do sales analysis in real time.

Many types of businesses, have found renewed business energy in the new distribution channel of the Web — with a bigger marketplace, faster analytical tools, and the ability to provide more customer satisfaction. Check out Chapter 13 if you want to see if your company is ready to do business on the Internet.

It Is an Essential Part of Growth

For most businesses, a Web presence has become increasingly essential. More and more people are going to the Web to shop, to learn, and to play. Business customers and consumers alike assume that your business has a Web site to which they can go to get contact information or look through a catalog of products or services, and maybe even purchase online.

The marketplace is dictating that a Web presence be a standard component of any business. Don't look at this dictate as a problem. Instead, think of a way to leverage the Web to support your growth, increase your traffic, and increase your sales. It certainly is a great way to begin to build relationships with your customers, suppliers, and distributors.

Think of technology as an investment in the future of your business — an investment in your competitive advantage. A Web site is one piece of technology that you can't afford to be without.

Chapter 22

The Ten Best Technology Resources on the Web

● ●

In This Chapter

▶ Finding the best online sites for business and technology

● ●

*G*reat resources on the Web are worth their weight in gold. Anytime someone refers you to a good site, bookmark it on your computer or keep the URL (Uniform Resource Locator, or Web address) in a safe place, because you're probably going to need it. Eventually, you'll have so many bookmarks that you'll need to organize them by category, but that ultimately saves you time. Who has time to surf the Web a lot to find all the good sites? Not us! We get them not only from friends and associates but also from the newspaper, magazines, and other media. URLs are everywhere, so keep your eyes open. We've put together ten of our favorite technology sites here, along with a description of each site's highlights.

Tech Web

Tech Web (www.techweb.com) is a portal for people interested in technology. On this site, you can find the latest technology news and products, as well as services you can tap into. There also are links to other sites such as Planet IT, which is a community site for people interested in technology. Tech Web provides information about all types of applications. You must register to access a lot of the information, but there is no charge.

Wired.com

Wired magazine (www.wired.com) has been a staple of the computer industry for some time. This site plays on the stereotype of the computer nerd by using funky language like "current hoo-ha" to describe its news section. It offers articles in categories from Med Tech and Women in Tech to MP3 Rocks the Web. It also regularly covers the Linux world.

What's good about this site is that *Wired* sends a daily e-mail to you with the latest headlines and a link to the corresponding article. Recently, the site ran an article about the Webby Awards, which were held on May 12, 2000, in San Francisco. Although these awards mimic the Oscars in recognizing the top Web sites in a number of categories, they allow their winners to use only five words for their acceptance speeches. If only the Oscars would do the same! Here are the "speeches" of three of the winners:

- ✔ "Three letters: I P O." — Adbusters (Activism)
- ✔ "Thanks — come talk to us." — Café Utne (Community)
- ✔ "Is this thing edible?" — Epicurious (Food) (referring to the award statue)

Slashdot.com

Slashdot (www.slashdot.com) bills itself as "news for nerds," frequently publishing articles about the latest technology news before the news hits the mainstream newsstands. At Slashdot.com, moreover, you can buy everything from a koosh ball gun for your Ultimate Office Sniping Arsenal (UOSA) to the Linux Fish car emblem. Even if you're not a computer geek, you'll become one after spending time at this site.

CNN.com Technology

CNN, the ubitquitous news site that shot to fame after the Gulf War, provides a first-class site for information on all areas of technology (www.cnn.com/tech/). Not only does the site contain articles, but it also has video and audio archives — and you can chat with your fellow sci-tech fans (science and technology) using CNN's message board.

CNN has several popular weekly technology TV shows. If you've missed a show lately, you can usually find it in their archives. The three shows are

- **Movers:** `http://cnnfn.com/services/fnonair/whatson/movers`
- **CNNdotCom:** `www.cnn.com/CNN/Programs/cnndotcom`
- **Business Unusual:** `http://cnnfn.com/services/fnonair/whatson/biz.unusual`

Fortune Small Business/Technology

Fortune magazine, long thought of as reading material geared only toward people interested in the Fortune 500 and 1000 companies, has leaped onto the small business bandwagon with its excellent site, FSB/Technology (`www.fsb.com/fortunesb`). One of the best things about reading FSB/Technology articles online is that they have embedded links to sites discussed in the article, so you can read about a company, click on its link, and you're there — then hit the Back button to go right back inside the article.

FSB/Technology makes it easy for you to search its archives to find what you want. Just enter what you're looking for and hit "go." Don't forget to go to FSB's main small business page to check out articles on all areas of your business.

ZDNet E-Commerce

If you're interested in e-commerce, ZDNet E-Commerce (`www.zdnet.com/enterprise/e-business/`) is a good place to go. Here you can find news, reviews, and opinions; look for companies and ISPs, do research on an industry and even get technical help. You can download software to help you build your storefront and buy e-commerce products in a special area where you can compare prices and take part in auctions.

ZDNet has also pioneered the concept of interactive case studies. At its E-Business Solutions Center (`www.zdnet.com/smallbusiness/filters/home`), it provides answers to questions related to opening up shop on the Web. You can also see how companies solved their technology problems. Using ZDNet's Internet X-Ray, you can see an actual interactive layout of a company's Web site. It lays out all the different machines and the connections you need to make them work.

On ZDNet's Best Practices site, you find reviews of Web sites, which are an excellent way to find out what you should and should not do when you build yours. They cover the best and worst in e-commerce.

CNET

CNET (www.cnet.com), like ZDNet, provides tech news, auctions, hardware and software reviews, helpful hints, Internet tools, and Web building tools. As a business owner, you can post jobs on the site to find the technical people you need. You also can find interactive Webcasts on issues in the news, and CNET puts out a newsletter you can receive by e-mail.

Another great service that CNET offers is a way to find an ISP (internet service provider). The interactive page asks for your zip code and the type of service you want — dialup, cable modem, DSL, and so forth. You can also filter your search by whether you want regional or national coverage, whether you want one or two-way bandwidth, and by any other criteria you might have. CNET rates the ISPs so you can compare them.

The Standard

The Industry Standard is a magazine devoted to the world of the Internet and e-commerce. The Standard (www.thestandard.com) is the online version, which contains a series of newsletters on various topics:

- *Wireless News:* Covers the business of mobile technology.
- *Box Office:* Covers the business of entertainment on the Internet.
- *Daily News:* Presents a snapshot of the latest Internet Economy news.
- *Beat Sheet:* Reports on the convergence of music and the Internet.
- *Intelligencer:* Analyzes the week's major Internet economy news.
- *Metrics Report:* Reports the key indicators affecting the Internet economy.
- *Net Returns:* Guide to products and technologies that create profitable Web businesses.

You can also find newsletters in German, Spanish, and French.

The Standard is a good source for statistics on the e-commerce industry as well. It even lets you download PowerPoint slides on various industry statistics, so you have an instant presentation. There's lots to explore on this site.

Free Websites Directory

They say that there's no free lunch, but some Internet companies are trying to prove that statement wrong. Free Websites Directory (http://find. freehosting.net/bixhosts.htm) lists free hosting services. That's right — free Internet hosting services. The Web site hosts that you find here are rated by reliability, features, ease of use, speed, and the size of the site they provide. Stars are the rating symbols, so the more stars a host has — the better that host is in terms of the criteria against which Free Websites Directory measures hosts.

Free Websites Directory has gone to great lengths to do an objective job of rating the sites. Each criterion has a numerical value, because some characteristics are more valuable than others. For example, a site that provides long, complicated Web addresses will get a low rating. On the other hand, if the site has lots of graphics to help users navigate through, chances are it will get a higher rating.

Microsoft bCentral

If you want to start a business on the Web, market your business online, or manage the business you have more efficiently, Microsoft bCentral (www.bcentral.com) might be the place for you. Microsoft's vertical portal for small businesses (a *vertical portal* serves one segment of a particular market — in this case, small business rather than everyone), bCentral is designed to be a full-service site with a technology focus.

Offering a marketing package that lets your company be listed on up to 400 search engines (only the top five are used with any regularity), bCentral also enables you to advertise on MSN (Microsoft Network) and send targeted e-mail to your customers — up to 5,000 e-mails a month. By going to www. driveway.com, you can store your files in an online drive accessible from anywhere. You also can get free custom quotes from www.imandi.com; all you have to do is pick the best deal.

bCentral can help you build your e-commerce Web site, providing site design and layout templates, so that all you have to do is fill in the details and add pages at will. It even lets you accept credit card orders from your site through bCentral's shopping cart program.

Appendix A

About the CD

. . . .

System Requirements

Make sure that your computer meets the minimum system requirements listed below. If your computer doesn't match up to most of these requirements, you may have problems using the contents of the CD.

- A PC with a 486 or faster processor, or a Mac OS computer with a 68040 or faster processor.
- Microsoft Windows 95 or later, or Mac OS system software 7.55 or later.
- At least 16MB of total RAM installed on your computer. For best performance, we recommend that you have at least 32MB of RAM installed.
- At least 450MB of hard drive space available to install all the software from this CD. (You need less space if you don't install every program.)
- A CD-ROM drive — double-speed (2x) or faster.
- A sound card for PCs. (Mac OS computers have built-in sound support.)
- A monitor capable of displaying at least 256 colors or grayscale.
- A modem with a speed of at least 14,400 bps.

If you need more information on the basics, check out *PCs For Dummies,* 7th Edition, by Dan Gookin; *Macs For Dummies,* 6th Edition, or *iMacs For Dummies,* by David Pogue; *Windows 98 For Dummies,* or *Windows 95 For Dummies,* 2nd Edition, both by Andy Rathbone (all published by IDG Books Worldwide, Inc.).

Using the CD with Microsoft Windows

To install the items from the CD to your hard drive, follow these steps.

1. **Insert the CD into your computer's CD-ROM drive.**

2. **Open your browser.** If you do not have a browser, we have included Microsoft Internet Explorer as well as Netscape Communicator. They can be found in the Programs folders at the root of the CD.

3. **Click Start➪Run.**

4. **In the dialog box that appears, type** D:\START.HTM. **Replace** *D* **with the proper drive letter if your CD-ROM drive uses a different letter. (If you don't know the letter, see how your CD-ROM drive is listed under My Computer.)**

5. **Read through the license agreement, nod your head, and then click the Accept button if you want to use the CD. You can choose to launch the HTML Interface or the PowerPoint Interface.** This action will display the file that will walk you through the content of the CD.

6. **To navigate within the interface, simply click on any topic of interest to take you to an explanation of the files on the CD and how to use or install them.**

7. **To install the software from the CD, simply click on the software name.** You'll see two options — the option to run or open the file from the current location or the option to save the file to your hard drive. Choose to run or open the file from its current location and the installation procedure will continue. After you are done with the interface, simply close your browser as usual.

Using the CD with Mac OS

To install the items from the CD to your hard drive, follow these steps.

1. **Insert the CD into your computer's CD-ROM drive.**

   In a moment, an icon representing the CD you just inserted appears on your Mac desktop. Chances are, the icon looks like a CD-ROM.

2. **Double-click the CD icon to show the CD's contents.**

3. **Double-click the License Agreement icon.**

   This is the license that you are agreeing to by using the CD. You can close this window after you've looked over the agreement.

4. **Double-click the Read Me First icon.**

   The Read Me First text file contains information about the CD's programs and any last-minute instructions you may need in order to install them correctly.

5. **To install most programs, open the program folder and double-click the icon called "Install" or "Installer."**

   Sometimes the installers are actually self-extracting archives, which just means that the program files have been bundled into an archive, and this self-extractor unbundles the files and places them on your hard drive. This kind of program is often called an .sea. Double click anything with .sea in the title, and it will run just like an installer.

6. **Some programs don't come with installers. For those, just drag the program's folder from the CD window and drop it on your hard drive icon.**

After you have installed the programs you want, you can eject the CD. Carefully place it back in the plastic jacket of the book for safekeeping.

What You'll Find

Here is a list of the great stuff you'll find on the CD that comes with this book, along with a description of each item.

Templates

Business Goals Statement

Every good plan starts with a statement of goals. This template gives you a place to store your vision, mission, and technology goals so that you can refer to them often.

Business Goals Worksheet

With this worksheet, you can plot your major goals and the strategies you will use to achieve them. With your business goals in mind, you're in a better position to look at your technology needs.

Information Needs Assessment Worksheet

This worksheet helps you identify the types of information you use in your business, who generates it, and in what form it's normally received.

Micro Business Processes Worksheet

This worksheet helps you identify all the business processes you have in your company and prepares you to discuss your business with the tech consultant and consider the types of technology that might be appropriate.

Information Components Worksheet

This worksheet helps you illustrate the information components that make up your business environment. Use it to better understand the information relationships in your business.

Technology Inventory Worksheet

You can use this worksheet to gather information on the current technology you have in your business. This will help you and your tech consultant look at your technology gap.

Technology Evaluation Packet

This packet of three templates helps you look at the current status of technology in your business, evaluate it, and decide the beginnings of an implementation strategy.

Technology Strategy Planning Template

This template walks you through the process of creating and documenting your technology plan, from analyzing your business to determining the technology gap to implementing the plan. It is based on chapters in the book and refers to them where appropriate.

Request for Quotes Template and Confidential Disclosure Statement

This template helps you structure a request for quote or proposal from a technology consultant and/or vendor. It includes a confidential disclosure statement because both parties will be revealing proprietary information.

Vendor Evaluation Matrix

This template helps you evaluate several tech consultants/vendors to decide which to interview (in the case of a consultant). It's a way of refining the decision-making process.

Technology Implementation Worksheet

Here you find an organized form for planning for the type of computer and network hardware you might need, as well as software applications. You can use it to begin discussions with your tech consultant and vendors.

Technology Questions

These questions can help you prepare for a meeting with your tech consultant. You can print these out and take them with you. We've given you space for you to write in answers.

Tech Lingo Guide

This guide will solve all your language interpretation problems by giving you Dummyesque definitions of commonly used technology terms.

Case Studies

We have included two short case studies on small businesses that were part of our research to illustrate how technology gets integrated into a business environment. They provide good examples of what it takes to design, implement, and maintain services that will be valuable to your business. They also demonstrate how certain technologies are used within different industries.

Microsoft Small Business Video Case Studies

The video case study looks at a small business and shows how it integrated technology into its business environment. You can watch it right on your computer. You get a good understanding of what it takes to design, implement, and maintain technology in your business.

Microsoft Publisher '98

We've included a version of Microsoft Publisher so you can test your ability at designing a Web page for your bCentral Web site. You can also use it to design and create all sorts of marketing materials for your business.

FrontPage 2000

The Microsoft FrontPage 2000 Web site creation and management program for Windows gives you everything you need to create and manage your Web site. This 45-day trial will enable you to create an attractive Web site even if you are a novice to the Internet. For more information, check out www.microsoft.com.

Internet Explorer

Internet Explorer, from Microsoft (Commercial version; Windows and Mac), is one of the best-known Web browsers available. In addition to the browser, this package includes other Internet tools from Microsoft: Outlook Express, a mail and new reading program; Windows Media Player, a program that can display or play many types of audio and video files; and NetMeeting 3, a video conferencing program. For more information, check out www.microsoft.com.

PowerPoint View 97

Microsoft PowerPoint Viewer allows those people who don't own a version of Microsoft PowerPoint to view PowerPoint files. It is a limited version that allows you to read only and not edit or take advantage of other valuable tools provided in the full version of the software.

If You've Got Problems (Of the CD Kind)

We tried our best to compile programs that work on most computers with the minimum system requirements. Alas, your computer may differ, and some programs may not work properly for some reason.

The two likeliest problems are that you don't have enough memory (RAM) for the programs you want to use, or you have other programs running that are affecting installation or running of a program. If you get error messages like Not enough memory or Setup cannot continue, try one or more of these methods and then try using the software again:

- ✔ **Turn off any antivirus software that you have on your computer.** Installers sometimes mimic virus activity and may make your computer incorrectly believe that it is being infected by a virus.

- ✔ **Close all running programs.** The more programs you're running, the less memory is available to other programs. Installers also typically update files and programs; if you keep other programs running, installation may not work properly.

- ✔ **In Windows, close the CD interface and run demos or installations directly from Windows Explorer.** The interface itself can tie up system memory, or even conflict with certain kinds of interactive demos. Use Windows Explorer to browse the files on the CD and launch installers or demos.

- ✔ **Have your local computer store add more RAM to your computer.** This is, admittedly, a drastic and somewhat expensive step. However, if you have a Windows 95 PC or a Mac OS computer with a PowerPC chip, adding more memory can really help the speed of your computer and enable more programs to run at the same time.

If you still have trouble installing the items from the CD, please call the IDG Books Worldwide Customer Service phone number: 800-762-2974 (outside the U.S.: 317-572-3342).

Appendix B

Tech Lingo Guide

• •

*T*o help you understand some of the language that is typically thrown around in technology circles and that may slip into your business when your tech consultant is around, we've created a dictionary of sorts that you can use to interpret what's being said. Feel free to adopt some of these terms into your own vocabulary to spice it up a bit.

access rights: A list of rights that explain what you can and can't do with network files and directories.

antivirus program: A program that finds viruses on your network and exterminates them or puts them into quarantine.

archive: Permanent long-term storage of data.

attributes: Personality characteristics assigned to files to designate whether they are read-only (look, but don't touch), archive (really old), hidden (you can't find them), or system files (don't touch these).

buffer: A memory area that holds data for a period of time while it's on its way to somewhere else, sort of like a hotel.

bus: Refers to the row of expansion slots in your computer. Also refers to a network topology where network nodes are strung out along a single cable called a segment. Boy, you really wanted to know that!

cache: A higher order buffer with more space, where a large amount of memory is set aside to hold data that you need to access quickly. For example, when you return to something you've been working on, you don't have to wait long for it to load up.

Cat5 cable: Different types and grades of cables are used to network computers. Category 5 cable is the most commonly used because of its reliablility for dealing with data.

CD-ROM: A high-capacity disk that uses optical technology to store data, including all that music you've been downloading from the Internet.

Certified Network Dummy: Someone who insists on installing his own network without the help of a qualified tech consultant.

client: As in client/server, a computer that has access to a network but doesn't share any of its resources with the network, sort of like some people we know.

Client/server network: A design that can be used what putting together a LAN. Several desktop and laptop machines all get connected in a network. A server is also connected to this same network and provides services and information to all machines.

dedicated server: A worker-bee computer used only as a network server to provide services to clients (computers connected to the network).

differential backup: Backing up only those files that have changed since the last backup.

domain: When referring to the Internet, domain is the name assigned to a host computer.

DVD-ROM drive: This drive has a much higher capacity than a CD-ROM drive. You can also run your favorite movies on your computer with this drive.

e-mail: An application that lets you exchange jokes with your employees.

Enterprise Solutions: Just a fancy term for applications that cover a medium-to-large business's complete computer needs for all its operations.

FAT: Something you get from eating too many of your tech consultant's Twinkies. Actually, FAT32 is a way of keeping track of disk files used with Windows 98.

fiber optic cable: A lightning-fast way of tranmitting data by using light rather than electricity. It's usually used as the backbone on large networks over great distances, although this technology is rapidly coming to an office near you.

file server: The computer that contains disk drives available to users on the network to share files and other types of information.

Frappuccino: The breakfast of champions.

FTP: *File transfer protocol,* which is a way of sending and retrieving files from the Internet. You don't need to know how it works; just that it's behind that button you clicked to download a file from the Internet.

gigabyte: About a billion bytes of disk storage (1,024MB, if you like precise numbers).

HTML: Language used to compose pages that can be viewed via the Web. When your browse the Web and enjoy the pictures, text, sound, and animation that's there, realize that all that has been programmed in HTML. When you use software like Microsoft FrontPage, you can create pages with all these things in a friendly Word environment, while behind the scenes, the software is converting what you do to HTML.

Internet: An enormous network of networks (and networks and networks) that circles the globe, providing access to pretty much anything you want or need, and even some things you don't need and shouldn't have.

Internet connectivity: The connection between your computer and the computer that is giving you access to the Internet; often your Internet service provider (ISP).

Intranet: Think of an intranet as a private Internet that only those people you designate have access to — sort of a private party.

IP address: A sequence of numbers used to provide a unique identifier for computers. Every computer must have its own address if it is on a LAN or WAN. Think of it like a driver's license — every number is unique.

ISP: Stands for *Internet service provider,* which is a company that provides you access to the Internet for a fee. You can also surf the Web to find the free providers.

LAN: A *local area network,* which just means that the network is a bunch of computers physically connected within your one office as opposed to many offices in many regional areas.

live long and prosper: The secret password to the local tech society inspired by Mr. Spock of *Star Trek* fame. You may find that you have to do that weird thing with your hand, though, that looks like an alien version of the hippie peace sign.

login: This is the process of getting access to your network by providing your login name (usually your own name) and a secret password (newer versions don't require the special decoder ring). This is also called your *user ID*.

logout: The opposite of *login*.

mail server: The place on the network where all that private e-mail you've been sending to coworkers that you shouldn't have is stored in perpetuity.

media: Disks, tapes, and CDs are all different forms of media. This may come up in conversation when you talk about the type of media you use to back up your data. Most common forms of media are 4mm tape, 8mm tape, Zip Disks, Jaz Disks, CD-R (recordable only once), and CD-RW (these can be reused). When it comes to storage media, the bigger the better, unless you like constantly changing disks, CDs, or tapes.

modem: A hardware device that converts signals from the computer to sounds that are transmitted over a regular telephone line and ultimately to another computer that converts those sounds back into a form it can read. In short, it's a way for computers to carry on a conversation.

network account: The only way you can get on a network is through an account that tells you what rights you have. Your system administrator will set up this account. If you don't log in to your account properly, the network may look like it has disappeared.

network administrator: In most organizations, this person is equivalent to a god. This person manages your network and keeps it going. *You do not want this job.*

network drive: A drive that is located somewhere on the network rather than on your computer, which is good, because everyone has access to it.

network hub: A small box that that connects all the network cables coming from the NICs (network interface cards) inside your computers. Hubs are used to physically connect servers and other computers within a LAN.

network interface card: Also known as a NIC, it is used to attach a computer to a network cable and then to another computer or network hub.

network server: The computer that stores all the information on a network. Think of it as a big vault.

node: A hardware device residing on the network; for example, a computer or printer.

offline: Things that are not available on the network.

online: Things that are available on the network.

password: The only thing standing between your files and someone trying to access them while pretending to be you. Not the best defense, but it works well if you change your password frequently and don't use the obvious: your birth date, social security number, and so forth.

pocket protector: This used to be the identifying sign of a true technology geek; today, it's the PalmPilot.

Relational database: A database with two or more tables that share information and are associated with each other. Although complex and difficult to set up, this type of database is powerful and often used for accounting or production information.

ScanDisk: A command in Windows 95 and 98 that does diagnostics on your computer's hard disk.

sneakernet: A network made up of tennis shoes tied together in a string. Just kidding. It's the cheapest type of network you can have because you manually transfer files via floppy disks. Higher-end sneakernet users have gotten good at sailing floppies over cubbie partitions. A hole in one is when you land your floppy right next to the floppy drive of your coworker's computer.

TCP/IP: The transmission control protocol for the Internet. You will have to deal with this term only if you're configuring your own dial-up connection, or other network connection, to the Internet (get your tech consultant to do it).

techie: Someone who knows more about technology than you do.

Trojan horse: The mascot of the University of Southern California — also a very nasty virus that reformats your hard drive. That means it erases everything you have on it.

uninterruptible power supply: Also known as UPS. This keeps your computer running when the power goes out. Too bad humans don't have something like that.

virus: An alien that gets into your computer without you knowing it and then spreads blazingly fast all over the place. It can actually destroy your computer.

Index

• C •

Notes

Notes

Notes

Notes

Notes

Notes

Notes

Notes

Special offer for
eBusiness Technology Kit For Dummies
readers!

IDG Books Worldwide, Inc., End-User License Agreement

READ THIS. You should carefully read these terms and conditions before opening the software packet(s) included with this book ("Book"). This is a license agreement ("Agreement") between you and IDG Books Worldwide, Inc. ("IDGB"). By opening the accompanying software packet(s), you acknowledge that you have read and accept the following terms and conditions. If you do not agree and do not want to be bound by such terms and conditions, promptly return the Book and the unopened software packet(s) to the place you obtained them for a full refund.

1. **License Grant.** IDGB grants to you (either an individual or entity) a nonexclusive license to use one copy of the enclosed software program(s) (collectively, the "Software") solely for your own personal or business purposes on a single computer (whether a standard computer or a workstation component of a multiuser network). The Software is in use on a computer when it is loaded into temporary memory (RAM) or installed into permanent memory (hard disk, CD-ROM, or other storage device). IDGB reserves all rights not expressly granted herein.

2. **Ownership.** IDGB is the owner of all right, title, and interest, including copyright, in and to the compilation of the Software recorded on the disk(s) or CD-ROM ("Software Media"). Copyright to the individual programs recorded on the Software Media is owned by the author or other authorized copyright owner of each program. Ownership of the Software and all proprietary rights relating thereto remain with IDGB and its licensers.

3. **Restrictions on Use and Transfer.**

   (a) You may only (i) make one copy of the Software for backup or archival purposes, or (ii) transfer the Software to a single hard disk, provided that you keep the original for backup or archival purposes. You may not (i) rent or lease the Software, (ii) copy or reproduce the Software through a LAN or other network system or through any computer subscriber system or bulletin-board system, or (iii) modify, adapt, or create derivative works based on the Software.

   (b) You may not reverse engineer, decompile, or disassemble the Software. You may transfer the Software and user documentation on a permanent basis, provided that the transferee agrees to accept the terms and conditions of this Agreement and you retain no copies. If the Software is an update or has been updated, any transfer must include the most recent update and all prior versions.

4. **Restrictions on Use of Individual Programs.** You must follow the individual requirements and restrictions detailed for each individual program in Appendix A of this Book. These limitations are also contained in the individual license agreements recorded on the Software Media. These limitations may include a requirement that after using the program for a specified period of time, the user must pay a registration fee or discontinue use. By opening the Software packet(s), you will be agreeing to abide by the licenses and restrictions for these individual programs that are detailed in Appendix A and on the Software Media. None of the material on this Software Media or listed in this Book may ever be redistributed, in original or modified form, for commercial purposes.

Installation Instructions

The *eBusiness Technology Kit For Dummies* CD offers valuable information that you won't want to miss. To install the items from the CD to your hard drive, follow these steps.

For Microsoft Windows users

1. **Insert the CD into your computer's CD-ROM drive.**

2. **Open your browser.**

3. **Click Start⇨Run.**

4. **In the dialog box that appears, type** D:\START.HTM

5. **Read through the license agreement, nod your head, and then click the Accept button if you want to use the CD.** You can either click to view the HTML Interface or the PowerPoint Interface.

For Mac OS users

1. **Insert the CD into your computer's CD-ROM drive.**

2. **Double-click the CD icon to show the CD's contents.**

3. **Double-click the Read Me First icon.**

4. **Open your browser.**

5. **Click on File⇨Open and select the CD icon entitled eBiz Tech Kit FD.** Click on the Links.htm file to see an explanation of all files and folders included on the CD.

6. **Some programs come with installer programs — with those you simply open the program's folder on the CD and double-click the icon with the word "Install" or "Installer."**

For more complete information, please see Appendix A, "About the CD."

IDG BOOKS WORLDWIDE BOOK REGISTRATION

We want to hear from you!

Visit **http://my2cents.dummies.com** to register this book and tell us how you liked it!

- Get entered in our monthly prize giveaway.

- Give us feedback about this book — tell us what you like best, what you like least, or maybe what you'd like to ask the author and us to change!

- Let us know any other *For Dummies*® topics that interest you.

Your feedback helps us determine what books to publish, tells us what coverage to add as we revise our books, and lets us know whether we're meeting your needs as a *For Dummies* reader. You're our most valuable resource, and what you have to say is important to us!

Not on the Web yet? It's easy to get started with *Dummies 101*®*: The Internet For Windows*® *98* or *The Internet For Dummies*® at local retailers everywhere.

Or let us know what you think by sending us a letter at the following address:

For Dummies Book Registration
Dummies Press
10475 Crosspoint Blvd.
Indianapolis, IN 46256

BESTSELLING BOOK SERIES